Praise for

I Didn't Sign Up for This

"It can be difficult to change patterns in your relationship. Dr. Tracy shows us real stories of how couples heal old wounds and develop deeper, more meaningful connections. A must-read book for anyone in a relationship!"

—**Dr. Shefali Tsabary,** clinical psychologist and author of
the *New York Times* bestseller *The Conscious Parent*

"*I Didn't Sign Up for This* offers relatable stories of real-life couples. Whether you are newly in a relationship, married with children, or navigating a blended family, you'll gain real tools to help you feel more connected with your partner."

—**Eve Rodsky,** author of the *New York Times* bestseller *Fair Play*

"Partnerships are tricky, especially when you are parenting young kids. *I Didn't Sign Up for This* offers an approach for how you can stay connected to your partner—and to yourself—as you navigate those early childhood years. Dr. Tracy weaves together real moments from couples therapy, honest stories from her own life, and direct teaching of coping skills so you can make meaningful change in your home."

—**Dr. Becky Kennedy,** author of the
#1 *New York Times* bestseller *Good Inside*

"At a time when everyone is asking themselves questions about their relationships, Dr. Tracy's insights into couples and their everyday dilemmas remind us that we are not alone in our struggles and that there are actionable tools we can use to feel closer and more connected to our partners. Thank you, Dr. Tracy, for being a trustworthy and compassionate guide."

—**Alexandra H. Solomon, PhD,** licensed clinical psychologist,
faculty at Northwestern University, and author of
three books, including *Love Every Day*

"*I Didn't Sign Up for This* provides an honest look at what couples struggle with while also highlighting that even therapists are not exempt from these struggles. Combined with her signature compassion and empathy, Dr. Tracy reminds us that struggling is part of what makes us human."

—**Amanda E. White, LPC,** founder of @therapyforwomen
and bestselling author of *Not Drinking Tonight*

"This book provides an honest look at what we commonly struggle with in our relationships while giving you one big insight: Even therapists struggle too. Combined with her compassion and empathy, Dr. Tracy reminds us that we are all human. *I Didn't Sign Up for This* is a must-read and must-have for your bookshelf!"

—**Chelsea Bodie & Caitlin Slavens,** therapists, authors of *Not Your
Mother's Postpartum Book,* and founders of @MamaPsychologists

"If you've wondered whether you're alone in the challenges you face in your relationship, *I Didn't Sign Up for This* will show you otherwise. Filled with relatable stories of the challenges of intimacy and the insights and tools you'd receive in the therapy room, Dr. Tracy's book is a must-read for all couples trying to build and enjoy a relationship in modern times."

—**Elizabeth Earnshaw, LMFT,** author of *I Want This to Work*

I Didn't Sign Up for This

A COUPLES THERAPIST
SHARES REAL-LIFE STORIES
OF BREAKING PATTERNS AND
FINDING JOY IN RELATIONSHIPS
. . . INCLUDING HER OWN

DR. TRACY DALGLEISH

Published by
PESI Publishing, Inc.
3839 White Ave
Eau Claire, WI 54703

Cover and Interior Design: Emily Dyer
Editing: Chelsea Thompson and Jenessa Jackson, PhD

ISBN: 9781683736622 (print)
ISBN: 9781683736639 (ePUB)
ISBN: 9781683736646 (ePDF)

Printed in the United States of America.

PESI Publishing
pesipublishing.com

To Gregory, who has held my hand
through all of the storms.

To Anderson and Eloise, may you always
know curiosity and compassion.

Contents

Introduction

While the cultural landscape of relationships has changed radically throughout the ages, the courtship phase has always been what inspires us to take the journey. It's the romantic part. The fun part. The part that makes it easy to put our best self forward. Flush with bonding and reproductive hormones, couples in the heady initial stage of a relationship seem to meet each other's needs effortlessly. Unless the relationship is derailed by significant potholes, momentum may carry them smoothly to the milestone of commitment. But all too often, several months or even several years down the road, they're pulled up short by an unexpected roadblock: The relationship no longer feels like the one they said yes to.

This is where I come in.

As a psychologist and couples therapist, I have been struck by the number of clients who show up in my office saying the same thing: *I didn't sign up for this.* The couple arguing about invisible labor and searching for the solution to a more even division of labor. The mother of three children, desperate to have her husband see her overwhelming reality and get on the same team for parenting. The remarried couple doing their best to blend families while navigating the interference of a toxic ex-partner. The man who ended his twenty-five-year marriage because he never felt like he could show up as his authentic self. The woman who went outside of her marriage to reawaken her desire because her husband wasn't willing to address his sexual difficulties. As different as these clients are, they have in common a longing for their "old" relationship—the one that felt easy, connected, fulfilling.

Their experiences echo words I once found myself thinking about my own relationship. My husband and I have been together for sixteen years and married for eleven, have two young children, and co-own a business. Despite the deeper love I felt for my husband with every warm cuddle or tender word he gave our children, I found myself resenting him as the years went on, in part for seemingly going about his life more or less the same way while my life and identity felt turned upside down. It is one thing to know intellectually that marriages change over time, but it's a completely different experience to be in the thick of those changes, repeatedly wondering how we got here and if it will always be this way.

What Is Keeping You Stuck?

Clients come to my practice eager for solutions to fix their flatlining connection. They want me to tell them how to redistribute the family chores, how to co-parent better, how to tolerate their in-laws, how to have more sex, how to stop having the same fight over and over again. Underneath these practical needs is a more fundamental question, one that loads every minor disagreement with existential doubt: *If we love each other, why can't we seem to solve our problems?*

I imagine it's something you've wondered too. Maybe you have committed to fair play, become fluent in your partner's love language, and learned everything you can about how to get the love you want, yet you remain deeply unhappy in your relationship and don't understand why.

Between my clinical practice and human experience, I've learned that none of the surface issues—the dishes, the in-laws, the kids, the sex—are the root cause of your relationship woes. For that reason, there's no one-size-fits-all solution—improved communication, chore charts, creative date nights—that will fix your problem. (If only it were that easy!) Humans are too complex for that. We show up to our relationships with our early childhood experiences, previous relationship histories, beliefs, and perceptions, trusting that our new love will resolve them all. But when challenges arise, we end up repeating old patterns that developed in our first relationships. After all, these old patterns are familiar, and familiarity feels safe (even when it doesn't feel good).

After fifteen years of treating couples in therapy and speaking with thousands more through my podcast, masterclasses, online educational programs, and social media platforms, I have come to believe that many of our repeated relationship conflicts stem from deep unmet needs, unfulfilled longings, and above all, the mistaken belief that dependency is bad. We live in a society where the value for individualism and self-reliance sends an ulterior message that needing someone makes you a weaker person. Indeed, clients often share with me that they worry about becoming too needy in their relationships. (Or worse, that their love actually reflects *codependency*, a popular psychology term that gets tossed around so easily in conversation or on social media these days.)

In fact, this tendency toward individualism is harmful to our mental and emotional health and, by extension, to our relationships. The focus on "I" abandons a human's natural, emotional, and even biological need for closeness and security, or what is known as *attachment*. According to psychologist and psychiatrist Dr. John Bowlby, the pioneer of attachment theory, knowing that we matter to others, that we are worthy to be seen and understood by those we love, is imperative to our survival. It is akin to a gravitational force: We cannot control gravity, nor can we control the coming together of relational bonding. Research now shows that loneliness and social isolation (i.e., disconnection from others) kills more people than heart attacks or cancer.

With that in mind, I suggest a solution for our relationships that goes against our cultural obsession with individualism: moving toward the creation of healthy *interdependence*.

What Is Interdependence?

Interdependence is about holding both personal autonomy and relational intimacy at once. *Autonomy* is concerned with maintaining independence, while *intimacy* focuses on finding healthy and successful ways to bring people close to us and share our experiences. Being interdependent requires recognizing that you and your partner are two separate people with your own thoughts, feelings, opinions, desires, and wishes while cocreating a relationship that meets each other's needs for connection and closeness.

Building interdependence begins with something called *differentiation*. Simply put, this is the process of defining oneself—one's needs, values, feelings, and boundaries—while remaining close and connected to those we love. I like to frame it as "I am me, you are you, and we are both okay." Differentiation enables us to navigate the difficulties that arise when we risk intimacy and allows us to self-soothe in the face of big emotions like anger, anxiety, and fear. It helps us see the connection between thoughts and feelings (rather than seeing them as the same). It empowers us to problem solve and make decisions in a way that is both authentic and empathetic. Counterintuitive though it may seem, differentiation offers us the ability to drop into someone else's experience. By giving ourselves the opportunity to be separate, we learn to honor and understand someone else's selfhood and experiences. This is how we reach true connection and closeness.

Emotional fusion is the opposite of differentiation. This is a term from psychiatrist Dr. Murray Bowen's family systems theory that indicates psychological enmeshment and codependency between partners or family members. It's having your thoughts, feelings, and behaviors entangled with another person's, such that at times it's hard to see two separate people. In this space, a person stops expressing themselves, abandons their own feelings and needs, and gives up what they desire with the hope of appeasing, fixing, or placating the other person's emotions. Fusion says things like, "I will do what you want so that you are not angry with me" or "I won't share my feelings because they'll upset you."

While fusion may masquerade as closeness, it ends up creating greater distance between two people. The more I fuse with you in my attempt to get close, the more you feel that this closeness is too much and end up pushing me away. We can see this at work in the parent-child relationship. When a child starts to develop healthy separation from their mother, they will push her away. If a mother is not attuned to her child's needs and insists on hugs and snuggles, the child will become distressed. In the same way, fusion in our adult relationships—having our sense of self impacted by our partner's moods or thoughts—builds resentment, which leads to disconnection and dissatisfaction until we practice separating their experience from our own lovability and worthiness.

(So far, I've used a number of clinical terms like *attachment, differentiation, emotional fusion,* and *autonomy.* Throughout this book, when I use terms to illustrate a situation, I'll explain these words or phrases the first time they appear. If you don't remember when you see it again, I've created a glossary at the back of the book that you can refer to as needed.)

I have seen firsthand that when clients start doing the work of cultivating interdependence—healing childhood wounds, disrupting negative patterns, and developing the ability to see the self as separate from the other—their relationships begin to change. I believe that you, too, can change what is happening in your relationship so that you can live a fulfilling and meaningful life with the person you love.

Stories + Strategies

In my clinical practice, I frequently use stories as part of the therapeutic process. I find that it helps people become less defensive and more curious and open to change. To help you examine your relationship and shift into new, healthier strategies, I've included five different case studies in this book. Each chapter focuses on snapshots of my sessions with three couples and one woman who, like many individuals I see, came to my office telling me that her partner wasn't ready for couples therapy. (Even if someone's partner isn't interested in therapy, when one person changes, the relationship can also change.)

What about the fifth case, you ask? Well, it's me.

Although I have spent over a decade researching attachment theory and emotionally focused couples therapy (EFT), I found myself struggling to find my way in my own relationship. My husband and I were both surprised by the difficulties we experienced in our entry into parenthood: navigating the invisible labor, setting boundaries with family members, and most of all, feeling resentful and disconnected in our relationship with each other. The potentially negative impact a child can have on connection and intimacy in a relationship is well documented. However, I don't think that the change in our relationship was solely the result of having children. I believe the unhelpful communication patterns and unhealed wounds were already there. Parenting simply catapulted them into consciousness.

While it is not standard practice for couples therapists to share personal experiences from their marriages, I believe that keeping myself out of these pages would be a disservice to you, the reader. The whole point of this book is to show that withholding our own vulnerability and authenticity creates barriers in relationships, breeding shame and self-doubt that drive couples further apart. It's also important to know that therapists are not perfect, nor are our marriages. It is my hope that by showing up as a human in these pages, I can offer a healing reminder that none of us are alone in our struggles.

While I share my own story as it really happened, the client stories you'll read are composite characters created from the core experiences of my real-life clients' stories. Identifying information has been changed to protect their confidentiality, but the details of their personalities, coping mechanisms, and presenting difficulties have been preserved to show the common issues and hardships that tend to bring couples to therapy. It is my hope that these stories will normalize the difficulties that you may have experienced and offer validation and hope that you, too, can make a change that brings you and your partner closer. At the end of each chapter, I've provided a brief exercise or journal prompt to help you apply the information and deepen your learning. These exercises can be done on your own, but I encourage you and your partner to explore your answers with each other.

◇◇◇◇◇

A Note to My Clients

You play an important role in these chapters and I want you to know that I hold your stories dearly. If you recognize yourself in these pages, it's because, to speak plainly, you are not unique. (I often sit in front of you and think, *I wish you could see the client that was here just before you.*) This isn't to dismiss the complexity of your inner life. Rather, it's to say that you are not alone in the struggles you experience. Your vulnerability has impacted and inspired me more than you'll ever know. It's because of you inviting me into your world that I have grown into the therapist and person I am today. I am forever grateful for our work together. Thank you for showing up.

PART ONE

<><><>

Aware

As humans, we look for a beginning, a middle, and an end when it comes to stories. However, as the stories in this section illustrate, change is not always so linear, and neither is therapy. The deeper we probe into the beliefs we hold and the patterns they've created in our relationships, the more we realize that our relationship problems started well before we made a long-term commitment. Before anything can change in the relationship, we need insight into the struggles we are having within ourselves.

CHAPTER 1

Emily and Matt

Our relationship disagreements are not really about the dishes, the in-laws, the kids, or even the sex. They're about the unmet attachment needs and longings that we all carry inside. Our inability to solve conflict in our relationships stems from repeated cycles of missed connection and miscommunication that result in us being unable to meet each other's needs. Learning to identify your negative cycle will help you to see the cycle as the problem instead of your partner.

◇◇◇◇◇

Please don't say it. Please don't say it.

The couple sitting across from me are as far apart from each other as my office sofa will allow, their gazes fixed on opposite ends of the room. I chose my office's pale decor scheme in an attempt to create calmness for my clients, but the effect is not working on Emily and Matt. At this point, it isn't working on me, either. We are stalled, and I am feeling frustrated.

Emily and Matt are a couple in their early forties who have recently had a baby. In fact, three-month-old Alice is here with us, swaddled and snug in Emily's arms. Having recently become a mother myself, I'm impressed by Emily's seemingly effortless command of the situation. Then again, she also supervises a large team in her role as a human resources executive; she's clearly no stranger to managing people and their challenges. However, her highly attuned professional skills are simply not transferable to romance. Directing her partner isn't getting her what she wants in her relationship.

Our session today starts exactly like our very first one several weeks ago, with Emily running through her laundry list of everything Matt doesn't do.

"Why can't he just do what I ask?" Emily wails. "I have to do everything—I'm the CEO, the mother, the partner, the chef, the housecleaner, the organizer. If I ask him to do one simple thing, he should be able to do it."

The emotional heat in the room is high. Small beads of sweat stand out on Emily's forehead as she purses her lips and raises her eyebrows, waiting for Matt to say something—anything. But it's a catch-22, and Matt knows it. Staying quiet too long could result in her storming out of the room, but saying the wrong thing could lead to the same outcome. He runs his hands through his hair and lets out a throaty exhale, as if he has been holding his breath up to this moment. Emily may long for a closer connection with Matt, but her anger pushes him further away.

As part of my couples therapy process, I meet with both partners individually to learn about the assumptions, beliefs, thoughts, and feelings they have about themselves and others that feed their relationship distress. It's also a time when I gather unfiltered data from each partner about the other, a practice that reveals discrepancies between how they show up as a couple versus as individuals. In our one-on-one session, Emily disclosed that she doesn't think she can continue in the relationship. In my experience, this is fairly unusual in a first session; after all, most people choose to be in couples therapy because they want to stay in the relationship. But Emily is not so sure. Torn between a yearning to keep her family of three together and a deep desire for equal partnership, she confides her doubt that Matt has it in him to be able to take responsibility for household and childcare tasks. At the same time, though, her exhaustion with the heavy load she's already carrying has made her determined to do no more than her share.

I appreciate that Emily has enough self-respect to recognize that this relationship doesn't feel fair, but I also see her self-protective stance as a withdrawal from her commitment. I'm desperate for her to not say, "I'm done; we're over"—words I can practically see hanging from the tip of her tongue in our session now. If she spits those feelings out in a fit of anger—and for those with a temper like Emily's, it's likely to happen—it will throw a grenade into our progress. Worse, Matt's response would be to spiral into depression, which would lead him to disengage even more from Emily and their family—the exact opposite of what she craves from him.

Emily is back to her script of recriminations. "I get home—it's the first time all week I've been out of the house alone—and he's made sausages. Sausages. This isn't what we agreed to when we discussed the weekly menu. I'm the one planning the dinners and he can't even follow simple instructions," she snaps.

"I did!" Matt exclaims. "I didn't have time to get out to the grocery store to make the lasagna you wanted, but I planned dinner out and I made it. But you didn't even give me a chance to put food on the plate before you jumped down my throat. Your expectations are impossible to meet." He lets out a big sigh and stares at the ceiling.

It's not lost on me that Emily likely has a point when it comes to Matt. I, too, sense the imbalance in their relationship around parenting Alice, tending to the domestic work, and making important decisions for the family. But if I focus on the minutiae of their fights—who left the socks on the floor, why the dishes aren't done, who is supposed to pick up the kids—I will end up in a "who said what" battle. We're trained as therapists to avoid focusing on the content of what couples fight about and instead focus on how and why something is shared in a particular way. But it's easier said than done because the urge to find the "right" approach is strong.

Emily doesn't explode at Matt, but she doesn't hold back the anger in her gestures and tone of voice—desperate for someone to see her overwhelming reality. Emily speaks to me instead of Matt. Now that I am the conduit between them, she views me as the safe person who won't immediately snap back at her when she expresses herself.

"I'm exhausted," she cries. "I can't keep doing it all."

So stop doing it all. I've had this thought several times in our sessions so far. At the same time, I don't blame her for getting angry. Carrying all the invisible labor of her relationship isn't something Emily landed in by choice. Societal pressure pushes many women into it. *In fact,* I think, *you can't imagine how much I relate to you on this, Emily.*

The fight I had with my husband last night flashes before my eyes. I was doing ten tasks at once while trying to meet the demands of our toddler-aged son, Anderson, when I looked over and saw Greg lying on the couch, ankles crossed, watching television, oblivious to what was going on around him. I told him he needed to help and he yelled, "I am!" I'm not sure how he could be laying on the couch *and* helping at the same time—is it a magical skill? It escalated quickly from there, with each of us trying to blame the other person and argue over who was and wasn't helping. When I woke up this morning, I felt exhausted at the idea of having to revisit the disagreement and resolved not to say anything, to let it go and move forward.

. . . But have I really moved forward? Or is resentment slowly burning in the background? Emily's description of her relationship dynamic rings disturbingly true for me: Why do *I* have to be the CEO in our family?

I blink a few times to refocus my thoughts back on Emily and Matt. I know I have limited time to shift the conversation in a more positive direction. It's important they leave the session feeling like they are in a better place. Feeling like I'm on the clock, I jump in.

"Matt, you feel like you're trying, right? You put dinner on the plate, but then you felt deeply unappreciated for what you did. Can you share more about that?"

"Yeah, well, I can never do it right for her," he repeats. "Maybe sausages aren't the best meal but at least I did something." Shifting his gaze to Emily, he blurts out, "You never see what I do. It's never good enough."

This is where Emily and Matt, like many couples I see, enter their *negative cycle*—that is, a pattern that stops couples from being able to communicate. Their particular cycle is of the *pursue-defend* variety: "I get critical because you are defensive" is met with "I get defensive because you are critical." Like 80 percent of women in this type of negative cycle, Emily falls into the pursuer role. She fears being a burden to others, so rather than ask for the connection she deeply desires, she forces it with laundry lists and to-do tasks. It feels easier to demand practical assistance than reach out for emotional support.

Meanwhile, Matt is afraid of failing and disappointing Emily, which is rooted in his childhood wound of being constantly told by his father that he was doing something wrong. So rather than risk making a mistake and feeling that pain of never measuring up, Matt waits to be told what to do. When his fear meets her overwhelm, Emily pursues with anger and biting commentary while Matt defends himself by calling her expectations unreasonable.

Both partners are clearly desperate to improve their relationship; the challenge is that neither is willing to talk about their own thoughts and feelings. Instead, they keep their focus on the other person's behavior. In therapy, we call this *externalization*. It's common for people to want to stay in their frustrations and blame something outside themselves, because going inward to identify our own painful thoughts and feelings isn't something we are taught. If we go to these hard places, we also need to trust that the other person is going to be open, be curious, and try to *get* it. When we fear that they won't, we avoid real vulnerability.

Opening up requires us to hold empathy for each other, to work together as a team, to fundamentally be on the same page. But when we're stuck in a negative cycle, we struggle to share our underlying feelings and core longings, leaving these deeper thoughts and emotions unexplored and unexpressed.

As a result, we are all living in two time zones, in a way. One time zone is our current reality, where our partner makes the wrong thing for dinner or comes home in a black-cloud mood. The other time zone is our childhood, where many of our emotional reactions were created by our parents' reactions (or lack thereof) to our behaviors, experiences, feelings, and needs. We all respond to stimuli in the present day through the template of what we experienced in childhood. We might act in the same manner as our parents did in their own relationship, respond in ways that our parents acted toward us, or act out the same coping patterns we used as children. This is because our brains crave predictability. There is comfort in routine, even when it's not helpful. But this cycle prevents us from developing a deeper connection with and understanding of our partner. Underneath the armor and weapons are unmet needs and desires. Instead of talking about these, we stay stuck wanting the other person to pick up the socks and make the lasagna.

Emily and Matt had different realities when they first met. Single and tired of waiting to find "the one," Emily decided to make a financial investment and purchased a townhouse. Meanwhile, Matt was living with two other men, a decision he made when his ex-fiancée told him that she wasn't happy anymore and dumped him two weeks before their wedding, leaving him heartbroken and without a place to live. Despite their differences (or maybe because of them), Emily and Matt instantly connected when they met through mutual friends during a weekend getaway. Emily said that Matt was funny, easygoing, carefree. She enjoyed being with someone whose approach to life wasn't always so planned out as hers—ironic, now that his inability to initiate and follow through with making plans is a huge point of contention. Matt was drawn to Emily's assertiveness, having struggled with decision-making and problem-solving in his own life. He liked that Emily knew what she wanted, though now her determination feels more like a measuring stick for his failures.

Being in their late thirties, they both knew what they wanted in a partner, and the relationship got serious quickly. Before long, Matt moved into Emily's home, despite the knock to his pride at not being a purchaser of the home they were going to share. About one year into their relationship, Emily discovered she was pregnant. Emily had always wanted a family. She longed for Matt to propose to her, not because she valued the tradition itself, but because she wanted to know that the father of her child was devoted to her. Matt, however, became distracted with a big work project. He was reaching for a promotion and had begun to focus even more on his career when Alice was born.

By the time they entered therapy, Emily still hadn't received a proposal. It remains one more item on her list of things that Matt isn't doing. Matt claims he will do anything for Emily but doesn't see the significance of getting married. After all, his first experience with proposing didn't pan out the way he had hoped. Matt's drive to be successful at work is ego-driven, a desire to prove his worthiness and to finally feel like he measures up. Yet, by prioritizing work, Matt fails to see the cascading impact of his actions as Emily is left to care for Alice for more than ten hours a day by herself, prepare all of the meals, tend to the household, and plan the family's activities. Matt's focus on work fuels her growing resentment, but her anger at taking over all the tasks (which she is good at doing) is at odds with her desire for control. The more Emily controls and demands from Matt, the more his childhood wounds of never measuring up are triggered. Now, with a three-month-old, there is a deep wedge between them. Their relationship no longer feels like it once did. They know something has to change.

While my first task is to break up the negative pattern they're in, simply shifting out of those patterns won't be enough. The end goal is to create healthy interdependence in their relationship. Characterized by compromise, flexibility, and an equal exchange of power, interdependence allows partners to enjoy their own autonomy while finding authentic ways to be intimate in their relationship. Getting there requires both partners to focus less on themselves as individuals and more on the quality of their relational connection—less of the "who did what?" and more of the "how can we move forward?" I need Emily to start sharing her softer emotions so that Matt can grasp why she demands to be behind the steering wheel but, at the same time, resents him for letting her do all the driving. I need Matt to tap into his vulnerable side so that Emily can see the support he's trying so hard to give her.

"Can you help me understand, Matt?" I begin. "You got defensive, but I heard something else too. What just happened for you?"

"It just feels like I can never do enough," Matt repeats, slower this time, looking at his feet. "It's like I'm failing her, and I will never get it right."

I attempt to nudge Matt further in this direction. "I'm wondering where else you have felt like you can never get it right." I've observed that Matt tends to stay in his *secondary emotions* (which are emotions about emotions, like anger and frustration) and avoids his *primary emotions* (which are softer, clearer, and describe the core of our experience, like pain, sadness, hurt, and loneliness). Whereas secondary emotions tend to push our partner away, our primary emotions help them understand our more vulnerable parts. By gently guiding Matt into his internal experience, he can access the core needs and feelings that will bring Emily closer.

Matt frowns and shrugs. Being put on the spot makes him uncomfortable; he would rather keep trying to find the solution that will please his partner. But this focus isn't working for him for two reasons. One, it fuses him with Emily's emotions and desires, sacrificing the differentiation between his autonomous self and hers. Two, Emily doesn't actually want him to solve the problem; deep inside, she is looking for a partner to be on deck *with* her, not for one of them to steer the ship alone.

Since Matt seems unsure where this feeling came from, I press a bit with what I know from his history. "A few sessions ago, you shared that same emotion—this sense of being a failure—only it was about your father." Sometimes, to create real change, I need to lead clients somewhere they'd rather not go. This is a difficult thing to do as a therapist, requiring me to brave my human dislike of having people be upset with me while finding a way to bring up the hard topics in a way that doesn't provoke them to reject the therapeutic process altogether.

Matt nods. "My dad would tell me that I'd never be good enough."

"What comes to mind when you think of your father telling you that?" I ask.

Matt takes a deep breath. "I remember this one summer when my dad was finishing the deck. It was a special project, this multilevel deck overlooking our backyard. I looked up to him, and all I wanted to do was help him hammer the nails. So I went out to help." He clears his throat. "But as soon as I started banging nails into the boards, he yelled at me to stop. I wasn't doing it right. I was screwing it up."

Old wounds like these keep us apart and prevent us from connecting. It's clear to me that the validation Matt longed for from his father continues to show up in his need for validation from Emily today. While Matt's vulnerability doesn't excuse his behavior of not stepping in, it can pave the way for understanding and compromise.

"So when Emily is upset, you begin to feel like you're failing." Matt's eyes start to well up and I keep going. "And it feels just like when your father would tell you, all those years ago, that you couldn't use the hammer right. He would tell you to leave when all you wanted was to be like him. To be liked *by* him."

Emily lets out a forced breath through pursed lips. "Here we go again. It's always about you and never being good enough. No one tells me that I'm good enough when I'm doing the dishes or taking care of Alice. Who is telling me that I'm doing a good job?"

"Wait." I put my hand up like a stop sign. "Emily, let's slow down. I see it's hard for you to hear that Matt doesn't feel good enough. In those moments, you need him to see you, to make the dinners, to just pull it together. Those are *your* needs. But for him, all he hears is his father saying that he can't do anything right."

I soften my tone and pace my words, hoping this will bring her with me.

"Matt is sharing what he learned about love and relationships growing up," I continue, dripping the words out slowly and gently so she can register them. "Anything he did was never good enough. And here, today, that feeling shows up with you. I hear that you *aren't* saying he isn't good enough, but can you allow yourself to see that younger part of Matt who struggles in these moments?"

Matt has a pleading look on his face. He doesn't do well opening up, and she's not giving him much reason to feel good about it now. Growing impatient, I shift gears.

"I wonder, Emily, what does this stir up inside of you? Is it that part of you that always needs to be in the driver's seat?"

She doesn't respond. We sit in silence for several seconds. I am comfortable in silence, but Emily shifts in her seat and glances at the clock.

"Well, look at the time. We're done for today," she says matter-of-factly. With Alice in one arm, she stands up, brushes off her dress, and walks to the door.

"Emily . . ." Matt gets up from the couch to follow her, picking up the diaper bag and Alice's car seat as he calls after her. "I need you to talk about this stuff here!"

Emily looks at Matt, then back at me. Her position—one foot out the door of my office—is an unsettling presence of the secret between us: that she has one foot out of her relationship. She knows it. And I feel it.

"See you next week," she says, walking out.

I watch the couple leave my office, chalking one up to Emily for having dodged talking about her deeper issues yet again. I question at what point they will stop attending therapy, or worse, when Emily will decide to end their relationship. I catch a glimpse of my weary face in the small black framed mirror hanging on the wall. Then, emotions stirring through me, I pick up my phone and start texting Greg. I feel sickness in my stomach but fury in my fingers. Before I can think about what I have just written, I hit send.

We need to talk.

Aware

Learning Your Negative Cycle

According to renowned couples therapist Dr. Sue Johnson, there are three types of cycles that couples get stuck in: (1) Find the Bad Guy (blame each other), (2) The Protest Polka (pursue-defend), and (3) Freeze and Flee (shut down). Head to www.drtracyd.com/cycles to learn more about each cycle, then take some time to explore these questions.

◈ Which relationship pattern do you and your partner get stuck in?

◈ What are the common issues that lead you and your partner to get stuck in this cycle? These might be "hot topics" (e.g., conversations about in-laws, sex, kids, household tasks), verbal or nonverbal messages, behaviors, or absence of behaviors. Identifying your common issues can help you recognize your cycle before it gets started.

◈ The first step in changing negative patterns in your relationship is to learn how to stop the cycle. Write out what you will do next time you and your partner escalate into your cycle (e.g., ask your partner to take a break, use humor or playfulness to break the tension, label the cycle with a playful name).

CHAPTER 2

Tracy

When you get stuck in a disagreement, your nervous system becomes dysregulated and overwhelmed. You can't resolve issues in your relationship when your body is in fight-or-flight mode or you have become frozen and shutdown. One of the first changes you can make in your relationship is learning to identify when you have moved out of a state of calm and how you can get back into it.

◇◇◇◇◇

There's a common belief that therapists have it all together. Thanks to their training and their study of human behavior, they understand relational patterns, recognize the motivation behind people's choices, and offer strategies and tools to overcome challenges, all with the goal of helping their clients live a more meaningful life. As a couples therapist, I shouldn't be struggling in my own relationship, right?

This could not be further from the truth. Even as I'm coming home from a day of helping couples find a way out of their negative cycles, I'm spinning through my own. Specifically, I'm seething over the fact that Greg hasn't replied to the text I sent after my session with Emily and Matt. *Not surprising*, I think. *This is what he does.* If it were up to him, every disagreement between us would get swept under the rug. Deep down, I know that he avoids hard conversations not because he doesn't care. It's actually the opposite: It's because he wants so badly not to upset me. But his lack of initiative to resolve conflict and work on our marriage only upsets me more.

As a therapist, I see conflict as an inevitable part of any relationship—handled well, it is actually very healthy. But for Greg, conflict is bad, full stop. To him, it's a sign that something is wrong in our relationship, and this makes him anxious and overwhelmed. In response, he *compartmentalizes*, literally tucking away potentially difficult information in separate compartments of his brain. This is a common defense mechanism for people when they are stressed or anxious. But when you try to avoid a negative emotional response from your partner by not bringing up something difficult, you guarantee that they will indeed be angry and upset. It's a *self-fulfilling prophecy*.

Understanding this about Greg doesn't make it any easier to deal with. My mind likes to whisper these "if-then" rules: *If* he brought these conversations up, *then* I would know I am important to him. Sound relatable? It's a conditional rule that many people (even therapists) get stuck in, and it doesn't work any better than compartmentalization.

Tonight, we clean up after dinner, put our son, Anderson, to bed (knowing that I will be up in a few hours to feed him), then sit in front of the television to watch our favorite show. Therapists call this *parallel play*, while the layman's term for it is "being alone together." Whatever you call it, it's a poor substitute for real connection. As a relationship expert, I know this side-by-side silence doesn't exactly achieve the intimacy I long for. But as an exhausted working mom, I'll gladly take it over initiating something different.

A nagging voice tells me that the reason Greg and I have been arguing so much is because parenthood has changed us, and we are no longer a good match. The research is clear on the impact children have on marriages: 67 percent of new parents will experience decreased marital satisfaction for the first three years after having a baby, and the first year is often said to be the hardest. Knowing that doesn't make it easy to be living in this unfamiliar space of deep disconnection. While I'd never admit it to any of my therapist colleagues, I genuinely believed that our love was different, that it was special, that we'd never get to this point.

Our romance started in a bar one Thursday night in Ottawa. It was the first year of my PhD program, and I had just turned twenty-two. Having moved across the province on the cusp of true adulthood and living alone in the city without friends or family made it easy to feel like a big impostor in my academic program. Fortunately, that year offered me a rare and important lifeline: a good friend. Her name was Lindsey and we quickly bonded over a mutual love of *Grey's Anatomy*, walks along the Rideau Canal, and (of course) psychology. After visiting a local pub one night, where we celebrated our survival of another grueling week, I was tucked in bed when I heard the familiar dinging of MSN Messenger from my computer. It was Lindsey messaging me that her roommates had just arrived at the pub—could I come out for "one more drink"? Despite the Interpersonal Therapy module looming early the next morning, I obliged.

I was just beginning to regret staying out late when I locked eyes with a tall man who was leaning against the wall in the corner of the dimly lit room, talking to Lindsey's roommates. He had dark hair and great shoes. I learned that he was twenty-seven, in town visiting his younger brother. He enchanted me with his stories of living near the Rocky Mountains, even boldly telling me he had visions of getting married there. His life and adventures excited me. He said I should visit him one day.

After seven months of on-and-off emails and phone calls, Greg invited me to visit him. I had never seen the mountains, and exploring them with Greg made them all the more exciting. More exciting still was how at ease I felt with him. Our conversations flowed like the white-water rivers we hiked beside. We talked effortlessly about family, work, and how we imagined our futures. Sipping coffee on a bench in front of turquoise-hued Lake Louise while taking in the view of the majestic snow-capped peaks, I had an inner certainty that I was sitting with my future husband.

This was very much out of character for me. As a psychologist and couples therapist, I don't believe in finding "the one." I believe that we bring our baggage wherever we go and that any relationship, no matter how magical it feels, requires us to sort through this baggage to make it work. This intuition of mine about our future together was not something I wanted to trust.

Still, Greg had a maturity about him that I hadn't seen in any of the men I had dated before. He wasn't playing games or giving mixed signals that could lead me into the kind of "are we or aren't we?" anxiety I'd experienced in past relationships. I was instantly attracted to that confident, straightforward quality of his; it made me feel confident and open in return. For his part, Greg always said that he was attracted to my drive, my empathy, and my indiscriminately kind and caring nature. While we didn't love the long-distance factor, it had the benefit of making us good communicators right from the beginning. We were forced to plan out the time we spent together, talk about issues, and articulate our hopes for the future. At the same time, the distance between us fed a subconscious avoidance. We didn't have to face the daily issues experienced by couples who cohabitate. We never had to consider that the things we were drawn to in each other could end up being the very source of our conflict. In the early days of a romance, who does?

Now, a few years after our wedding and several months after the birth of our son, I feel a distance growing between us. When I step back from the minor mundane irritants to examine what is happening in our relationship, it can be summed up in one word: imbalance. I'm confronted with it first thing in the morning when, amid a flurry of diaper bag packing, baby bottle preparation, and anticipation of a thousand possible needs our son might have while I am out, I watch him leave the house for work without a backward glance. The imbalance is on full display again when I'm rocking our son to sleep for the fourth time because Greg is out golfing with friends. My life has been radically changed by the weight of managing the household *and* our marriage; meanwhile, Greg's life appears unchanged.

Both research and my own clinical experience make it clear that women tend to shoulder the domestic load in a relationship. But despite having counseled hundreds of couples on this very issue (including Emily and Matt just hours ago), I don't see any easy way to change my situation. I am slipping further into resentment and Greg is burying himself in avoidance, just like the couples I see in therapy. The division of the invisible labor continues to grow unfavorably for me, and so does the distance between us.

I feel the return of last night's anger start to rise inside me as I check on Anderson one last time before heading to our bedroom for a heart-to-heart with Greg. *This isn't the way to enter into a conversation,* I think. *You know this—you're the couples therapist!* The thing is, I've been a human a lot longer than I've been a therapist. I know what anxiety feels like when it grips my chest so tightly that I think I'm going to collapse. I know the leaden weight of grief at the bottom of my stomach. I know the ache of loneliness in my bones. I know the bitter temptation of taking the easy route—either giving into my own reactive patterns or shoving down my feelings to avoid a conflict. Even for therapists, knowing better and doing better are two vastly different things.

I double-check the locked doors and turn off all the lights in the house, all the while building up courage for the conversation we need to have. But when I get to our bedroom, I find that Greg has fallen asleep, iPad still perched upright on his chest. Back in our honeymoon stage, his uncanny knack for passing out while holding an object in his hands was funny to me. He once dropped a book on my forehead as I was resting my head on his chest, and it became our inside joke for years. But now his ability to fall asleep at the drop of a hat, even at a moment when we are disconnected from each other, is the opposite of funny to me.

I advise all my clients that no good ever comes from discussing big issues right before bed. But I'm not taking my own advice tonight. I am no longer in my *window of tolerance*; I am ready to fight. I flop heavily onto the bed to make sure Greg feels my presence and say, my voice a little louder than normal, "You're just going to sleep, then?"

The window of tolerance is the space in which we can make sense of our feelings, think logically, and work through our problems. When we are outside of our window of tolerance, our stress response system can get triggered more easily by escalating conflict. According to *polyvagal theory*, the autonomic nervous system can react to this conflict by going into a state of mobilization, in which our sympathetic nervous system mobilizes us for action (commonly referred to as fight-or-flight mode), leading to anxiety and anger. Conversely, we can enter into a dorsal vagal state, in which our parasympathetic nervous system immobilizes us, leading us to freeze, collapse, and shut down.

Greg jolts awake. Fear flashes in his eyes, and he quickly apologizes for passing out. "You know how tired I am," he pleads, fear turning into defensiveness. The weight of the fight we had last night is heavy in the room. If I'm honest, the feeling for me isn't just about the fight. It's about how it seems like we're arguing all the time. It's about how I don't feel close to him anymore.

At the same time, my internal anger is not ready to back down. *He's asking* me *to be understanding?*

I turn my back to Greg so he doesn't see my eye roll and, changing the topic, I ask, "What do you have planned tomorrow?" Even as I say it, I know it's a passive-aggressive move, the kind we all make in our relationships rather than using direct communication to work through what is at the heart of the issue. *Why do I do this?* My therapist brain has the answer: It's because entering into a deeper conversation about whether I am important enough to my partner means that he could confirm my fears of being a burden to him.

Greg doesn't reply immediately, his interest seemingly more drawn to the news site that he was scanning on his iPad. I sense that he's searching for the right words to steer this conversation down the smoothest possible path.

"Okay, just tell me," I press, an unsettling feeling beginning to well inside of me as my mind jumps from one disjointed thought to another. These moments of not knowing what Greg is thinking remind me that there could be something that I am missing. Maybe something is fundamentally flawed with me. Maybe Greg is on the verge of saying, "I'm not going to be with you anymore."

This particular insecurity dates back to my first love, a classic case of emotional unavailability. One night, while my high school boyfriend was driving me home in his Pontiac Grand Am, he looked over and announced, over the melodic aggression of Blink-182, that he was breaking up with me. He told me that it was my fault, that there was something wrong with me, that I wasn't easygoing enough. Even after I learned the truth—that he'd been cheating on me—his awful words remained burned into my unconscious mind. That feeling of sole responsibility for my relationship unhappiness has lingered ever since.

As a psychologist, I know the impact of our earlier experiences on our present-day life. Our early romantic attachments in particular form our understanding of who we are in the world and act as subconscious guides for how we interact with future partners. If those relationships were traumatic, those negative response patterns may repeat themselves, often at an unconscious level. The joke of it all is that I am conscious of my own negative pattern, yet it feels safer to stay in that pattern than share my insecurity with Greg. As a result, I ping-pong between blaming Greg for our problems and wondering if the problem is me.

Honestly, if there were ever a time to wonder this, it's now. There is no time as vulnerable for a woman as the months after giving birth, myself included. My body is softer and my skin is loose. My daily "look" consists of whatever forgivingly stretchy clothing item is handy. I'm sleep deprived. My libido is nowhere to be found. After having worked with several mothers through this transition to motherhood, helping them explore and redefine their identities, I am taken aback at how this experience has rocked me to my core.

"I'm going to play golf tomorrow," Greg finally mutters.

My relief at his response is quickly swallowed up by anger. "I thought we were going to spend time together. We've barely been able to hang out lately," I say, not ready to tell him directly that I'm struggling to feel important to him.

"We never confirmed it," he shrugs, putting the responsibility on me for not asking what he was doing the next day.

"Okay, so your golf games are more important than spending time with me, and us as a family." Heat grows inside my body as I realize that the round of golf also means I'll be spending the weekend parenting by myself. Again. "I'm tired of this. I'm left to clean up the house, plan the meals, and care for Anderson. Why do I have to keep doing it all?" Disappointments from the past few years are flashing before my eyes— the lack of date nights, the poor boundaries with his family, the meal prep and house cleaning falling on my shoulders. I'm spiraling and I can't stop.

He sighs in exasperation and shifts on the bed, noticeably uncomfortable. "I think you're blowing this out of proportion," he says. He might have thought this would defuse the situation; instead, he's poured gasoline on the flames. I grab my pillow and the baby monitor and huff off to the basement bedroom. Pulling the duvet up to my neck, I squeeze my eyes shut, trying to make this argument go away, trying to remember how it even started.

I hear footsteps down the stairs, followed by weight on the edge of the bed. I feel Greg place a heavy hand on my leg. My back turned, I tell him I don't want to talk, secretly wanting him to stay and fight for me.

We sit in silence for what feels like an eternity. Finally, Greg speaks.

"What does this mean for us?" he asks nervously.

I turn over and make out the sunken look on his face, fear in his eyes, lips quivering. Matt's face from earlier today flashes in front of me, the same fear in his eyes as he longed for Emily to validate him. I feel my body loosening against the anger. The flames start to go down.

"Nothing," I whisper, trying to reach for something softer inside me. *It's not about the dishes, Tracy,* I remind myself, *just like it wasn't about the sausages for Emily.* "We're going to work through this," I resolve, more to myself than to him, and reach for Greg's hand to pull him close. Hugging is an act of *co-regulation*—a way of soothing both our nervous systems in times of distress.

As Greg holds me, I see my phone light up on the bedside table. A photo has popped up, one that I took shortly after we came home from the hospital with our newborn baby. My heart stops for a moment. What should be a tender memory is instead a reminder of the first time Greg broke his promise to protect me, his wife and newly the mother of his child. We may have made it through tonight's tension, but this photo reminds me that we're far from finished with our conflict.

Aware:

States of (Dys)regulation and Learning to Regulate

The vagus nerve is the longest bundle of nerves in the body, running from the base of your skull to your digestive system. Polyvagal theory suggests that there are three states activated by the vagus nerve: *ventral vagal* (a state of calm and connectivity), *sympathetic nervous system* (a state of fight or flight, anger, anxiety, mobilization), and *dorsal vagal* (a state of shutting down, depression, collapse, immobilization). By identifying the state that you are in, you can find coping mechanisms to help you return to feeling calm and connected.

◈ We all get triggered sometimes. This is the autonomic nervous system's way of protecting us from real or potential threat. We can get triggered by our thoughts or feelings (internal experience), how we perceive something from the world (external experience), or something that our partner does or doesn't do (relational experience). Spend time observing yourself over the next week and write out when you move into different vagal states. (We'll talk more about triggers in chapter four.)

◈ Write out the internal experience that you have in each vagal state. This will help you identify when you have moved out of a state of calm and into a state of activation or shutdown. This awareness will help you avoid getting escalated into your negative cycle and allow you to get back into a state of regulation. Use the following prompts to explore how you respond in ventral vagal, sympathetic nervous system, and dorsal vagal states.

  ◇ My thoughts are . . .
  ◇ The feelings that show up are . . .
  ◇ The sensations that happen in my body are . . .
  ◇ The color that I give this state is . . .

◈ It's important to remember that you cannot resolve your issues if you are *dysregulated*, meaning that your nervous system is in a state of physiological overwhelm. Here are some go-to strategies for getting back into a calm state when you are in a sympathetic nervous system or dorsal vagal state:

◇ *Self-regulation* (i.e., strategies for soothing on your own)

- Movement: Go for a brisk walk, do jumping jacks, run in place, or do a few minutes of intense exercise.
- Music and sound: Put on your favorite song and dance, sing, or hum along.
- Temperature: Squeeze an ice cube, hold a cold washcloth under your chin, or put a frozen water bottle on your neck.
- Progressive muscle relaxation: This practice involves tensing and releasing different parts of your body. Starting with your toes, squeeze and tense your muscles for five seconds, then intentionally release. Move on to the muscles in your calves, thighs, buttocks, shoulders, biceps, fists, and face.

◇ *Co-regulation* (i.e., strategies for soothing with your partner)

- Hug each other until you feel relaxed.
- Place your foreheads together and focus on each other's eyes and your breath.
- Put your head in your partner's lap.

CHAPTER 3

Ashley

As a child, you learned strategies to stay safe and adapt to your environment. But these old behaviors may now lead you to remain stuck in unhelpful patterns in your relationship (e.g., people-pleasing, caregiving, avoiding, taking on a victim role). Intimacy in adult relationships asks you to put aside your self-protective patterns and learn adaptive strategies for managing difficult emotions.

◇◇◇◇◇

I like to observe how people show up in my office, often embodying what they do in their life. My new client Ashley presents the picture of a put-together wife and mom: Hair styled neatly in a bun, with yoga leggings, a soft cardigan, and designer shoes, she sits in the middle of the couch, legs crossed at her ankles. She is neither taking up space nor moving things around; instead, she almost sinks into the couch, as if trying to disappear. *From what or whom is she hiding? And how is this serving her?* Already formulating questions and hypotheses, I ask the question I put forth to all my new therapy clients: "What brought you here today?"

"My husband says I need to figure out a way to deal with my stress." Ashley speaks quickly, holding her worried gaze on me. Despite being a couples therapist, I see many solo clients whose partners aren't ready for therapy, aren't interested in engaging in the process, or believe their partner is the problem.

Ashley doesn't continue. She waits for me to prompt her. Meanwhile, I'm wondering about why we're starting with what her husband thinks. "Okay," I respond, though I don't really mean it's okay. "Tell me more about the stress you're experiencing."

"Well, it started last year, or maybe even before then," she begins. "I was at work, preparing for my maternity leave. I was thirty-three weeks along. I was rushing, I know—I had so many things I needed to get done, and I was trying to get a document on my boss's desk. And then I felt a sharp pain. It almost knocked me over. I ran to the bathroom and there was blood. I thought I was going to lose my baby." Ashley pauses, blinking several times and pushing her lips together to hide her emotions, quite a contrast to the clients who cry within moments of beginning a session. "I wasn't even done grieving the miscarriage I'd had right before I got pregnant again."

Ashley stays close to the facts and doesn't share the pain that she must have felt in that moment, alone in the washroom. "We weren't ready. We didn't even have the nursery set up. I went into early labor and delivered Liam the next day. Our lives changed in twenty-four hours. We were going back and forth to the NICU. I was trying to heal after giving birth while also trying to care for our two-year-old at home." She lets out a sigh, again brushing away any sign of emotion that starts to rise up.

Some clients start therapy holding their emotions at bay, fearing that they will never be able to come out of the pain if they open up. But the reality is that emotions are more like waves: They come in, crest, and recede. Our job is to ride the wave—allowing ourselves to get uncomfortable, listening to the discomfort rather than fighting against it, and using the information within that discomfort to find the real need under the feelings. Neuroscientist Dr. Jill Bolte Taylor has shown that emotions tend to flare up and fade within just ninety seconds if we identify the internal experience, name the emotions, then allow them to flow. But when people use unhelpful strategies to deal with emotions, it tends to make them last longer and feel more powerful. I can see that unraveling this unhelpful strategy will be my task with Ashley—to slow her down and get her attuned to what is happening inside of her.

I start by reflecting the grief and loss that Ashley must have felt. Not only had her plans for motherhood gone out the window, but she had lost the control that we as humans like to hold onto. The desire to foresee any negative outcome gives us a sense of security, but it's a false security that, when it backfires, tends to create more anxiety and tension. Ashley's son is now fifteen months old, and she's recently returned to work. She struggles to uphold her responsibilities as a mother, wife, and full-time executive assistant. Daily decisions burden her. She sometimes breaks out in a full sweat trying to decide what to make for dinner each night. Her jaw is sore from clenching so much, and her stomach is constantly in knots. When her husband gets home, she is often irritable and short with him. She has a hard time falling asleep, knowing that in a few hours she will have to wake up to nurse her son. I recognize these as the classic symptoms of generalized anxiety disorder.

"After the birth, I felt like I couldn't get it right, like my body had failed my son by not staying pregnant," she continues. "I still feel that way—like I'm constantly failing. Someone is always upset. In those earlier days, Owen, our then two-year-old, would be hitting me and biting me, and I would get so irritated that I would yell at him 'Just stop!' and he would run off crying. What kind of mother yells at her child?"

An overstimulated mother, I answer in my head.

"I just keep worrying about everything," Ashley continues. "It doesn't matter what I do. Liam is so fussy." In a dimmed tone, she adds, "And right from the beginning, he preferred Daniel."

I sense the tension with Daniel, her husband, by her inflection when she says his name. I shift gears. "Tell me about your relationship with your husband." After all, there must be some reason she chose to reach out to a *couples* therapist. While anxiety and stress management are her presenting issues, the question that always exists in my mind is, *What is this person like in the context of their life, with their significant other*, and *Are there patterns or coping strategies in their relationship that contribute to their stress and anxiety?* Our emotional experiences and our mental health do not exist in silos. Research shows that depression and anxiety influence relationship satisfaction and vice versa. It's a chicken and egg situation: Some people become depressed and anxious, and this impacts their partnerships, while others first experience relationship distress that goes on to impact their mental health.

Ashley responds in a high-pitched tone, "It's good!" Then she hesitates. "I mean, it's not like he's absent. He helps with the kids and does bedtime. But he doesn't know what it's like to have anxiety or to be a mother. He tells me I'm making a big deal of things when there is nothing to worry about. But our relationship is fine."

To be blunt, I don't believe that, especially as Ashley continues to limit her disclosure about her marriage to factual information, as if she's reading from an event calendar. She met Daniel shortly after moving to France, where she had accepted a job to get away from the confines of her hometown. He was an expat like her, and she was comforted by spending time with someone who was also away from their home country, as well as attracted to the intensity of his ambition. Ashley's mother, who regularly guilted her for moving abroad, was even more upset when Ashley started a family in France. When their first child was thirteen months old, the couple recognized the old adage that it takes a village to raise a child and decided to return to Canada. Their decision to live closer to Daniel's family, a twelve-hour drive from Ashley's family, only added to her contention with her mother.

Even with these details, I am still unsure how Ashley's husband fits into the dynamic of her life and her ability to cope with stress. Instinctively, I shift gears toward the mention of her mother.

"Your mom had a lot of feelings about you not being close to her," I reflect. "Tell me more about what it was like growing up for you."

Ashley responds promptly, "It was good. I had a good childhood."

Except, as she elaborates, I can see that it wasn't all good. (It never is.) Ashley tells me that she grew up in Spain, with parents who fought constantly. As a young child, she didn't know that relationships could look different; she assumed this is what people did when they loved each other. But when she was just five years old, her father left the family. She remembers the awful night when her father abandoned them: her mother leaning over the kitchen table with tears streaming down her face, her father standing at the door with his brown leather suitcase, Ashley standing in the middle of the living room with her arms outstretched, as if she might be able to hold them together. Her father said he loved her and that he would see her later. She didn't see him again for years.

Soon after that, Ashley's father met another woman, got married, and started a second family in a different country. When he visited, all he offered Ashley was fun: weekend trips, days at the museums, ice cream. But he wasn't around when real-life issues—her tonsil removal surgery, her first dance competition, her frequent fights with her mom—came up. Ashley felt used and betrayed, like her love was something that could be bought for a weekend. Ashley and her mother later moved to Canada to be with extended family. Meanwhile, Ashley began feeling obligated to care for her mother, who was now a single parent trying to keep them afloat with shift work.

I ask Ashley to describe her mother using five words. Her hesitation is so sharp it could cut through glass.

"Well, she's loving, caring, maybe a bit of a perfectionist like me." She rubs the silver button on the cuff of her cardigan with her thumb and forefinger, her gaze shifting to the ceiling before returning to me. One of her crossed legs is quietly bouncing up and down. "But . . . she's also self-focused. And she is . . . combative." Another pause. "But I'm not saying she was a bad mother. She was great."

31

By now, I'm pretty sure that she's trying to protect her mother—or her memories. If I suggest that her mother may not have been supportive and responsive to her, she may shut down completely. I tread carefully. "Tell me more about 'self-focused' and 'combative.'"

"I'm more of an introvert and I need alone time. My mom's the opposite. She's an extrovert—and actually, so is Daniel, now that I think about it. But for me, I do better when I have time for just me." It is not lost on me that Ashley uses the word *time* twice in the span of a few seconds. Time for themselves is what many of my clients need. "In middle school, I would get home at the end of the day and she was always there, just waiting for me in the front foyer. She would ask me so many questions, like 'How was your day? Whom did you talk to? Is there anyone you like? Did any boys talk to you?'" She mimics her mother's high-pitched, excited tone.

"How would you respond?" I ask.

"Well, if I told her I didn't want to talk, she would guilt-trip me. She would get upset and say that I was treating her poorly and not thinking about her feelings."

I note that her mother slipped into the victim role and made Ashley's needs about her, as if they were some form of rejection or personal attack. This is just one of the ways parents engage in emotional fusion and maintain codependency in families (the opposite of trying to teach children to build differentiation and interdependence).

"I remember this one time . . ." Ashley pauses, as if the scene is playing like a film in front of her. "I had gotten into a big fight with my best friend, and my boyfriend and I had broken up. I was crushed. When I got home from school, my mom was standing there at the doorway smiling, completely oblivious that I had been crying. So I told her, 'I want to be alone.' She didn't listen. She told me to stop being so selfish, that I was always thinking of myself, and then stormed off."

"I imagine this must have been hard for you," I say. "Your mother didn't see you—she didn't understand what you were feeling or needing.

Your emotions were just as important in that moment." I instill the idea that she and her mother are two separate people with separate wishes and desires. What I don't say is *Does this mirror what your husband does now, sending you off to therapy to deal with your stress on your own?*

"I learned not to upset her. It wasn't pleasant when she was angry. She would cancel our plans, like getting my favorite dinner or seeing friends on the weekend, or she would threaten to take my things away," Ashley explains. "It was just easier to answer all of her questions rather than telling her I wanted time alone."

We develop a sense of self in childhood through micro moments such as these where we experiment with expressing our feelings and needs. The way our caregivers respond to these expressions matters. If a parent perceives these moments as a rejection and they place their anxiety onto the child, or if they respond inconsistently, the child learns that their own feelings are not important. In response, they may start to either *hyperactivate* or *deactivate* their needs. A child who is hyperactivated may frequently demand proximity to the caregiver and struggle to feel soothed by this closeness. Alternatively, a child who is deactivated may minimize their emotions and needs, and push away from their caregiver. This is how insecure attachment develops.

I push a bit harder, guessing that what she does or feels with her husband is similar to what she learned to do with her mother: engage in people-pleasing.

"That's a hard lesson," I affirm. "Teenagers long for independence. They want their alone time and, more importantly, they need their parents to hear them." I understand the narrative that she's telling herself—that other people's feelings and needs are more important than hers. An indication of emotional fusion.

My work with Ashley will be to bring awareness to her tendency to fuse with others. She is used to pushing her wishes deep down inside of her because she thinks she'll be rejected if she speaks up. But this has left her with anxiety, as it usually does, as well as a constant need to seek approval and validation from others to demonstrate that she is good enough. She'll need to unlearn her people-pleasing tendencies and actually assert herself, which is part of interdependence. By discovering her voice and learning to identify and share her own thoughts and feelings, Ashley will be better able to develop a healthy style of connecting with others, quite possibly her husband.

I sense that Ashley sought a partner she could take care of, just like she had to do with her mother. Freud called this *repetition compulsion*— our unconscious need to reenact early childhood traumas as a way of working through them. Ashley will need to see the repeating pattern she is engaging in with her loved ones and start challenging her core beliefs around what it means to be loved. She'll also need to learn to give herself validation, instead of continuing to seek it by performing for others.

My thoughts are interrupted by the ticking clock on the bookshelf, a reminder that it's not possible to get to everything in the first appointment. I give Ashley my initial impressions and end our session by leading an exercise to help her get grounded and present using all of her senses.

It's clear to me that Ashley has anxiety, and it's no wonder. Her father abandoned her, leaving her without a male figure in her life and feeling obligated to her mother. She learned to carefully monitor her mother's moods and be a "good girl" to avoid the punishment of her mother's emotional outbursts. Experiences like this keep us hypervigilant to any potential threat in the past, present, or future. Our brain is constantly on alert for something bad that could happen, even when the possibility of it happening is actually quite low. With anxiety, we also overestimate the outcome of this projected misfortune and underestimate our ability to cope.

Still, Ashley does have some resilience in the face of difficult emotions. After all, she found a way to deal with her father leaving, as well as her own move away from her birthplace and later to a foreign country. But something changed for Ashley when she met her husband

and became a parent. What is her anxiety protecting her from? What does her partner do that makes her anxious? I can relate to Ashley—I too have spent years pushing away my own needs in hopes of making my relationship work—but I suspect there's something else at play for her. I am still missing the answers to my questions around her marriage. I sense that Ashley may have a secret.

Aware

Identifying Your Safety Behaviors and Adaptations

Part of your healing journey is coming to understand what you have learned about love and relationships in your formative years, as well as the strategies that you used as a child to adapt to your environment and avoid difficult experiences. Let's explore these here.

◇ How would your parents or caregivers react when you expressed difficult feelings and needs? Thinking about their reactions, was this what you wanted? If not, did you ask for what you needed?

◇ What did you learn about emotions from watching other people? For example, how was anger expressed in your family?

◇ When someone experiences insecurity in their relationship, you've learned that people can react by hyperactivating their needs (e.g., upping the ante, over-seeking reassurance from their partner, needing their partner to soothe them, protesting against boundaries) or deactivating their needs (e.g., shutting down, not turning toward their partner, keeping to themselves, numbing out, staying independent, not sharing their feelings). Take a moment here to write out what strategy you use during times of distress in your relationship.

◇ Considering your tendency to hyperactivate or deactivate, what are some ways you try to protect yourself from experiencing hard things (e.g., avoidance, playing the victim, making comparisons, people-pleasing, caregiving, self-criticism)?

CHAPTER 4

Karine and Peter

We all have triggers that set off difficult emotions. You can't eliminate these triggers, but you can learn to identify them, see when they are taking over, and respond to them differently. Being compassionate and curious when your partner is triggered can be a healing experience.

◇◇◇◇◇

"I was standing in the middle of the parking lot at his office, ready to explain myself." Karine talks to me first, then hesitantly addresses her partner, Peter. "You came storming toward me. I knew you were upset with me." Her eyes grow into wide circles while she squeezes her delicate hands.

"I told you it wasn't a big deal that you were late. Why can't you just believe me?" Peter snaps. I'm momentarily distracted by Peter's appearance—neatly styled dark brown hair, a crisply pressed blue shirt, and polished brown shoes that impatiently tap against the floor. Despite my effort to suspend judgment, it's not a stretch to imagine that this buttoned-down appearance goes along with a controlling character.

"But you barely said two words to me," she objects, scrunching her eyebrows together. "You got into the car and you were just . . . huffy."

Peter crosses his arms. "You're making a big deal out of this," he brushes her off. "We're good. Our relationship is fine. Why can't you trust me?"

Never in the history of relationships has it worked well to tell your partner that they're making too big a deal out of something. (It does, however, offer an entry point into my new clients' conflict.) Instead of being curious about the other person's emotional experience, they assume it's a reflection of themselves. "Why can't you trust me?" and "You were mad at me" are common things that people say when they experience emotional fusion. Despite how close their relationship is, they have lost the ability to build understanding and connection.

For Peter to see and validate what Karine is saying would require differentiation—for him to acknowledge that her emotions are different from his and to allow room in their relationship for both to exist at once. It doesn't help, as he stated right at the beginning of our session, that Peter doesn't "do" emotions—or, at any rate, not the kind of emotions that Karine is asking from him to fill her leaky emotional bucket. Karine's need for constant reassurance is a sign that she is overreliant on Peter to fill a void within her. What I'm curious about is why that frustrates him. *Does his frustration reflect a personality trait*, I wonder, *or a communication skill that he doesn't have?*

"Before we go forward, I have to know: What *was* going on, Peter?" I ask.

He sighs, reluctant to answer. "It's Charlotte. My ex-wife. She's always causing problems in our relationship."

Like all couples, Karine and Peter's romantic histories play a key role in their current situation. At the time they met, Peter had been divorced for five years, and it had been almost three years since Karine's divorce from an ex-husband who spent most of their marriage directing hostility and contempt toward her. She was worried that she hadn't shown her children (ages ten, thirteen, and fifteen) a model of a healthy marriage, which made her reluctant to date anyone new—what if she made the same mistakes again? Eventually, though, Karine's girlfriend introduced her to Peter. "You have to meet him," the friend had said. "He is kind and caring and he also has a kid. You'll really like him." Karine felt ridiculous being set up at the age of forty-five, but with this endorsement, how could she say no?

Her friend wasn't wrong. Peter, a fifty-year-old father to a nine-year-old daughter, was indeed a catch—good looks, subtle charm, a stable career amplified by a successful side business. They met for coffee and developed a quick connection. Peter was attracted to Karine's caring nature, which aligns with her profession as a nurse. Karine appreciated Peter's thoughtfulness—he liked holding the door for her, ensuring she wasn't cold, and making dinner reservations. During their courtship phase, he had appeared emotionally open and willing to really listen to Karine, a sharp contrast to the irritability and frustration he shows her now that they are committed (though not married) life partners. Karine's fear of repeating past mistakes has returned in full force; she often wonders if she was duped.

In a way, she *was* duped, though I doubt it was Peter's intention. Unhealed wounds from childhood don't necessarily show up in the honeymoon stage. Instead, they are more likely to emerge once we grow more settled into a relationship, catching us by surprise. Karine and Peter are playing out old parts of themselves in their relationship. It's also common in blended families for co-parents to revert to their old relationship cycle when things get stressful. After all, these are the patterns that drove apart their first relationships.

A look of annoyance crosses Karine's face as she looks at me. "Peter doesn't tell me about the emails Charlotte sends him. That day, she emailed him demanding that he send back clothes from our house. Clothes that *I* bought for his daughter. Charlotte is always trying to control him, and Peter lets her walk all over him."

"Peter, would you agree? That Charlotte controls you?" I ask.

"Not at all," he states. "Karine is just looking to blame Charlotte."

Karine lets out an audible sigh.

"What happens for you when you get these requests from Charlotte?" I ask. "It sounds like you came out of the office angry and upset."

"I'm just looking out for Brielle, my daughter," Peter says. "If I don't respond to Charlotte, she makes shared custody ten times worse than it already is. I don't want my daughter to have to deal with her mother's toxicity. It's easier to just give in. I told you that, Karine."

"I know—whenever Charlotte wants something, you are there for her. But you aren't there for me in the same way. You get home late. You go to your office early. You never tell me when you are changing plans. You just leave me hanging." Karine's exasperation is evident, a contrast to her naturally gentle demeanor. Her pale cheeks grow to the hue of an apple.

"I'm not there *for* her," Peter refutes.

"What do you do, Karine, when Peter does this?" I redirect them out of the semantics to learn what roles they are playing in their relationship.

"I ask questions—lots of questions—to get information from Peter. I also make sure the kids have everything they need. And I try to be flexible. Isn't that what a good partner does?" she asks.

To a certain extent, I think, *but not if you're stuck in a difficult pattern that isn't really working for you.*

Being in a relationship means navigating the tension that comes with being a separate self *and* an intimate partner. When our fear of being alone or abandoned outweighs our fear of losing ourselves, we find any way possible to merge with our lover, even if those actions don't really work for the greater good of the self and the relationship. One common dysfunctional pattern that can emerge from this is the *overfunctioning-underfunctioning* dynamic. In this dance, the overfunctioning partner tends to take more control over planning, provides caring (sometimes too much), and tries to fix things for others. Meanwhile, the underfunctioning partner relies more and more on their partner to make plans and decisions on their behalf, doesn't complete a fair share of household or childcare tasks, and procrastinates or frequently asks for help. While this dynamic works in the short term by letting each person remain in their comfort zone, in the long term, partners end up feeling disconnected and resentful.

I suspect this is what is happening between Karine and Peter. Still, I get the sense they have a good foundation. They began the session by echoing to each other that they wanted to build stronger communication now that they are four years into their relationship. They even exchanged a look of admiration as they shared this detail. Karine had reached out to hold Peter's hand as she said, with hope in her voice, "We want to improve the way we talk to each other about our feelings. We want to show our children what it means to be in a loving relationship—not like what happened in our first marriages." It's good to see that their emotional foundation is still intact, even though there is real distress in their relationship. The house may have some broken windows and could use a new roof, but the structure is sound.

I ask about Karine's core emotions when Peter came storming out of the office that day. I want to know what she does to cope and whether or not that coping is functional. Does it bring her closer to Peter (and to differentiation and interdependence) or further away from him (and to fusion)? I also want to suss out whether her timid affect includes any fear of him getting physical when he's upset.

Karine confirms what I suspected: While there's no physical violence between them, she feels fearful of Peter's anger but never tells him so. Her reluctance to disclose her true feelings doesn't bring them a sense of connection, though. It only leads them further away from differentiation. Hiding one's experience doesn't lead to a separate self or the understanding of the self and the other.

"Peter comes out and says there is nothing wrong, but you believe something different," I suggest, wondering if this response derives from her individual experience or a past event with Peter. "I'm wondering, did you consider that his anger might not have been about you? From what you're telling me, you didn't do anything wrong. What reasons would he have to be upset with you?"

Karine shakes her head and looks at me blankly. One more sign of her fusion with Peter is how she carefully monitors his feelings; she needs him to be okay before she can feel secure. I look to Peter to see if he can help dispel her belief that she must be the source of his irritation. He stares back at me expectantly, not sure what to say.

I go back to Karine. "How do you tell Peter what you need? Do you let him know, 'Hey, I need to be considered here too' or do you keep quiet?" I have noticed that partners tend to operate from one of two positions: either *I'm going to ask for my needs* or *I'm going to see if you can guess what my needs are.*

"No. I don't say anything about my feelings and needs," she replies. "If I can tell he's angry, I'm not going to share. I just go and problem solve on my own."

Karine tells me that in these difficult moments, she goes for a run or focuses on her work or the kids. As I described in chapter two, the flight response is one of the ways our nervous system responds to stress and conflict. This coping strategy begins to make sense as she shares her early childhood experiences. Most days, her father would come home and, in her words, "rage for hours." When he wasn't angry, he was in bed, unable to play with her. She recalled going into her father's room one day and asking him to look at the solar system project she completed at school, only to have him dismiss her. She didn't understand—how could she have?—that her father was suffering from undiagnosed depression.

Karine adds that her mother was so focused on her father's moods that she didn't notice what Karine was feeling. Karine's mother would frequently tell her, "We just need to make Dad happy" or "Daddy is sad today. Why don't you go help him be happy?" These were her mother's ways of being fused with her father, implicitly teaching Karine to do the same thing with significant others. Instead of being validated, Karine became skilled at de-escalating her father's volatility and hiding her pain from her mother. This evolved into an unconscious habit of reading the moods, gestures, and facial expressions of everyone she encountered for signs of emotional discomfort. Sometimes this ability has proved to be a strength, like when Karine sits at the bedside of ICU patients who can't tell her the suffering they are in. But it's a liability in a relationship where this coping mechanism isn't necessarily needed.

Karine can't see the ways she has fused with Peter because no one helped her to be autonomous as a child. My work with her will be focused on separating her feelings and sense of lovability and self-worth from Peter and teaching her what it means to create healthy intimacy with another person.

"I don't understand why you can't just come to me if you're upset," Peter mutters. This is his way of expressing empathy.

I ask Peter what he feels in these moments when she doesn't come to him.

"Frustrated!" he says. I'm soon to learn that Peter likes this word—we'll stay at "frustrated" for several sessions. Peter was referred from another colleague, so he knows what to expect from therapy: Go inward, share feelings, talk about the hard stuff. But I sense he isn't going to dig deep. Not yet, anyway.

"I hear you feel frustrated, Peter. Help me understand what you mean. Is it frustrated-sad? Frustrated-disappointed? Frustrated-alone?" This is a trick I learned to help my clients uncover more about their emotional experience. It's not that Peter doesn't have other emotions; it's that he doesn't allow himself to explore other aspects of his interiority.

He thinks about my question for a moment. "Frustrated-sad." He shifts in his seat, pulling his shirt collar away from his neck, then unexpectedly softens. "I love this woman. Why can't she just come to me when she's upset?"

Karine looks more open to listening when he talks about sadness. This will be important in our work together. His secondary emotions of frustration and anger remind her of her father and her ex-husband, both of whom always put their own needs before hers. She has described her ex as a narcissist who told her that nothing she did was ever good enough and who always guilted her for doing anything for herself. But here with Peter, I will help her see the softer parts of him that he is just beginning to reveal.

"But you were angry," Karine says. "You were angry *at* me. That's why I didn't talk to you on the way home." Wrinkling her brow, she blurts out, "And this is what is so frustrating, Dr. Tracy. No one sees me."

"No, you're getting it wrong." Peter's frustration kicks back in. "That's not what I said at all."

"I think I understand what's happening," I interrupt. Being a couples therapist requires me to be attuned to the dance that is happening between them and not get caught in the content of their back-and-forth. Sometimes I have to play traffic cop, redirecting partners before they get sucked into their negative cycle. "Peter, you were angry because Charlotte sent you an email about your daughter. But Karine, when you saw Peter's face and external expression of emotion—his anger—you were triggered. It stirred up self-blame and self-doubt because you thought it was about you, right?"

"How else am I supposed to take it?" She literally cannot consider another reality.

"Peter, what was going through your mind at that moment?" I ask, giving him the opportunity to disprove her unhelpful beliefs right here and now.

"I was so angry at Charlotte," he answers. "She threatened to say something to our daughter that would make me out to be the bad guy for not allowing her to go to a last-minute concert with her mother. This is our weekend with Brielle—it's part of our co-parenting agreement. But Charlotte is constantly trying to change our arrangement."

"And when Karine picked you up, you were in that headspace. It wasn't about Karine." I turn to her. "Karine, can you let it sink in that Peter wasn't angry at you, but instead was having his own internal experience?"

This is the concept of *mentalization*, which is the ability to see and understand the self, the other, and the self in context of the other. It's important in our relationships to acknowledge that our loved ones can have entirely different experiences than what we are perceiving from them, and that their outward expressions, emotions, and needs are not necessarily about us.

To be clear, I'm not saying that anyone should have to be okay with their partner's inappropriate expression of anger just because it doesn't have to do with them. What I am saying is that a healthy relationship requires allowing your partner the space to have their own experiences and feelings. This allowance must coexist with your own boundaries and needs. If your partner is angry and raging at you, you have a right to say something like "Love, I see you had an awful day. It's triggering when you slam the cupboards; it reminds me of my dad's anger. I need you to find a different outlet" or "I see that you're angry and it's not okay to yell at me." Statements like these can sometimes feel foreign for people who struggle with differentiation and boundaries, but with practice, they can be very empowering.

Next, I shift to helping Peter understand what happens for Karine in these moments by sharing the concept of *flipping the lid*, as described by psychiatrist and author Dr. Dan Siegel. When we are triggered by something, whether it's an email from an ex or an argument about the kids, the emotional part of the brain (the amygdala) takes over and the rational part of our brain (the prefrontal cortex) goes offline. Because our bodies feel these triggers before we can think, we are no longer able to regulate ourselves or even think rationally in these moments, let alone express our needs in a comprehensible and appropriate manner. This makes it very hard to stay connected, even when that's what we want most. Instead, we "flip our lid" by lashing out, people-pleasing, running away from the source of the trigger, or engaging in other unhelpful coping strategies.

Peter nods as I explain this, but I'm not completely sure that he fully registers the impact of his behavior on Karine's brain. In her childhood and her first marriage, Karine wasn't allowed to make mistakes. Now with Peter, a man who seems to allow imperfection, her old coping skills are no longer effective—she can't appease him by overfunctioning, so instead she withdraws, afraid of what his emotions mean about his love for her. Meanwhile, Peter is used to coping by shutting down his emotions. When he met Karine, he felt himself opening up, but when Karine started spiraling into insecurity, he quickly returned to what felt more familiar. This only contributes to Karine's uncertainty about the security of their relationship. The more she feels unloved, the more he shuts down in defense—and on goes the cycle.

Peter must learn that Karine's unhappiness is not related to his adequacy (another assumption that indicates emotional fusion). She is allowed to be upset, to have her own feelings and reactions. In some ways, Peter takes a similar position to Matt (from chapter one) in his relationship cycle—getting defensive, shutting down. But unlike Matt, Peter doesn't need constant validation of his worthiness. What he does need is to get less "frustrated" when Karine is unhappy.

I assign them the simple homework of talking about one emotion each day over dinner. Peter raises his eyebrows and clears his throat. On his way out the door, he announces, "I told you before, Dr. Tracy. Emotions are a waste of time. It's Karine that needs the help here." I look at Karine, who widens her eyes in disbelief. Both of us wonder if he wasn't listening for the entire session.

Peter thinks that Karine needs to be "fixed," but creating healthy interdependence is going to require both of them to do the work. When one partner doesn't believe they need to change, my work is even harder, especially if the hypothesis I'm forming about Peter is correct: that Karine may have chosen yet another partner who repeats the patterns in her past.

Aware

What's Triggering You?

A trigger is an experience, either internal or external, that ignites a reaction, often anger or frustration. Some triggers are familiar and can be easily identified; others may be discovered in a new stressful experience. Take some time here to reflect on your triggers.

◈ Think back to your last fight—what started it? Was it something your partner did or said? If you can't think of the last time you disagreed or argued with your partner, try thinking of the last time you felt triggered by your kids or a work colleague.

◈ What did you start to think or feel in the moment you became triggered? What perceptions of your partner or the situation did you have? What assumptions did you make about your partner's behavior or the motivations behind their actions?

◈ Now imagine yourself as a child experiencing this same moment of friction and consider what others (e.g., parents, caregivers, teachers, friends) would do in the following two scenarios: If you acted the same way your partner (or kid or colleague) did, how would others around you respond? If you reacted the same way you did when you felt triggered, how would others around you respond?

◈ Practice placing a hand over your heart and saying to yourself, *We all get triggered. We all have difficult experiences. This is what makes us human. I am learning to be compassionate to this part of me that gets triggered. I am learning to be kind to me.*

CHAPTER 5

Tracy

You must accept that your partner will perceive the same events differently than you do. These differences stem from early childhood experiences that lead you (and your partner) to have certain assumptions and interpretations about yourself and others. The ability to understand that your partner has an entirely different experience than you is an important part of building differentiation.

◇◇◇◇◇

About a year into our relationship, when I knew that Greg would become my future husband, I sat down and carefully crafted an Excel spreadsheet called "My Life" that mapped out the next ten years in two columns. In my Significant Life Event column, I included my dissertation proposal, data collection and defense date, clinical residency, PhD graduation, Greg's proposal, and our wedding. And in the Date Expected column . . . Well, you get the picture.

Based on my clinical training, I knew this wasn't a healthy strategy for planning out our future as a couple. Nevertheless, I emotionally clung to those columns when life felt tumultuous, never considering that my one-day husband might have different plans. Having such a rigid view of what my life should look like, including my marriage, meant that just about anything Greg did was bound to disappoint me. Setting up my expectations so early in the relationship only set us up for disconnection down the road.

In the first session with couples, I ask, "When did the disconnection begin?" For some, the exact moment rolls off both partners' tongues, with the familiarity of the narrative only exacerbating their relationship distress. In other situations, one partner identifies the disconnection while the other doesn't see the problem, whether it's because they're living in ignorant bliss or because they have completely different needs. Some of these couples have experienced an *attachment injury* in the relationship, in which one partner violates the expectation of providing security and care for the other partner in times of distress. The attachment injury can also come in the form of infidelity—sexual, emotional, or financial. For many people, cheating is where they draw the line, a cue to end the relationship. What people fail to understand is that infidelity is not just about the person who cheated. As shown by the work of psychotherapist Esther Perel, infidelity is a sign that something is missing in the relationship, that some need within the cheating partner is not being met. But for both men and women who show up in my office with an affair to disentangle, both the offender and the injured partner are less interested in the cause of the infidelity than in answering the question "Should I stay or should I go?" The answer is never clear-cut. I have seen people heal in ways that they couldn't have before the infidelity, empowering them to do the hard work of building a new relationship.

I have also worked with couples whose disconnection has led them to *conscious uncoupling*, a term created by psychotherapist Katherine Woodward Thomas in 2009 and popularized by Gwyneth Paltrow that reflects a mutual decision to amicably end a commitment. Some of these couples have been married for twenty or more years and then, once the kids are gone, decide they no longer want to be together. Other couples identify a slow unraveling that results in suddenly waking up to find their connection is "lost at sea," leaving them confused as to when their co-captain abandoned ship.

Nearly all these couples echo each other when they describe their goals for therapy: "We just want to feel like we did when we first started dating." What they really mean is they want to feel the same way they did when they first recognized "their person" in each other—the one who checked off every box on their spreadsheet, who made them say "Yes! Sign me up!" Everyone longs for the excitement that comes with the honeymoon period (or the limerence stage, as we call it in the world of relationship studies). The text messages that say, "I can't wait to see you tonight." The lingering kiss that sends tingles through your body. The inside jokes, the shared memories, the easy flow of conversation. While we don't ever go back to the same feelings of this particular season, we can continue to build excitement and deepen our connection by doing what we did back then: sharing our authentic and vulnerable selves. Strangely, it's a lot easier to do this with someone we're just getting to know than with someone who has proved to be more complicated, more human, than the dream-come-true we signed up for.

Before Greg and I had our son, I knew that relationship satisfaction plummets in the first three years after having a baby. I guess I thought that forewarned is forearmed, so it is a shock to realize that I have become part of this statistic. It's not only shocking, it's confusing. I feel a deep sense of gratitude and connection when I sit quietly on the living room chair and watch Greg zoom cars back and forth with Anderson, catch him before he falls, bring him from tears to laughter in mere moments, and teach him that it's okay to feel all of his feelings— messaging that many men didn't get while growing up. Yet at the same time that I melt at Greg's outpouring of love for our child, I struggle to feel the same closeness toward him that I used to feel.

The one thing I know I shouldn't do is keep hiding my struggle. The trouble is that others see me as floating easily through life; they presume that I have no difficulties. I left my childhood hometown to attend the university of my choice. I was among the 5 percent of applicants accepted to the PhD program for clinical psychology. I finished the degree (even though I never felt like I was good enough) and landed not only a top-ranked residency but also the dream post-grad job. To top it all off, I found a partner who committed to spending his life with me, we welcomed the first grandson of both families, and now I have the "perfect family." I, too, can see that it certainly looks like I "have it all," so if I'm still struggling, there must be something wrong with me. At least, that's what my inner narrative keeps telling me.

No one knows that motherhood has made me feel like a discarded toy, placed in a dark cupboard and just waiting for someone to play with me again. When I show up to family events, family members either pay attention to my son or critique my parenting choices. Strangers stop me to ask, "Is he a good boy? Does he sleep for you?" Even my massage therapist didn't see me as a patient needing support. Instead, as she dug her thumbs into my shoulder blades, she asked me what key ingredients I believe a couple need to make a healthy relationship. (I provided a vague response, instantly regretting that I told her my profession but not about to abandon a good massage.)

Today, we're supposed to be having one of those Instagram highlight reel kind of days together at the neighborhood park, but I can't shake this feeling that all this "smiling family of three" business is more like a performance, another check mark on the to-do list. Nevertheless, I dutifully play my designated role of Happy Mom, cheering Anderson on as he pulls himself up to the red tunnel. The last thing I want is for this day to go awry—this is my chance to connect with Greg, something I've been needing deeply. With him having to work on Saturdays, Sunday is our only day together as a family, and I feel a lot of pressure to make the most of it.

Greg doesn't seem to feel that pressure, though. He's sitting on the park bench, staring intently at his phone. I remind myself to be patient, that it's probably something work related, that I'm better off leading with compassion for his workload than with my anger at his company's demands.

"Did something stressful happen?" I ask, leaning back on the park bench. I attempt to nudge Greg to bring up things that he doesn't think to share with me. Some people can give a play-by-play of their days with every minor detail of what they did and thought. Others, like Greg, give the minimum. After all, responding to this question requires going inward, recalling short-term memories, identifying thoughts and feelings from the day, putting them into words, and speaking them out loud—and that's without knowing whether they'll even be met by someone who is open to receiving the information. While all this comes easily to an external verbal processor like me, a more withdrawn individual hesitates: *Last time I opened up to you, were you receptive? Curious? Understanding? Because if you weren't, if I felt a hint of judgment or rejection, then I might not want to share right now.*

Here's my pro tip for avoiding this particular pothole: Find really specific questions to ask your loved one, such as "Tell me more about that," and become a really good listener. It's classic behavioralism as shown by B.F. Skinner's experiments with rats and dogs: If you want someone to repeat a behavior, provide positive reinforcement—and lots of it. By giving attention to your partner's disclosures and showing that you are interested in them, they are more likely to continue to share more with you next time.

Still, despite knowing all this and wanting to be a good and active listener in my relationship, I wait passively as Greg shares a tense experience he had with a customer. If I'm honest, I don't really want to hear about his day at work. I want the conversation to move to *us*. As soon as I find a moment to insert myself, I ask, "Why don't we plan a day trip to the beach as a family next week?" Making plans is a strength that I bring to the relationship, but I long for Greg to take over this task, even though it's not his forte. For me, it would mean that he's thinking of me, that he's excited enough about spending time with me to think ahead and plan this for *us*.

He nods at the idea. Then his pocket buzzes and he pulls his phone out.

My cheeks flush and my leg begins to bounce up and down with impatience, but I'm quickly redirected by wails from the playground. Anderson is face down in the woodchips; my heartstrings tighten. Just over a year old, he's still a little wobbly on his feet. But with some soothing words and brushing off, he returns to climbing on the play structure.

I look over at Greg. He's still on his phone. My jaw clenches.

I used to look at this man with nothing but admiration and passion. I was captivated by just being beside him. Despite being apart for weeks or sometimes months during our courtship, we both had a sense of knowing the other person; whenever we reunited, our conversations flowed with ease. After we got married and Greg moved to Ottawa, where I was based, we settled effortlessly into a natural rhythm of daily life. We took turns making dinners. We grocery shopped together. We still had our own separate activities and interests that brought us joy, but we were always eager to come back together and share our experiences. We had more than just desire; we had time and intentionality.

That everyday intimacy is a far cry from our relationship today. Instead of long chats on the couch with our feet nestled in each other's laps, we have nightly scrolling sessions conducted from separate chairs. Instead of leaping with excitement to hear about his day, my heart hardens with grim speculation about whether I will be doing bedtime with our son again and, if so, whether Greg will at least wash the dishes while I'm in the nursery. Instead of the warm fulfillment I hoped for from this family day at the park, I feel irritated by him being here with us yet not truly present.

For a while, I refocus on Anderson and start playing a game of peek-a-boo through the holes of the tunnel. But when Anderson stops paying attention to me, I take my seat beside Greg again. He looks up from his phone. "I got an email from the head office this week about our annual work trip."

I keep my eyes averted as he groans about the drudgery of having to sit through several days of meetings and presentations, and point out that his work trip isn't *really* that hard for him. Yes, there will be meetings, but there will also be sunshine, beers, and multiple rounds of golf. Irritated, Greg insists that he misses us while he's away and would much rather be at home. I nod and try to sympathize, but it's difficult for me to digest his complaints about this type of trip. When he's gone, I'm left to carry the burden of the household and childcare while managing my own busy work schedule. He is either minimizing what his trip means for me or he's oblivious to it. Either way, it's infuriating. It takes me back to a place I try to avoid, a memory that has been playing in the background of our relationship ever since I gave birth to our child.

At forty-one weeks of pregnancy, my labor finally started. Contrary to everyone's "You'll be early" predictions, I was past my due date, and the long, sharp contractions came as a relief—finally, I would get to meet our son. (Not to mention, be able to sleep on my stomach again.) I texted Greg to notify him that I was in labor and he replied with, "Are you sure?" At my insistent "YES," he raced home and started packing the car in panic mode. In no time, our birth plan turned upside down. Instead of a non-medicated birth with my midwife in a dimly lit birthing room, it was blazing lights, a team of hospital residents, and the obstetrician giving me my options while I signed a consent form between contractions. When my water finally broke at nine centimeters dilated, my midwife's internal exam revealed a little baby bum. My baby was a surprise breech, which meant I would be transferred from my midwife to the care of obstetrics. In what Greg would later call my first act of being a brave, fierce mother, I opted for an urgent cesarean section to ensure the safe delivery of our baby.

I spent several nights in the hospital, overcome with exhaustion and disappointment. The incision through the layers of my abdomen was a glaring reminder that my body had betrayed me. I spent weeks feeling like a failure as a mother—how had I not known that my son was in the wrong position? The post-surgery care and pain that followed me home added insult to injury by forcing us to accept help from my mother-in-law. On the first night in the hospital, she rightly told Greg that it would be "a lot to recover from major surgery with a newborn" and offered to come and stay with us. Despite our initial wishes of having no overnight visitors in our home while we bonded with our son in those first days as parents, we agreed with a tired yes.

The overwhelm didn't ease with the addition of hands. On the second day home, we decided to give Anderson his first bath. It was one of the "firsts" that I was especially looking forward to. Throughout my pregnancy, I'd dreamed of this special bonding moment with my new baby, and the idea grew even more sacred when I was hidden away pumping milk for twenty minutes at a time while Anderson was lovingly passed between Greg and my in-laws. The photos from that time show everyone else snuggling with my sleepy newborn. I was alone in the nursery, crying about how my life had just been turned upside down.

But at last, the moment I'd dreamed about came. I slowly lowered Anderson into the warmth of his shallow bath, ran the washcloth over his wrinkly skin, and gazed into his big blue eyes as he gazed back into mine. The pain in my abdomen grew quiet with the rush of joy that came over me, and my heart warmed with confidence that we could be a good team together.

He started to cry, letting me know he was done. Keeping one hand on his belly, I reached with the other for a towel. It wasn't there. Suddenly, in one quick swoop, my mother-in-law wrapped my son into her arms, snuggling him into her chest and whispering into his ear. She'd had the towel the whole time.

My heart pounded loudly in my ears. My stomach churned. I felt robbed—the ending of the first bath felt literally stolen from my arms. Searching for words but coming up empty, I glanced over at my husband and begged him with my dropped jaw and wide eyes to step in, to ask his mother to pass our son back to me.

Instead, Greg stood across the dining room with a deer-in-the-headlights look. My eyes started to fill up. As my mother-in-law continued to coo in my son's ear, I made my way to the bathroom. Tears overflowed from my eyes as the word *abandoned* kept repeating in my head.

Greg taps me on the shoulder, bringing me back to the park. I blink a few times at him and give a smile that we both know is forced. Whether he realizes it or not, Greg's work trip, and even his way of characterizing it as a drag, is a big trigger for me, one that picks at my not-feeling-seen scab. It's a familiar feeling, pulling up a core belief—that I am not lovable, that there is something wrong with me—and mapping it onto today's events. But knowing where the feeling comes from doesn't stop it from appearing anytime we are fighting about the dirty dishes, the mismatched socks, or the demands of extended family during the holidays. The fights may get resolved, but they leave me questioning how long I will feel invisible in my marriage. *When will my husband start putting in the same effort as me? How can I release this anger once and for all? Why can't I seem to use my training as a couples therapist to improve my own marriage?*

I tell my clients that change is uncomfortable. But I'm beyond uncomfortable right now. I'm unsettled by these questions and the feelings they stir up in me. Still, I'm not sure I'm ready to risk the vulnerability it will take to change our direction. Recognizing that family day has run its course, we pack up Anderson and head home.

Aware

Healthy Individuation and Separation

To understand individuation and separation, think of yourself and your partner as two separate boxes. Inside your box, you have your own thoughts, feelings, opinions, desires, wishes, and values. Inside your partner's box, they have their own thoughts, feelings, and so forth.

Me	You
Thoughts	Thoughts
Feelings	Feelings
Opinions	Opinions
Desires	Desires
Wishes	Wishes
Values	Values

These boxes represent healthy separation. When we are fused, we lose the lines between you and me. As two separate people, we must remember that we are not responsible for the internal experiences of another person. Your job is to communicate and be responsible for *your* internal experiences.

◊ When your partner is upset, can you practice seeing them as having a separate experience from you? Write out a mantra or statement of radical acceptance that would help you remember this.

◊ Do you have a ritual of connection? Distressing moments are unavoidable in relationships. When the kids are pulling for your attention, dinner is burning on the stove, and stress levels are rising, sometimes we snap or say hurtful things to our partner. In these moments, practice a ritual that will help you see your partner as a teammate rather than as another source of stress. Here are just a few ideas:

　◊ Hold hands and squeeze them while looking into each other's eyes.
　◊ Use an expression like "I got this one."
　◊ Remind yourself or say out loud, "We're on the same team."

CHAPTER 6

Lydia and Sam

Beneath the disagreements, there is an inner child with deep wounds. These unhealed childhood wounds replay in our relationships today. Instead of being able to differentiate from our partner, we become fused together, trying to get the other to give what we truly wish for. But this inevitably backfires. As one person tries to get closer, the other moves further away, creating a never-ending cycle of abandonment and rejection. To get what you want from your partner, you must first become responsible for your internal experiences.

◇◇◇◇◇

"You come highly recommended, and we need to talk to you about our marriage," Lydia, one half of my new couple, blurts as I open the door. She's clutching her leather briefcase under her arm as she hurries into my office, long orange-red hair flowing behind her. Her husband, Sam, is noticeably less hurried. He saunters in from the waiting room, taking in the art on the walls before moving the couch pillows to the floor and taking a seat far apart from his wife. What is Sam's reason for distance? Is he a willing attendee, ready to engage? Or is he aloof and unaware of the difficulties in their relationship? I've barely had the chance to welcome them, yet I can already tell that there is an unspoken pressure—scratch that, an expectation—to solve their problem.

"Why don't we start at the beginning?" I suggest.

Lydia launches in, no holds barred. "Sam decided he wants out." Her approach to starting our work together is like pushing her husband off the deep end into an icy pool. Unsurprisingly, Sam says nothing.

"There must be something that changed, then. Otherwise, you wouldn't be here today," I say, trying to draw Sam out.

Sam looks at both of us as if to gauge what is required of him. Finally, he speaks. "We have a long history together," he shares. "It's not something that I want to just throw away."

I learn that Lydia and Sam first met in high school while sitting beside each other in class. They didn't date then and often spent time outside of class with different friend groups. However, Lydia liked that Sam was different from her. He was in the high school band and worked his best dance moves in drama class performances. Lydia was "book smart" and aspired to be a physician. When she didn't get into a competitive pre-med program in university, she promptly changed directions and pursued law.

Lydia and Sam reconnected after high school on social media. At the time, Lydia was studying for her LSAT exams in Kingston, while Sam was bartending and making his way from culinary school into top restaurants in Toronto. The romance that developed from their online chats took them both by surprise. Unlike many couples, the two-and-a-half-hour drive proved not to be a barrier for them, and they found ways to have romantic getaways across the US border: exciting weekday adventures, sunset walks along the lake, long dinners out after Lydia had been studying all day. Sam would stay in her apartment for days at a time, then return to Toronto on the weekends for work.

Hearing their story, my mind flashes to the long-distance relationship that Greg and I endured. While it was filled with passion and adventure in the honeymoon stage, it eventually turned to struggle and grief. We didn't get to have dinner together on a whim. Family events were separate. Our calendars had to be aligned and flights scheduled in advance for us to have the shared spontaneous experiences that most couples enjoy during the courtship phase. Strangely, our difficulties connecting only intensified when Greg finally moved within driving distance of Ottawa. I would express a wish for time together, but he dreaded the two-hour drive (a new conflict for us, as the travel never bothered him back when I was a four-hour plane ride away). We ended up seeing each other less, and our time together didn't feel rewarding.

It seems Sam has been feeling a similar wedge intruding on their closeness. "This feeling—a lack of joy between us—has been going on for a while," Sam continues. "I feel like I simply exist beside Lydia. She's never home. She works long hours. Her work is number one and I feel like I don't have a say in what our life looks like. We don't do anything together. She comes home tired and talks about everything that is stressful: her clients, her cases, the firm. Where do I fit in?"

Lonely and desperate to connect, Sam finally spoke up last month. After serving bowls of rice and green curry chicken, he took his seat across from Lydia and, as she lifted a fork full to her mouth, blurted out, "I'm done." Pausing mid-bite, Lydia demanded they seek therapy together. Sam admits that his announcement was more an act of desperation than a real ultimatum. He was trying to get Lydia's attention—and it worked. Actually, it rocked her world. She had been living in denial, believing her partner was fine. Yes, he seemed a bit down, but don't we all have melancholy stages? With the problem thus rationalized, she had continued to prioritize her job—working late, taking on more cases, answering emails at all hours.

"I want to make it work," Sam expresses to me.

"No," Lydia interrupts, shaking her head. "Sam *needs* to make it work."

This is a common refrain I hear in sessions: the idea that a marriage *must* be saved. While the intention to uphold a commitment is a good one, I hear less of a heartfelt desire in this statement and more of an absolutist form of thinking that is often tied to wounds from a person's

61

childhood. I ask Lydia what she means by this, as Sam stares up at the ceiling.

"I'm the breadwinner. I bring in the money for our family so Sam can pursue his *other* interests." Her eyes harden and narrow into slits. The way she emphasizes the word *other* is not lost on me; she seems to be intentionally choosing her words to send a message to her husband.

I sense Lydia holds the power in this relationship, which is an important concept to examine and understand between two people. Sometimes in a relationship we give up our power intentionally; other times, it is taken over by the other person. These clearly delineated roles—leader and follower, manager and assistant—can be beneficial to a degree, simplifying the process of making big decisions (e.g., when to move, navigating finances, parenting approaches) and even little decisions (e.g., what to do for dinner). The problem is when these roles get so familiar that their expressions become extreme, one partner becomes aggressive ("I'm going to hold all the power") and the other becomes passive ("I'm going to give up my autonomy"). Power dynamics taken to the extreme are simply unsustainable in a healthy relationship. The person with no power will eventually try to find some way to feel and express their autonomy—it's a basic human need.

The attempt to control another person disconnects you from finding the *we* in your partnership just as much as people-pleasing does. Both approaches lack the differentiation necessary for an authentic, healthy bond between two people. I'm curious about what other attempts at control are being played out between Lydia and Sam.

Sam looks at Lydia, his skin deepening in color. "You know that isn't fair, Lydia. You know I struggle with this part. I want to be able to contribute equally to the family, and I try to show up in other ways. I do everything for you—I make the dinners, I look after the house—all so you can keep pursuing your career. My career is different, and you know it can't take off here in Ottawa. But of course you didn't even consider living somewhere else—I wouldn't expect that from you."

This last sentence, laced with contempt, tells me that Sam has a long history of repressing his needs. *This couple should have been here a long time ago*, I think.

It is clear that Lydia and Sam are struggling with some common communication patterns that can devastate relationships. As described by relationship experts Drs. John and Julie Gottman, these communication styles are known as the "Four Horsemen" because they often lead to the destruction of a relationship: *criticism, defensiveness, stonewalling*, and *contempt*. The existence of any of these patterns is a major red flag for the health of a relationship. According to their research, couples who use these negative ways of communicating are at greater risk of separation and the dissolution of their relationship. Lydia and Sam are no exception.

Lydia argues back that she is trying to be supportive to Sam, that she wants him to do whatever fills him up, that she finds him attractive when he's doing things to light his spark. As proof, she begins listing out all the things he could be doing in Ottawa to fulfill himself creatively.

"You're doing it again," Sam interrupts her. "You're pontificating. TEDx-ing. Lecturing." Despite the fact that they're arguing, it's a good thing that they're talking to each other. It means that I can play a more objective role in their work. "Dr. Tracy, she's always telling me what I *should* be doing instead of actually hearing what I want to do," he adds to me. "I'm not some court case to be solved. I'm not a client needing professional guidance. I'm her husband."

Lydia explains why she's trying to help him, and her reasoning is sound: It's uncomfortable for her to be thriving in her career while Sam is floating at sea trying to find a port. I deeply relate to how she feels. I have frequently found myself shifting into solution mode with Greg, proposing ideas for what he should do to get out of the career rut he complains of. I do it from a place of discomfort of being unable to make someone change, from a need to grasp control of the outcome of our lives, but it never works in my favor; Greg just shuts down. I imagine that when Lydia sees Sam feeling good, she also feels at ease (a classic example of emotional fusion), but she doesn't see the negative impact her unsolicited problem-solving is having on her husband's listlessness, much less the relational cost of their fusion.

That said, the dynamic between Lydia and Sam runs much deeper than their circumstantial power imbalance. Lydia shares a key moment in the early days of their relationship, when both were in their late twenties. After dating for two years, Lydia thought that Sam would soon move to Kingston to be with her. Instead, Sam announced that he was moving back to South Asia, where he was born. He wanted to put a true effort into developing his culinary skills while connecting to his roots. Feeling duped and derailed, Lydia lost trust for her partner and began to wall herself off, working longer hours and throwing herself into her cases. Law was the only thing that brought her a sense of control and certainty.

Sam had made his decision based on the feeling that he needed this trip for self-discovery, even if it meant putting his relationship on hold. But after several months of lonely isolation in his home country, Sam decided to return to Kingston. He arrived home with a surprise: taking Lydia to their favorite secluded bench along the lake, he asked her to marry him. Lydia was ecstatic and said yes. However, their happy reunion had the side effect of masking the unhealed wounds from their pasts that they both brought into the marriage.

This couple holds a strong history together, clearly wanting to make it work. They are both engaged in life in their own ways and their overall functioning doesn't appear to be impaired by anxiety, depression, or any other mental disorder that could impact how they relate. That said, Sam could be at risk for developing depression if he continues to slip into his *anhedonic behavior* (a fancy therapeutic term for a precursor to depression) and detach from things that are meaningful to him. I also question the extent to which Lydia has healed from her felt sense of betrayal when Sam chose himself by moving away; her long hours at work seem like a way to bury her emotional pain.

We start our relationships making our partner feel like they are the sun to our Earth, and the safety we feel with them fosters a sense of comfortable familiarity. But this comfort can be precisely what changes passionate lovers into indifferent roommates living parallel lives. One thing I know to be true is that if we don't continue to make choices *toward* our relationship—spending intentional time together, sharing, getting curious, playing—it will wilt like an unattended houseplant.

Wanting to better inform my conceptualization of their problem, I meet with Sam separately the following week. I learn that, even though he was the one who gave the ultimatum, Sam actually wants the marriage to work. Despite being different from him in how she approaches life, Lydia has an intensity that he is drawn to: passion for her career, fearlessness in speaking her mind, a sense of purpose and drive that anyone would admire. (All traits, I note, that are opposite to him.)

When I ask about his upbringing, Sam tells me that he never felt adequate in his family. The youngest child of four, Sam was constantly measured against his brothers and their accomplishments. Specifically, his interest in music and food was a stark contrast to his brothers' pursuit of science, medicine, and engineering. Along with belittling Sam for his artistic desires, his mother would escalate into anger over the smallest infractions, like an untucked shirt or a toothpaste lid not replaced on the tube. These are all examples of how a parent doesn't allow for a child to build healthy differentiation from family members. This ends up lowering the child's self-worth and ultimately impacts their ability to be an autonomous individual or build healthy intimacy. Our relationships with our parents are our first models of what it means to connect with others, and I hear in Sam's stories a child yearning to be seen and accepted by his mother.

Sam discusses how his childhood experiences continue to follow him today, as he is under constant scrutiny for the ways he expresses himself (and his autonomy) that are counterintuitive to his parents' desires, including his passion for creating extravagant five-course meals. But cooking isn't the only way Sam tries to express himself. Last month, he made a rash decision after a few short sailing lessons and bought a boat, despite Lydia saying she wasn't interesting in spending her leisure time on the water. Sam's impulsive purchase has created a greater rift between them. He tells me he always wanted a boat, but I don't completely buy it; to me, it seems like an ego-driven cry for attention. I know that people with this tendency often escalate their behavior, making bigger and more outrageous moves as time goes by. Is Sam trying, even unconsciously, to create a crisis in his marriage?

A few weeks pass before Lydia reenters my office for her individual session, her briefcase tucked under her arm as though she is appearing in front of a judge. As she states the facts of her marriage, her school experiences, and her family, I find it no surprise that Lydia ended up in law. Throughout her childhood, she had to excel to gain her parents' approval. When she brought home near-perfect grades, her parents asked where the other 5 percent was. Their push for excellence made their daughter self-assured yet left her unable to celebrate her accomplishments. No child can see that they aren't supposed to be perfect, and Lydia always felt like there was more she should be doing because she wanted them to be proud of her.

But then Lydia's life was turned upside down at the age of thirteen when her father abruptly left the family. Despite the years of discord between her parents, she had assumed their arguing was normal and never thought that either of them would leave. She blamed herself for not being good enough for him to stay and questioned her own lovability. After all, how could a father leave his own daughter if there wasn't something fundamentally flawed with her? Her mother, lost in her own grief and needing help with managing the house, wasn't able to provide Lydia reassurance that his abandonment wasn't about her. She never seemed to see that Lydia was still just a child.

As soon as she was old enough, Lydia got a job and started contributing financially. When she left home at age seventeen, she took her habit of *self-abandonment* along with her. It now shows up in her relationship with Sam. For example, Lydia never shared her true feelings with Sam about his choice to go to South Asia; she just put her head down and worked harder. She hasn't admitted to Sam that she wishes he had more ambition or took more initiative with his talents. These days, every time she comes home from work and Sam is there with dinner waiting, she represses the knowledge that, even though she loves Sam, she's no longer excited by her relationship with him.

It's not uncommon for people to experience periods of dissatisfaction with their partner—it doesn't necessarily mean that it is a failed relationship. But Lydia's upbringing has given her a black-and-white understanding of success and failure, making it difficult for her to not see the normal challenges in her marriage as a complete crash-and-burn. It has also given her a misunderstanding of how to be close to someone that now hinders her ability to feel real intimacy. She continues to play out the role of provider in her marriage, not seeing that Sam is looking for something else entirely. He wants her to tap into *being* with him, but she wants to keep *doing*. After all, it's what she knows best.

Lydia bounces her leg and interlocks her arms over her body as though she might come undone if she releases her squeeze. With only a few minutes left of our one-on-one session, my gut starts to turn at the heavy silence between us. I intuitively feel a secret in the room.

Finally, it comes out. Lydia releases her arms, leans over her legs, and collapses her head into her hands. "I'm having an affair," she blurts out, lifting her head and running her hands back over her frizzy hair. "Or I was. I'm not anymore. I ended it a few weeks ago when Sam agreed to couples therapy." She takes a deep breath. "It was a man I went to school with. We happened to both be in court one day, and . . . I don't know, he's charming and engaging, and one thing just led to another. But it's nothing and I want my life to be with Sam. It's over," she repeats, more to herself than to me.

Oh shit. In contrast to my internal upheaval, my exterior stays still. I will my face to express empathy and warmth, even as I get right to the point.

"What was the draw for you? Sex? Or emotional connection? What did this relationship fill up for you that you were missing with Sam?" I ask.

"It was sex," she replies, without giving it thought. "Or maybe connection. I'm not sure."

After having met with Sam, I imagine it was likely both. Sam seems aloof and disengaged; having pushed down his passion for life, he takes a back seat and lets Lydia drive. But Lydia desires someone who, like her, has their own ambition.

Affairs aren't meaningless. According to psychotherapist Terrence Real, people engage in affairs for one of two reasons: They have a grandiose personality that leads them to believe they are entitled to the affair, or they are seeking something that is missing in their relationship. People who choose an extramarital partner are often searching for something they don't have in their current relationship: appreciation, power, feeling desired, being treated like they are special. When we find ourselves drawn into a romantic dynamic with someone outside our current relationship, it's important to examine what the attraction promises to give us. This can offer us an opportunity to see what is missing in our relationship so we can communicate our needs to our partner, an imperative for restoring connection and achieving the intimacy we desire.

Interestingly, dealing with the fallout of her affair feels less urgent for Lydia compared to the prospect of moving her relationship forward in an important way: After trying to conceive for over three years, Lydia has recently begun fertility treatments. In other words, she's making the decision to layer her commitment to Sam by pursuing having a baby. At some level, Lydia seems to intuit that the vulnerability of pregnancy could prompt Sam to step up and support her, restoring their connection.

Lydia tells me that she doesn't want to tell Sam about the affair. Even as a couples therapist, it is not my job to disclose it, but I advise her that secrets like this can get in the way of healing a marriage. It's ironic: Sam experienced Lydia's disconnection so deeply that he threatened to end the relationship, while Lydia, who insisted on couples therapy, has been pulling away with an affair. I'm starting to get a clearer picture of their struggle: two adults committed to each other, each trying to get the other to give them what they truly long for, but having it backfire, as fusion and codependency inevitably do. Each of them has deep inner child wounds calling the shots. Lydia fears that Sam will abandon her, just like her father did, while Sam struggles to feel accepted by Lydia for who he is, just as he struggled with his mother. As one person tries to get closer, the other moves further away, creating a never-ending cycle of abandonment and rejection. Our work in session will be to create healthy interdependence. Finding true connection with themselves will reignite the passion they once felt for each other.

◇◇◇◇◇

After my clients are done for the day, I exit my office to the waiting area. I share office space with several other clinicians, and this area has become our designated location to unwind after the clinic closes and to consult each other about difficult moments in our therapeutic work. Consultation with colleagues is important for therapists to maintain a high standard of care. It's worth noting, though, that while we talk about the process of therapy, various interventions for specific presenting issues, and places where we are stuck in session, we don't share identifying information of our clients.

"A secret affair. Tell me what I'm supposed to do with that?" I ask my colleague Meagan as we settle into our respective seats. We all hold secrets in our relationships to some degree—this is where trust comes into play—but this particular kind of secret puts a couples therapist in the difficult position of holding information that one half of the couple doesn't have. If Sam knew this information, it could change the course of their relationship.

Meagan helps me explore my options. I can encourage Lydia to tell her husband, but she could decide that this breaks our alliance and seek out a new therapist (and perhaps not tell that therapist of her affair at all). The other option is for me to hold this secret and help the couple navigate toward a stronger connection as best I can. From a clinical perspective, does it help or hinder to push this secret into the open?

Meagan wisely advises me that my first order of business is to calm my own discomfort at sitting with this secret. My selfish wish is that Lydia would open up about her affair, if only so that I don't have to sit in this tension every session.

"Remind me that we have good partners," I say to Meagan, only half joking.

"We have good partners." She swirls her water glass with a smirk. "*And* we get to feel annoyed when they can't find their keys or take initiative at home."

That's the thing about being a couples therapist. It can bring up issues in your own relationship or, just as easily, remind you of just how grateful you are for your partner. Right now, I'm feeling the latter. However much Greg and I have to figure out, it's comforting to know we aren't having secret affairs. We have a deep trust in each other today. More than we used to, in fact, because we've already tackled an issue like the one hiding between Lydia and Sam.

During my PhD, I went through a time when I was frequently frustrated and critical. Greg, meanwhile, was growing more and more defensive. Every conversation we had devolved into an argument. I was angry that we weren't living in the same city, angry that my PhD was taking over my life, angry that we weren't yet engaged and moving forward in our relationship. On the phone one night, Greg said he couldn't keep fighting and broke up with me. I spent the next few weeks collapsed on the floor of my one-bedroom apartment, heartbroken and stunned. This wasn't part of my spreadsheet! My old narratives about being defective, oversensitive, and not laid-back enough kept running through my mind like a horror movie playing on repeat.

After a six-week break, Greg called me and wanted to get back together. We had an emotional night of talking things through and setting new terms for our relationship. But later, while he was in the shower, I sneaked a look at his phone and discovered a series of text messages with another woman. Did I break his privacy? Yes. Had my gut intuition been right? Also yes. It turned out that before we broke up, Greg had been having an emotional affair with a woman he met in a bar. Texting with her became an escape from the tension in our relationship—she was easy to talk to, the connection felt exciting, and he felt less lonely. In short, it offered everything that had been slowly trickling out of our relationship. I finally understood why, for weeks, I had been feeling like I was pulling him toward me against something that was pulling him away. It was because that's exactly what *was* happening.

Discovering the infidelity was painful, yet we chose to stay together. But my trust with Greg was absolutely broken. I spent months needing frequent reassurance about our relationship. Fortunately, Greg was willing to own his mistake, and his responsiveness helped us heal. For my part, I had to get past my initial shock and hurt to go inward and take responsibility for how I'd contributed to our disconnection. My life felt so full of demands that I hadn't had the bandwidth to be an attentive and giving partner. I couldn't entirely blame him for seeking emotional comfort elsewhere. With time came the realization that it wasn't really anger I was feeling before our breakup. It was loneliness and loss of control. It was like the stressors of life were pelting down from the sky and I couldn't get my umbrella to open.

Today, when moments of insecurity arise (as they still do), I turn to Greg and say, "I feel distant and I have the urge to check your phone. Do

I have anything to worry about?" He replies, "No, love. I'm with you." Instead of choosing to linger in self-protective distrust, I believe him and lean into gratitude that we are on this journey together. This is what marriage asks of us: to choose each other over and over again, despite each other's past mistakes and ongoing challenges. I believe Lydia and Sam have what it takes to do this. The question is whether they're willing to be completely open with each other about the secrets they keep.

Aware

How Do You Abandon Yourself?

Self-abandonment contributes to depression, anxiety, and relationship dissatisfaction. People learn to abandon themselves as children when they live in hostile, critical, emotionally neglectful, or physically harmful environments. Explore the following questions to see how you might be abandoning your needs and *values* today in order to protect a relationship. While these questions are not diagnostic in any way, any that you answer yes to can shed insight into the specific ways you engage in self-abandonment.

◊ Do you struggle to trust your own thoughts and feelings? Do you ask others what they think before making a decision or double-check with a loved one?

◊ When you want to do something that matters to you but your partner is not interested, do you change your mind and decide not to do it?

◊ Do you feel unworthy or unlovable? Or that you have to prove your lovability to others?

◊ Are you highly self-critical or do you say mean things to yourself when you make a mistake? Is making mistakes painful or difficult for you?

◊ Would others call you perfectionistic? Do you self-identify as a perfectionist?

◊ Do you focus on meeting the needs of your partner? Do you ignore or dismiss your own needs?

CHAPTER 7

Ashley

Resentment is a toxic emotion that will erode the health of a relationship. It often reveals feelings and unmet needs that are not being shared. When you feel resentment rising up inside you, you are faced with a decision: Will you open up and share your feelings with your partner, or will you find other, less healthy ways to cope?

◇◇◇◇◇

"The red wine was *on* the couch. It was two a.m. Daniel had fallen asleep in some kind of drunken state. I was furious, but what could I say in the middle of the night? I sent him up to bed and tried to clean it the best that I could." Ashley rolls her eyes and lets out a heavy sigh from her chosen position in the middle of the couch.

When I asked her why she didn't get her husband to clean it up, she said that he probably couldn't do it right, so she just did it herself. This is a common response from clients, particularly female clients, that not only leads them to take on more than half of domestic responsibilities and *invisible labor* but also creates a precarious precedent in the relationship. The more one partner overfunctions by carrying the burden of household and childcare labor, the more likely that the other partner will underfunction, not taking on or even seeing the labor that needs to be done. Likewise, when a partner underfunctions, the overfunctioning partner feels they must fill in the gaps. When one person steps into criticism and overcorrection, the other feels undermined and inadequate. The cost is burnout, resentment, and deeper disconnection.

Eve Rodsky, author of *Fair Play: A Game-Changing Solution for When You Have Too Much to Do (and More Life to Live)*, describes three parts to a task within the family unit: conceptualize, plan, and execute. She states that women are more at risk for developing resentment when they only offload the execution of a task. I see this often in my practice. One partner—usually the husband—will say, "Just tell me what you want me to do and I'll do it!" And then they don't understand when their partner—usually the wife—is frustrated that she now needs to add telling him what to do to her list.

Is it a lack of engagement from Daniel that leads Ashley to do it all? If so, this could stem from a variety of sources: absence due to work (like military personnel, shift workers, or first responders), incompetence, or an overall disinterest in this role. (To be clear, none of these are good reasons for one partner to do it all.) It seems that "all of the above" apply in Ashley and Daniel's situation. Ashley describes frequent situations where Daniel is unaware of what needs to happen at home or in what sequence—for example, registering the kids for daycare, preparing their backpacks, responding to emails related to childcare.

The night of the wine spill, Ashley heard Daniel get home from his work event well after midnight, but she fell back into a light sleep. When she woke again, there was only darkness coming through the curtains and the spot beside her was cold. Tiptoeing down the stairs, she discovered Daniel passed out on the couch, still in his suit, head tilted back, and his mouth wide open. There were papers strewn across the coffee table. And of course, the tipped wine glass, still loosely held in his hand.

The next day, Daniel didn't say anything about the couch spill. Instead, he beamed about the social that followed his presentation, waving his arms around as he retold the events of the night. Ashley, barely keeping calm, nodded along while Daniel elaborated on the feedback from upper management. Ashley describes several more moments of not expressing her needs in the days that followed. She agreed to go to the park with the kids when she really needed quiet time in the house but didn't want to upset her husband by sending him alone. Whenever Daniel got home from work with furrowed brows and heavy sighs, she didn't ask for help with dinner and cleanup. Barely keeping her eyes open one night, she listened to him rant about office politics.

When we are distressed, we lean harder on familiar coping mechanisms, even when they are not helpful. Ashley's emotional fusion with others means she focuses on their happiness and doesn't vocalize her feelings or needs to anyone—her boss, her family, or her husband. As a result, her struggle with anxiety persists. She walks a tightrope, balancing feelings of burnout while continuing to please others. In the moment, anything feels better than anxiety, but avoidance only leads her feelings to come back even stronger. It's a vicious cycle.

I shouldn't be surprised that, despite attending regularly scheduled appointments with me, Ashley resists engaging in the strategies I suggest. It feels like she is playing baseball. She comes to the field with a problem in session, and we toss around different perspectives, strategies to deal with the anxiety, or invitations for self-compassion, but once it's time to go to bat, she just walks off the field, only to show up the next week wondering why things are so hard to change.

Admittedly, I'm struggling with Ashley. Now that we're several sessions in, Ashley discloses more effortlessly and with less prompting, which tells me we are building a *therapeutic alliance* (that is, how positively a client feels in the relationship with their therapist). Yet, from what I can tell, we aren't moving forward in any significant way.

This is a process. Adjust your expectations, Tracy. You'll get there, I think, taking a grounding breath and releasing the tension in my jaw. I remind myself that I need to be a safe place for Ashley, that if I impose my desired goals ("Share your feelings! Speak up for yourself!") too forcefully, she'll land in the same people-pleasing role with me.

Still, despite my impatience, I'm also deeply touched by Ashley. I recognize myself in her—I want to be liked, I want to belong, I tend to say yes to opportunities so that I don't disappoint others. I also recognize the profoundly human dilemma of understanding how I should behave yet feeling unable to do it when it matters most.

Ashley jumps to another story, even as she checks the time on her gold watch. Storytelling in therapy can be a way for clients to skirt around exploring their emotional experiences, but I'm allowing it today. Maybe something different will be revealed that will help me nudge her forward.

Ashley tells me that last night was "a disaster." The children were screaming up and down the hall after dinner, waving their pajamas in the air. Her favorite pink blouse had already been ruined at dinner when their youngest child spilled his bowl of beef bourguignon. She wanted to treat the stain, but after seeing Daniel checked out and on his phone during the pajama escapade, she resigned herself to focusing on getting the kids in bed so she could be officially "off duty" from parenting. Daniel eventually engaged in this two-person task, helping her get the kids settled in their separate rooms. Collapsing on the living room couch after, Ashley longed for comfort from Daniel. Instead, seeing her exhaustion, he snapped, "Other people can cope, so why can't you?"

I internally cringe at Daniel's response. He missed Ashley's *bid for connection*—her desire for attention, support, and affirmation. Instead of turning to her with kindness ("This was a hard night, I get it"), he turned to her with criticism. This type of dismissiveness breeds separation and feels like a smack to the face.

"I imagine this felt like a gut punch. You're exhausted, and your husband doesn't see all that you are doing." If she can't see how much she is doing, I will hold the mirror up for her. "What did you say to Daniel?"

"Nothing," she replies. "What's the point? You know I don't spend a lot of time on my feelings," she adds dryly. *Indeed, I do*, I silently agree. According to Ashley, Daniel's interest in her feelings is nonexistent.

Why would she make herself vulnerable if she believes that Daniel doesn't care?

Silenced by their exchange, Ashely took her blouse to the laundry room, scrubbing the stain over and over again as she questioned why she wasn't like all the other mothers who (she imagines) put their cooperative kids to bed as a team with their spouse, followed by wide grins and high-fives as both parents happily snuggle on the couch. Instinctively, she paused from scrubbing to reach into the back pocket of her jeans. With a few swipes and taps on the smooth, cold glass of her phone, she enjoyed a brief moment of satisfaction—she was the new owner of another pair of black knee-high boots.

Sharing this, Ashley bites her lower lip and averts her eyes. "Well, you see . . . I have a secret credit card," she confesses, clearing her throat. "With $10,000 of debt. Daniel doesn't know." Her secret spills out into the room like the bowl of beef stew her son splashed onto her blouse.

I hold my jaw and keep my gaze soft, the opposite of what I feel inside. Humans: We're so interesting that I'll never stop being surprised. This woman sitting in front of me, with her mild temperament and her mom-life look, has found a way to let out a little steam. Her husband is utterly blind to her anxiety and exhaustion—and to the major credit card debt she's racking up as a way of coping. Why use spending as a salve? Does it compensate for the emptiness in her marriage? Possibly. The anger of having to clean up after him? Definitely. But she's not attuned to her repressed anger, and I suspect there is more.

I run through memories of how she's appeared in previous sessions. Her designer shoes. The various watches. A different purse each time. Ashley's secret shopping is the opposite of what therapists would call an *adaptive coping strategy*—this would look like sharing her feelings and needs assertively with Daniel to help him understand them, and then setting and holding boundaries. These are the components that make up interdependence—the goal of building togetherness while also balancing autonomy. Instead, she engages in *maladaptive coping*. She receives quick dopamine hits by spending money on expensive items. This is her way of coping with Daniel's dismissiveness and lack of emotional connection.

Without shaming her for her decisions, I want Ashley to verbalize and acknowledge what this behavior is doing for her. I have to ask more questions and avoid making assumptions or interpretations. "Why that moment? Why did you buy the boots then?" I ask.

"I wanted them. I've been eyeing them for a while and have thought about buying them," she shrugs.

"Could you have talked to Daniel about purchasing these boots?" I need her to see that it's not just about the boots.

She replies without missing a beat. "What's the point? He doesn't listen. And he'll probably tell me that the boots are ridiculous, or that I'm being selfish for wanting something."

So there's judgment attached to the footwear. It's normal to want something, but what is most interesting is that she purchases it right after he *dismisses* her. The moments where she feels small, unseen, and rejected are the moments when she hits the "buy now" button.

"Could you share the credit card debt with Daniel?" I inquire, knowing that keeping a secret can inadvertently increase the distress in her relationship.

"Oh gosh—no," she replies. "This would break his trust. Besides, I have a plan to stop spending money. I know I need to stop. I'll slowly pay off the debt without him noticing." She checks her watch again and stands. We still have five minutes before our time together is over, but Ashley has once again ended our session early. I wonder if she feels any remorse for her financial infidelity.

Each session that follows focuses on a different topic with the same theme. (Daniel isn't emotionally or physically available, Ashley puts her needs to the side to please him, and she ends up feeling distant and burned out.) An image comes into focus of Ashley as a solo parent trying to manage her husband's difficulties, his long hours at work, and his alcohol abuse. (It turns out that the night after the work event was not a one-time thing—it happens once a week.) Even though they try to parent as a team, Ashley feels like she lives a parallel life to Daniel. They both take the kids to swimming lessons, go to the park together, and do family dinners together, but it's not building any sense of togetherness. I continue inviting Ashley to become aware of her learned patterns; finally, there's a shift. Ashley comes to session identifying a theme that keeps showing up for her.

"I keep caring for others, doing all of the things. I said yes to my boss to working overtime last week. I returned the phone call to my mother, even though I wanted to sit and read my book. I listened to my husband complain about his day. I'm lonely. I'm tired. Most of all, I want a partner I can lean on. This isn't what I signed up for." Her lips press together and I can see her throat tightening. "I resent him."

Resentment is a toxic emotion that slowly erodes the health of our relationships. It's also one of the most commonly expressed experiences I hear from the women I work with. A complex emotion, resentment is anchored in bitterness, rejection, lack of recognition, the feeling of being taken advantage of, and envy. It boils over from feelings of abandonment, boundary violations, and unmet expectations. These things don't exist in a vacuum—women who are taught by society to remain accommodating and caring often experience a buildup of anger and resentment instead of asserting their justifiable anger. For my part, I often feel a slow burning heat move throughout my body when I see my husband choosing to sit down and scroll on his phone while I am in the kitchen wiping down the counters, or when I'm left to pick up the toys and tidy the living room while he's already lying in bed. Resentment often stems from long-standing unmet needs, which can happen if someone has never expressed what they need, or their partner hasn't met their need or isn't capable of doing so.

Ashley's pattern of not expressing her feelings started early with her mother, even before her father left the home. With her father gone, there wasn't any space for Ashley to have her wishes heard, and she began to feel responsible for her mother's happiness. It wasn't just that she felt it was her duty; if she told her mother that she didn't like the lunch she'd packed for school or the clothing her mother had picked out for her, she was scolded for being ungrateful. Because she was punished by her mother whenever she tried to assert her needs, Ashley learned to stay silent.

As we dissect the different ways Ashley can express herself to her husband in the here and now (rather than living as if she is still with her mother), I remind her that change doesn't happen overnight, that finding just one moment to tell her husband what she wants would be a big step for her. She'll be creating a new way of thinking, shifting from *It's not okay to share my needs* to *I'm allowed to express myself.*

We both know that just speaking up isn't enough to change her exhaustion, but we have to start somewhere. When moms tell me how overwhelmed they are—navigating all of the things—I like to tap into the notion of "small things frequently." We are really good at going from one task to the next without acknowledging the impact each task has on us. We wouldn't let our cell phone battery drain to 10 percent before jumping onto a big meeting. We plug it in, multiple times a day. But we often let our own energy battery drain to empty. Recharging can be as small as a five-minute activity: grabbing a tea, putting your feet up against the wall while laying on your back, or taking ten slow, deep belly breaths.

I hope Ashley will take a chance on expressing herself and that Daniel will make space for her feelings. But therapists have to accept that when we close the door at the end of a session, we have no control over our clients' actions. Will they continue to follow their instinctive urges, or will they try something different? With Ashley, I'm left guessing. What neither of us know is that her world is about to be turned upside down.

The Road to Resentment

There are several ways that resentment can build in a relationship. Take a moment to reflect on the different ways listed here—do any of them help you recognize how this feeling developed for you? Remember, both partners can experience resentment but for completely different reasons. It can be worthwhile to explore these ideas in a safe way with your partner.

◈ Your partner is emotionally unavailable.

◈ There is an imbalance in your relationship, stemming from parental, relational, or household responsibilities.

◈ You feel like the default parent.

◈ You struggle to communicate and ask for your needs to be met.

◈ There is a breakdown in trust and respect in the relationship.

CHAPTER 8

Tracy

Anger is an important emotion, yet people tend to ignore the messages that come with it. Do you stuff your anger down until it explodes? Or do you unconsciously indulge your anger through rage-filled words and behavior? You need to acknowledge the impact your anger has on those you love, whether you are venting it out or keeping it hidden.

◇◇◇◇◇

It's Friday morning, and my colleagues and I are assembled on the waiting room chairs for our weekly consultation before we start our day. This week, I need help with my frustrations over Emily's outbursts in sessions with her partner, Matt. Specifically, I need help answering the oh-so-important question: *Is this a client thing or a me thing?*

"Her anger is so palpable," I tell Meagan and Melissa, two of the psychologists in my group practice. "It takes over the room and leaves no space for her partner. Sometimes I want to tell her *stop—just stop.*" I take a slow sip of my morning coffee as Meagan and Melissa nod in sympathy. "I think what's hard is that I get why she's angry. But if he is trying his best, as he says he is, doesn't she need to also be able to see that?"

"Do you think her anger is disproportionate to what is happening with her partner?" Meagan asks.

I tell them that Emily's anger makes sense based on her history and on having a partner who needs to step up. I look at anger as a roadmap, one that we aren't reading correctly most of the time; it's almost never about the socks or the sausages. While there is still debate among researchers and therapists whether anger counts as a primary or secondary emotion, my clinical perspective is that it's both. As a primary emotion, anger tells us that we've been wronged and hurt, or that something is unjust. When anger shows up in this form, it needs space to be released and processed (versus being stuffed down, which we are commonly taught to do). But as a secondary emotion, anger serves to protect us from experiencing softer, more vulnerable feelings like sadness or loss. That protective factor makes sitting in anger feel familiar, and thus comfortable, for many people.

Either way, it's important to acknowledge anger because it carries important messages about what we experience. However, as psychologist and author of *The Dance of Anger* Dr. Harriet Lerner puts it, women are taught to either be nice and sweep their feelings under the rug (which builds unconscious anger and rage), or they are viewed as bitches for expressing and venting anger. So women learn to stuff it down, fearing and denying their anger. But this only leads anger to come out in other ways, as all emotions do: a focus on things that are not actually the problem, externalization, a wish for others to change, depression, anxiety.

In Emily's case, her anger stems from having too much on her plate and things feeling unfair. She vents at Matt in an effort to change him, but instead it pushes him away. Ultimately, her anger only maintains the status quo: Matt's behavior never changes because Emily's rage ends up taking all the focus.

During my PhD program, I was fortunate to have Dr. Sue Johnson as my mentor and research supervisor. Dr. Johnson is the cocreator of emotionally focused couples therapy (EFT), which works on strengthening the attachment between partners. Instead of trying to solve a couple's argument, she always pointed us to each individual's underlying needs and longings. As she repeatedly told us, "You have to see past the anger."

As trainees, our client sessions were recorded on video. Once a week, we'd gather and review the tapes. After watching me work with a particularly volatile couple who yelled throughout our entire session, my fellow trainees asked me, "But how are you so *calm*?" At the time, I'd credit the insights I gained from Dr. Johnson but, in fact, my formative experiences made me something of a specialist when it comes to anger. I learned from an early age to observe and be quiet in the presence of this particular emotion. While I can't recall what my parents' arguments were about, I do remember their results: a pushed over kitchen chair, a slammed door, hurtful words in heated tones. I never saw my parents make up (what therapists call *repair*), but I did see them behave lovingly toward each other again once the fight was over. As an adult, I can appreciate that they likely finished their arguments in private or else simply let things go. As a therapist, I know that it's not possible to resolve every argument.

That being said, some kind of restitution, like a hug, an apology, or an agreement to do better next time, is needed for a relationship to remain healthy—and for children to learn how to be close again after a fight. Being able to see my parents apologize to each other, or at least having been told about their repair, would have been a significant chance for me to learn about loving resolutions and how to let go of anger. Still, becoming a mother has given me much more compassion for my parents. Now that I understand from personal experience all the stressors (work, marriage, kids) they dealt with when I was young, I can see my parents as good people who did their best. I've also seen them become more accepting of each other's flaws and continue to grow as a couple as the years have gone on. To this day, they still struggle with their negative cycle from time to time, but like two lake stones repeatedly thrown against each other by the waves, my parents keep smoothing and softening each other by working through the hard moments and making connection a priority, whether it's through big gestures like time away together or small moments like playing a board game while the kids are in bed. (My mother once disclosed to me that had it not been for their yearly "just the two of us" vacations, she doesn't know how they would have made it through the hard times.) My parents' example is proof that, while we can't avoid conflict or feelings of anger, we can overcome them by finding ways to remain friends and to like each other.

My clients' difficult experiences with anger don't scare me. What does scare me is that their conflict might be too deeply rooted for me to help them. Relationship difficulties can't get solved in a handful of sessions; after all, they don't arise from just a handful of bad fights. Unresolved conflict and disconnection get repeated and reinforced in micro moments each day, from terse morning exchanges to staccato texts about the kids' schedules to thinking about sex but deciding to not bring it up after being shot down the last ten times. Even the best repair won't work if we don't feel seen for the anger we feel.

Which brings me back to my dilemma about what to do next with Emily and Matt. Sensing that I need reassurance, Melissa reminds me of the incredibly challenging part of therapy, the part that both therapists and clients need to remember: "You can't make them change." The reminder lands squarely in the intersection of my professional and personal consciousness: *You alone can change yourself, but only if you want to change.*

"Can she see how she impacts him and step into his world? She needs to be able to see that and to maybe lean back and ask herself how she is influencing this dynamic," Melissa suggests. "But it sounds like he also needs to step into her world. If he can see that there is just so much to do, he might be able to see her anger differently."

Meagan checks her watch and stands up, signaling the start of our day. I take one last sip of my coffee, musing further about my next steps until I hear my first clients arrive. Perhaps it isn't just Emily's anger that I am looking to change. Maybe I'm really questioning how my own emotions are working for me in my marriage. I have to face the reality that I have unhealed wounds and that my anger, even when it's justifiable, has become my way of ignoring them.

Aware

Learning About Your Anger

Explore your experiences with your own anger and how it might impact your relationships.

◈ What did you learn about anger? As a child, who expressed anger in front of you? Who didn't express it but walked away or shut down their anger? Who was angry with you? What did your parents do when you got angry?

◈ Take some time to reflect on how you experience anger today. Do you allow yourself to feel it? Do you stuff it down or fear it? Do you vocalize your anger? Or vent it out?

◈ How do others respond to your anger? When others are angry, how do you respond to them?

Commit today to finding a healthy way to process your anger. Instead of getting critical at your partner and yelling at them, or shoving your anger down until it boils over, follow the steps here. Some people can complete these steps when they notice they are angry, while others might need to go for a walk, journal, or do some progressive muscle relaxation exercises (like the one at the end of chapter two).

◈ Recognize when you are feeling angry by noticing it in your body.

◈ Say out loud that you are feeling angry.

◈ Ask yourself where you feel anger in your body.

◈ With a slow deep breath, practice asking the anger what it needs in this moment.

PART TWO

◇◇◇◇◇

Acknowledge

In this section, my clients are building on their awareness and working to change and heal unconscious patterns, wounds, and core feelings and beliefs. Through therapeutic interventions, they are learning how to go from fusion and codependency to differentiation and interdependency. The chapters that follow will illustrate strategies that you can use to make similar changes in your own relationship.

CHAPTER 9

Emily and Matt

What you see on the surface is not always what is at the core. You must learn to mine for your core experiences and emotions because this invites your partner into your world to build understanding and compassion.

◇◇◇◇◇

"I took Alice to a play group," Matt beams. The sun is hitting the picture frame right behind him, bouncing back light that makes his proud-dad glow even brighter. Matt is sitting with his body turned toward Emily today; I wonder if taking initiative as a parent has helped him feel more empowered in the relationship. Matt goes on to share other personal victories since our last session: He's been having a weekly check-in to plan the nights he will make dinner, taking Alice for a walk when he notices Emily feeling overwhelmed, and asking Emily to share more about her stressful day. He has also been stopping their fights by saying, "Wait, we're spinning in the washing machine." Using a metaphor is a great way to pause and bring awareness to our negative cycles, which is all the more important when kids are involved. As one colleague described it, yelling at each other in the presence of children is the equivalent of taking a hammer to a vase. Anger and high conflict impact a child's brain development and their ability to self-regulate.

Sadly, his light is quickly put out by Emily's eye roll. Still facing away from Matt, she hasn't yet said anything, but I sense she has a tally of what Matt *didn't* do since our last session. Her grim expression and stiff posture speak to her determination to avoid looking inward, all of it heightened by the absence of a baby in her arms. In recent weeks, Alice had started fussing when her mother would get angry or upset, feeling Emily's emotional dysregulation. At my recommendation, Emily and Matt have begun leaving her with a trusted caregiver during their therapy sessions. Without Alice there, Emily's cold severity is on full display.

I validate Matt for stepping up to his parenting responsibilities while simultaneously cringing inside. As a working mom, I can't help but think that taking his daughter to play group should be the bare minimum. Intellectually, I'm with Emily—*Do more, Matt!*—but emotionally, I can't help but side with Matt—*Emily, can you just give a little positive feedback?* Her refusal to see his first fledgling efforts could discourage him from trying any further.

True to form, Emily snaps back, "I'm not going to give you gold stars. No one gives me any." I notice her tone is extra sharp today, her arms tightly crossed over her body as if to stop herself from internally combusting. *Okay,* I think, *what is actually going on for you?*

Matt looks at me, eyebrows pushed together. "I'm not asking for a sticker on a reward chart, geez. I'm just sharing with Dr. Tracy what I did since our last session. Am I not supposed to do that?" He brushes his hair to the side and lets out a sigh.

Emily looks at me with raised eyebrows. "What am I supposed to say? He's doing what a parent *should* be doing. He's not helping *me*— he's parenting *his* daughter."

Matt throws his arms up in the air, then slaps his knees with heavy hands. The gesture seems to light a spark to Emily's short fuse. "You know," she adds, glaring at Matt, "I told my mother this week that Matt took Alice to the play group. She said, 'Is that all he did?' These are minimum requirements and don't even come close to all the things I have on my list. Mom says I'm better than this."

Emily is really flame-throwing now and even bringing in a third person to support her side. This ploy, known as *triangulation*, is a common challenge that shows up for partners both at home and in the therapy room. We enter our couple partnership with the goal of "us"—you and me—but when that connection begins to break down, we sometimes throw another person into the mix in an attempt to ease conflict within the dyad. Triangulation can create an illusion of harmony by helping us build a case against our partner, but all it really does is prevent us from dealing with conflict head-on and ultimately create a wider divide in our relationship, especially if we are not careful about whom we're bringing into the conflict.

For Emily, the comfort of knowing how her mother will react to a situation with Matt feels better than going to an unpredictable source who might point out that Emily is part of the problem. But every time Emily turns to her mother for support instead of Matt, she adds to her relationship's ongoing struggle. By creating a situation in which her mother can only see Matt's weakness and mistakes, she sets her mother up to enable the behavior and thought patterns she's here in therapy to change. In therapy, we refer to this type of relationship as a *trauma bond*. It's characterized by an attachment with people who either cause us harm or enable a behavior or thought pattern we want to change.

Rather than ask Matt how he feels about Emily's mother's opinions—I don't want to reinforce the triangulation that Emily has been allowing—I ask how he feels hearing that Emily shares their relationship with her mother.

"I'm not surprised," he admits. "She's told me before that she talks to her mother and her friends. I mean, what am I supposed to do? I'm made out to be the bad guy." The light that beamed bright at the start of the session has been snuffed out. It's incredibly hard to be a team with your partner when they've thrown you under the bus to their family of origin or group of friends.

I call on what Melissa said earlier and step in with empathy. "You're right, Emily. No one is giving you stickers. Matt, you did something important and it felt good for you. But Emily, when you hear Matt asking for acknowledgment for how he is showing up in this family, you feel enraged because he doesn't give you accolades. You need gold stars too."

We've spent several sessions with Emily sitting in anger. I need more from her, but I have to be careful. If I reflect to Emily how her anger works against her, I could trigger her guardedness. This is always the balance with clients like Emily: wanting them to see how they impact their partner, but also not wanting them to shut down with me. The squeaky wheel partner can easily feel blamed for all the issues in the relationship: "So I'm the bad person because I vocalize my wants and needs?"

Like Karine, Emily instinctively personalizes her partner's words and actions, failing to appreciate that he has feelings and experiences that are different from hers, that he doesn't need to approach things in the same way as she does. This type of codependency hurts the healthy interdependence in their relationship. As I've said before, we want to aim for "I am me, you are you, and we are both okay." This is in sharp contrast to the way fusion plays out for Matt (which sounds like "If you're upset, it means I'm never good enough") and Emily (which sounds like "If you're upset, that's your problem. My feelings are more important").

Behind this dismissive attitude, though, there is a deeper shame at work. People like Emily who are quick to blame and criticize others have a really good reason for doing it: Blame lets the emotional brain discharge uncomfortable emotions, such as the shame and vulnerability we feel in the moment of making a mistake. I can think back to many moments when I have resorted to blame, often in response to little things like being late, making a mistake, or feeling afraid of what a situation's outcome will be. These are hard experiences for me, thanks to my tendency toward perfectionism. Instead of acknowledging my softer emotions and needs ("I'm so scared that I made this mistake and I'm not sure what other people will think of me"), it feels more comfortable in the short term to point fingers at Greg for how he could have prevented the whole thing ("If you'd have just gotten home when you said you would, I wouldn't have messed up dinner"). If you're on the receiving end of this communication style, I encourage you to try to see what your partner is feeling *underneath* the hostile comments. Behind it, there is often pain and feelings of being unlovable and unworthy.

Interestingly, blame is a natural part of brain development. The Swiss psychologist Dr. Jean Piaget asserted that between the ages of two and seven, children are developing memory and imagination but have difficulty thinking outside of their own perspective. A child in this developmental stage will fall and shout "You tripped me!" at someone who wasn't even close to them. The ability to see both self and other isn't fully formed until the prefrontal cortex is done developing at the age of twenty-five. No wonder our brains are focused on our own perspective during childhood.

For Emily, blame is a form of *projection* she learned from watching her mother blame everyone else. Having learned from her mother's example to cast responsibility for her uncomfortable emotions onto others, it's only natural for Emily to put her fears and desires onto Matt. Even though it creates conflict in her relationship, it's easier and feels safer than looking inward and asking herself, *How do I contribute to this?*

The key to improving our relationships is the consciousness that we always have choices. One of the most powerful things we can do in a moment of conflict is pause, allow ourselves to take a breath, and notice that there is something happening, either internally or externally. Then, seeing that we are in this dynamic *together* with our partner, we can ask ourselves whether we want to choose connection and closeness or keep focusing on "winning" the argument. This practice of pausing and choosing is essential to reach a conscious, interdependent relationship.

If Emily were willing to consider the impact of her actions on Matt and take accountability, she'd discover the power that comes from choosing. Instead of waiting for him to be "perfect" enough to change their relationship, she could use her power to begin shifting their pattern herself. Matt also faces this choice in how he responds to Emily—namely, by reminding himself that Emily's feelings are not fundamentally about him. My early work with him was focused on his reactive defensiveness so that he could intentionally choose how he communicates. Stepping outside of defensiveness—with responses like "I see you are upset right now, and your feelings are important to me. Can you try telling me again using a softer approach?" or "I hear you. I want to understand you, but it's hard for me when you are angry. Can we talk about this at another time when we are both not escalated?"— lets your partner know that you see them (as we all long to be seen) while setting loving limits for how they approach you.

Notice that I didn't use the word *boundary* in any of the suggested lines above. A sure way to add fuel to the fire is to blurt out, "You're crossing my boundaries!" Using this term, rather than telling your partner explicitly what you wish or don't wish to happen, can come across as scolding and aggressive. It focuses on the other, when boundaries are actually about the self. True understanding comes from statements like "I feel ____ when you ____," with a description of how you feel when the other person exhibits a particular behavior.

Seeing how deeply Emily needs to be acknowledged, I say, "It must be incredibly hard to not be acknowledged for all that you do in the family. Each session, you have a laundry list of things that you do during the day but don't feel seen for. It feels like you're steering this ship all alone, and you want your co-captain to come on board with you. Where else have you experienced this, Emily? This feeling of being on the ship with no one by your side—did you feel it with your mom?"

Using metaphoric imagery like this is part of an EFT intervention known as *evocative responding*, which can help clients access softer primary emotions. If you struggle to access or process a feeling or can't seem to describe an emotion to a loved one, try using an image or a metaphor to help you and others understand your experience. By being able to name what you are feeling, you are helping yourself regulate the internal experience you are having.

Emily's shoulders slump forward as she looks away. "Of course, it's tied back to Mom. Isn't it always the mother? It's one of the things I fear with Alice. Will she grow up to blame me for all her own difficulties in relationships? Am I screwing her up?"

This is all too relatable. I think many parents fear their children will repeat their negative patterns, myself included. But we can't change these patterns when we don't access or understand what these patterns, and the issues that bring them to light, are really about. Our emotions are like an iceberg: All we see from the surface are the secondary emotions like anger, frustration, or resentment. My job is to uncover the rest of the iceberg, the hulking mass under the surface where we hide our softer primary emotions like sadness, pain, hurt, fear, disappointment, depression, and loss. For once, Emily is allowing me a look below the surface.

"We don't get to control what our children end up doing," I remind Emily gently. "We only get to choose how we interact with them and how we model what it means to have a healthy relationship."

"Yeah . . . You know, my sister doesn't struggle with the domestic load like I do. It's such a difference between us." She raises a relevant point: Her younger sister is in a same-sex marriage, and research shows that gay couples don't tend to experience the conflicts that come from normative societal sex roles. Sensing that there might be an opening here, I press more.

"You needed your mom to see you, but she didn't," I suggest. "You were all alone, like you were invisible." I'm intentionally heightening Emily's core, or primary, emotion (another EFT intervention) with the hope of helping her become aware of her own feelings, connect them to her attachment need (i.e., her longing for connection and belonging), and eventually share them with Matt from a place of vulnerability rather than resentment.

Sure enough, Emily's voice is softer, her eyes beginning to well. "I was always on my own. I did so much for my family. Mom wasn't there—she was busy looking after Dad—and if she was there, she was enraged about the injustices in her marriage, how Dad never did anything as a family with us, how he was always working on the farm. So I stepped in. I helped my younger sister and around the farm. I made breakfast and lunch for me and my sister. I made sure the table was set and cleared every night. When I did those things, Mom didn't get angry. But my sister didn't have to do any of it, and she didn't have to experience Mom and her turmoil. It was all on me, even though I was only five years old. If I was having a bad day, no one noticed. I just kept doing it all."

I feel contented that Emily is expressing more vulnerable emotions, though at the same time there's a pit in my stomach as I think of five-year-old Emily feeling scared of her mother's anger and just trying to feel okay in her world. It's clear that Emily was a *parentified child*, shouldering household duties and emotional burdens that adults should have been managing at a time when she needed to play, explore, and make mistakes. No one acknowledged that she played this role, much less that it shouldn't have been hers to take on. Even worse, her attachment figures—the adults from whom she needed to seek comfort and security—couldn't see that she was struggling, that she needed to be acknowledged for all that she was doing, that she needed someone to say, "Hey, this isn't your work to do." Unsurprisingly, the feeling that it was her responsibility to care for everyone cultivated an overwhelming desire for control. Control is what allows her (back then and now) to create a false sense of security and comfort.

As Matt listens to Emily, he places a hand on her leg. Watching him, I see real potential for Matt to be the secure partner who can step into Emily's emotions. Hoping to help him stay focused on the younger part of Emily, the part that longs to be acknowledged, I reframe Emily's tendency to be the CEO today as the little girl who was trying to stay safe from her mother's rage. To my relief, Matt doesn't go into his usual frustration or defensiveness with Emily, which shows me that he is changing. He tells Emily that he sees all that she does for their family and admits that they wouldn't be the family they are without everything she does.

"Emily, what does Matt's acknowledgment offer you? Him seeing you leads you to feel . . ." I let the question hang.

She gives a half smile. "I don't know. Maybe that I'm not companionless." She turns to him. "I'm lonely, Matt. I'm up with Alice in the middle of the night all by myself. I'm overstimulated by dinnertime and I just wish you would say, 'I've got this' and take over sometimes. I don't want to be alone."

Matt leans in to hug Emily. Her confession of this core emotion helps him to see more of her, bringing him closer, where her anger used to push him away. She allows him to wrap his arms around her but remains still and closed off.

Most often, when I'm listening for the attachment needs and longing in partners, women tend to speak more to the loss of connection (that is, feeling they are abandoned and unimportant), whereas men tend to speak more to feelings of inadequacy (feelings of failure and not-enoughness). When a man goes into fixing mode (or its evil twin, defensiveness), he isn't unwilling to hear about his female partner's struggle. Rather, he's looking for a solution out of fear that he will fail his family. Many women are shocked to hear this and, at the same time, relieved that their partners are struggling in their own way. It's a reminder that we all want to be seen for what is happening for us.

Emily and Matt have made an important shift today, and Emily has shared more about her early childhood experiences than in previous appointments. Considering this progress, I give Emily and Matt homework for our next session: I want them to each write a letter to their inner child. The goal, I tell them, is to develop an understanding of the wounds they bring to their relationship that contribute to their negative cycle.

I want them to improve. Maybe I want it a bit too much; I see so much of my own relationship in their dynamic. But I also see possibility. I know that when partners put in the effort to turn toward each other in between sessions, stop their negative cycle, and share their feelings and needs from a vulnerable place, they can make real, meaningful changes. But I couldn't have foreseen the consequences that would come from the homework assignment.

Acknowledge
What Does Your Iceberg Hide?

Think back to the iceberg analogy earlier in the chapter. Take a moment to examine the emotions that often lurk below the surface level of everyday life.

◈ What primary, or core, emotions do you tend not to share with your partner?

◈ Thinking of your past, what would other significant people do when you shared those emotions?

◈ Thinking of the last time that you got into a disagreement with your partner, slow down the event. Ask yourself, was this a primary emotion that you shared with them? Did it feel raw, vulnerable, or newly discovered? Or was it a secondary emotion, a reaction to a deeper emotion or to your partner's emotion?

◈ What bodily sensations come with your primary emotion (e.g., nausea, clenched jaw, tight shoulders)?

CHAPTER 10

Karine and Peter

In a relationship, each partner will process information differently. One way that partners may differ is in the extent to which they process internally or externally. This is often connected to their individual attachment style. Learning about your attachment style can help you understand your behaviors with your partner, particularly during conflict. Do you seek closeness in times of distress, or do you shut down and need space?

◇◇◇◇◇

"I just feel frustrated," Peter states matter-of-factly, as if it's the first time he's said it. We're at the familiar spot in session where Peter doesn't "do" emotions. The rain pelts on the office window and the cuffs of both partners' pants are wet from the downpour outside, yet Peter's hair remains untouched. I have secretly wanted to mess up that perfectly styled hair, as if loosening up his put-together appearance could also release his grip on "frustration" and open up his internal emotional world.

Karine and Peter report that between sessions, they have been practicing mentalization and stopping their negative cycle at home. Though there have been small shifts, Karine is still getting swallowed up in her feelings of insecurity while trying to connect with something deeper in Peter. Meanwhile, he still isn't sharing emotions, persisting in wanting Karine to trust his love for her even when his actions don't reflect it.

Karine starts our appointment today by relaying a recent event with Peter's daughter, Brielle. At Peter's encouragement, she decided to take Brielle shopping for a new pair of shoes. Hoping to build her relationship with her stepdaughter, Karine tried to make small talk over lunch in the food court, but Brielle gave minimal responses as she picked away at her food. At the shoe store, Brielle clung to a designer high-top shoe (what teenager wouldn't?) that was way beyond Karine's price limit. Karine wanted to be sensible and fair to what she spent on her own children, so she recommended that Brielle look for something more affordable. In response, Brielle sulked and refused to talk it through or pick out another pair of shoes, and instead glued her eyes to her phone. They left the mall empty-handed.

When they arrived home, Peter was frustrated at Karine's choice and told her that she should have bought whatever Brielle wanted. Karine hadn't known that Peter didn't mind spending more on his kid's shoes than she did on her own children. Did Peter's decision to say this in front of Brielle mean he didn't love Karine? She pushed to get an answer from him until, becoming increasingly defensive, Peter finally confessed that his ex-wife, Charlotte, had sent him an angry text saying that she was "disgusted" by Karine, scolding him for his partner's "poor decision-making" and demanding that Peter "make it right."

Instead of working through the triangulation created by Charlotte's text, Peter retreated to the basement den, drowning himself in work and computer games while giving Karine the silent treatment. This lasted for the next three days. Karine was crushed. She had wanted Peter to stand up for her, but instead he punished her.

I want Peter to see the impact of his behavior on his partner. Even though he might not have a broad vocabulary for his emotions, doing his best to share what he was thinking and what was triggered in him is the only way to break the patterns that are hurting his relationship. By shutting down, he is pushing his partner away. At the same time, I tread carefully, as I suspect that pointing out Peter's mistakes may trigger a shame spiral. Shame makes people feel like they are bad and unworthy, which leads them to shut down, hide themselves, and stop being vulnerable. This lack of vulnerability, as professor and author Brené Brown describes it, breaks the interpersonal connection between two people. Vulnerability is like crossing a bridge to understand your partner, whereas shame causes the structure to crumble. Rolling into shame leads partners to feel further apart.

Like many of the other men I work with, Peter has a propensity to wall himself off in the face of difficult emotions. For him, "bad" feelings like pain, fear, sadness, and depression are not merely uncomfortable; they are considered unacceptable, often because of messages men receive while growing up, which emphasize the need to be "tough" and to ignore their emotions. So Peter finds ways to crop emotions out of the frame, as it were. The difficult conversation he had with Charlotte where he felt undermined and diminished? He told himself that it wasn't that bad and decided to focus solely on his daughter. The Sunday family dinner where he'd have to endure his father's awful comments about his appearance? He decided to go and said nothing. The argument he had with Karine where he felt small and discounted? He retreated to the den to play computer games. He deals with the discomfort of his emotions by pretending they aren't there.

You might recall from chapter two that shutting down and withdrawing in the face of conflict is a survival response to an over-whelmed and *flooded* nervous system, reflecting a dorsal vagal state. When someone becomes dysregulated to this point, they are no longer able to stay engaged in the conversation at hand. In Dr. John Gottman's research, couples were asked to talk about a recent conflict while hooked up to physiological monitoring systems that measured markers like blood pressure, heart rate, and oxygen levels. As they discussed the conflict, the men's physiological markers skyrocketed while the women's tended to stay more even. This evidence runs radically contrary to the popular idea of the stoic male, showing that men are, in fact, experiencing a great deal of emotion during a disagreement, even to the point of physiological overwhelm. They may congratulate themselves for being more "rational" than women, but bottling up their emotions makes them even more susceptible to irrational responses.

People like Peter who avoid communicating may believe they are sidestepping conflict, but this tactic doesn't work in a relationship. If you asked a question to a loved one and they said nothing, which would you feel—calm or unsettled? It's safe to say you'd feel uneasy. This reaction to withdrawal is natural and instinctive, as shown by psychologist Dr. Ed Tronick's "still face" experiment, in which infants and toddlers exhibited extreme distress when their caregiver's face became blank and unresponsive. It is also supported by studies showing that suppressing your own emotions increases your partner's blood pressure.

A person who goes quiet in the face of conflict may tell themselves that they have avoided blame in the interaction—after all, they're not adding to the conflict by ranting or getting loud—but by shutting down and not sharing their emotions and thoughts, they are contributing to the negative cycle of "The more you shut down, the angrier I get" and "The angrier you get, the more I shut down." (Recall the Protest Polka from chapter one.) If this describes your experience, here is what you can do instead: Offer to come back to the conversation after you take some time to calm down, and use physical connection (anything from a hug to a hand squeeze) to help everyone become more regulated.

Hoping to uncover the origins of Peter's propensity to shut down, I ask him to tell me about his early years. Peter shares that, as the youngest of six, he felt invisible growing up. I also suspect, based on Peter's personality, that he was what child psychologist Dr. Becky Kennedy calls a "deeply feeling kid," the kind who is acutely aware of their environment and easily flooded by their emotional experience. His sensitivity was compounded by his controlling, verbally abusive father. He recalled being upset when his father couldn't attend his baseball tryouts. The letdown was such a big deal for Peter that he ended up striking out and not making the team. Feeling crushed, he burst into tears. That evening, his father caught sight of Peter's distraught expression and snapped, "Get over it, kid," reinforcing the cultural messaging that boys shouldn't cry and that hard stuff isn't talked about.

Learning to bottle up his overwhelming feelings worked well to keep Peter safe from his father's criticism. However, it set up a pattern of lack of vulnerability in his romantic relationships, to the point that he took on the role of his father with his own loved ones: closing himself off, rarely expressing his needs, focusing on work as an outlet. He also chose partners who were emotionally distant or, worse, abusive and belittling, just like his father had been.

Given his history of being criticized, I am quick to validate how hard it must be for Peter to feel stuck between his ex and the partner he deeply cares about. As I say it, I hope that Karine is taking notes. While I don't want her to stop sharing her feelings with Peter, I do want her to see how getting the openness she wants from him can only happen if she offers space for him to share without being primarily concerned about her feelings.

Next, I move toward a perspective shift. "It's natural to feel almost as if your ex-wife had a tantrum about the shoes, and tantrums are uncomfortable for us. We feel flooded in our own brains when someone else takes control or overwhelms us with a massive meltdown; we just want it to stop. But to stop Charlotte's outburst, you turned against Karine."

"Charlotte is intense," he sighs. "She makes so many threats. I was just trying to do what was right—I saw Brielle upset and she really wanted those shoes . . ." He trails off. "I'm not sure what else to do. I try to tell Karine I love her. It's frustrating that she doesn't trust me."

I lean back in my chair, not quite satisfied with his response. *Love isn't about just telling your partner*, I think. *Your actions and your words need to match each other.*

105

"What are you getting from this unhealthy dynamic with your ex-wife?" I ask. I want him to be accountable for his behavior; looking at what he gets from it underlines the fact that he's making a choice. At the same time, I have to make sure that in doing so I separate his actions from his inherent worth as a partner. This is the bottleneck effect of a therapist's work: balancing empathy with accountability.

Peter glares back at me. "Do you have kids, Tracy?" His voice oozes hostility. He isn't genuinely asking this; he's challenging me so he can avoid looking inward. I give myself a moment, not wanting my own annoyance to show.

Rather than take the bait, I reflect it back to him. "I sense I asked a hard question, Peter. It's hard to look at why we do the things we do. I want to emphasize that the choices we make don't mean anything about us as people. We all make mistakes."

"All I'm saying is that if you did have kids, then you would know that you would do anything for them." His tone tells me that he feels like he's won.

"I get that your daughter matters to you," I say. "It also matters what you show her. It's one thing to teach her to be kind to others. It is much more powerful to demonstrate what it means to be a respectful partner who takes responsibility in the service of building connection. Seeing this helps children internalize a template for a healthy relationship. I think this is what you hope Brielle learns from you. As you've said here, you don't want her to repeat your mistakes." Seeing no hint of response, I try to explore Peter's behavior from another angle. "After that text exchange with Charlotte, what led you to stay quiet for so many days?"

He shrugs. "I needed to work through it on my own. My ex has a way of twisting my actions and words to make Brielle think I want to keep her away from her mom, or that I don't want to spend time with her. I just needed to figure out how to deal with the situation so she didn't put Brielle in the middle again."

"And did you?" I ask.

"Yes," Peter replies without offering additional details.

I keep pushing the conversation forward. "So there's this big bang between you and Karine. It doesn't feel good, it's not what you want, but it happens. We all have times when we blow up at the ones we love in some way." I'm normalizing the experience for Peter, walking a wide path around his shame spiral so he can stay working with me, even in his limited way. "In that situation, you go inward. You work through it internally and deal with it on your own. But Karine . . ." I turn to her. "You need to process externally, meaning *with* Peter."

Karine looks at Peter and reaches for his hand. Despite his tendency to wall Karine off, she keeps her nurturing stance for him. She doesn't turn away from him, like Emily does to Matt.

"I don't think there is a right way here," I continue, "but I do think you need to communicate what you want in those moments. It clearly doesn't work to wall each other out. Maybe, instead of going into the details of the issue, you could talk about the *process* of what is happening for you." I offer Peter a potential script for the next blowup. "In the instance of what happened with Charlotte, you can let Karine know that you see you made a mistake, as we all do, then tell her that you need to take some time to reflect on your own."

"I think this would help me, Peter," Karine jumps in. "I could give you space to think on your own. I can respect that—I just need to know. It's like when my patients are in pain—I need them to verbalize it so I can give them the necessary treatment."

Resigned, Peter says, "I guess I have to."

It's clear to me that Karine and Peter have opposite attachment styles, which makes meeting each other's needs incredibly difficult. I hear Karine's anxious attachment style in her cries for Peter to share with her: *Are you there for me? Do I actually matter to you?* Meanwhile, Peter is avoidantly attached, bottling up his emotions and keeping his needs hidden in moments of stress (this is the deactivation strategy I talked about in chapter three) while wondering if he will always fail Karine: *Am*

I ever going to get this right? Why can't you believe me? What's important to remember about someone with an avoidant attachment style is that they have the same internal emotions as others, but rather than invite their partner in to understand those emotions, they shut down, making their partner feel less close to them. Meanwhile, people with an anxious attachment style seek closeness and constant reassurance that they are lovable and worthy. The distance that results from disagreements can feel torturous to someone with anxious attachment, to the point that they will hyperactivate their needs to get any response at all. This leads the avoidant person to create more distance, and it all culminates in a classic pursue-distance cha-cha.

Couples therapy can sometimes feel like a house of cards, and when a partner who is eager to change is paired with another who is more passive or even digs their heels in, that imbalance can send the whole house crashing down. I'm feeling frustrated—Peter's catchall term is rubbing off on me—until I hear a familiar voice whispering in my head: *Do you know how to do this? Are you even a good couples therapist? How can you help people make real changes in their relationships if you can't get your own relationship on track?* I've spent countless hours training, researching, working with world-renowned clinicians, and watching tapes of couples interacting, yet my *inner critic* is as relentless as it's ever been. It always shows up with impeccable timing to make me question if I am actually good enough.

I tell my impostor syndrome to take a back seat and bring my attention to the present. It only takes one person to change a relationship dynamic—if I can't reach Peter yet, I can at least keep working with Karine. I highlight her tendency to become emotionally fused with Peter and how it stems from her father's emotional absence and her narcissistic ex-husband's abuse, as well as society's expectation that women should bear the emotional burden while men remain impassive. I talk about what trusting herself looks like, and how building her own sense of self will empower her to step into uncomfortable experiences *and* feel confident afterward that she acted with the best information that she had. I nudge Karine to consider that Peter's response came from a place of stress; this doesn't make his behavior okay, but it can help her build compassion for him and lessen her fears of being abandoned. It's important to balance her fears that Peter is just like her ex-husband with evidence that he is a supportive partner. I encourage her to practice seeing the positive parts that exist in their relationship, like the moments when Peter makes plans for them to go to the theater together (not his thing, but he goes to be with her), coordinates the weekend family event (he knows how important this is to her), or snuggles close on the couch to binge-watch their favorite show (a way that they feel close together). Recognizing these gestures will strengthen their bond, making it more resilient in moments of turmoil.

I also remind both of them that the goal of a relationship is not to keep our partner eternally happy. Constantly focusing on the happiness of someone else means giving up something within ourselves, which only builds resentment. I encourage Karine to practice saying to her partner, firmly and lovingly, "This is what I chose because it felt right in that moment. I understand that you are upset about it. I did my best." Simply remembering that there is a difference between hurting someone intentionally and acting in a way that they don't like can be Karine's entry into getting unstuck from their fused relationship.

◇◇◇◇◇

Despite all my encouragement, in their next session, Karine keeps slipping into her insecurity while Peter continues to avoid accountability for his actions. Despite his repeated assurance that he loves her, her distrust in their relationship continues to build with each connection opportunity he misses. Even while holding Peter's hand in session, Karine discloses that her difficulty trusting him is impacting other parts of their relationship. To be blunt, her sexual desire has flatlined.

"I know he wants more sex, but how do I do this when I can't lean on him?" I watch as she squeezes Peter's hand, as if to mitigate his reaction.

Peter pulls his hand away. "This isn't going to work in our relationship. Sex is important to me. To us." His shoulders round forward as he looks to me to solve this.

Ah, the mother of all couples therapy issues: sex. There's no debate that physical intimacy is important, though it goes beyond just intercourse and orgasms to include long hugs and deep kisses. Physical touch releases oxytocin, known as the cuddle hormone, that keeps us feeling close and bonded. Yet many people fail to understand that our emotional connection with our partners is intrinsic to our sexual connection. In other words, sex doesn't just happen between our legs; it occurs in our minds.

Research by psychiatrist Dr. Rosemary Basson has shown that the desire and arousal system is different for women compared to men, which is why female Viagra has yet to hit the market. Basson's studies have found that although women's genitals do in fact have increased blood flow in response to erotic stimuli, women do not report *feeling* more aroused. In other words, blood flow does not equal excitement.

When it comes to understanding what leads people to be aroused, sex educator and author Dr. Emily Nagoski uses the analogy of a car to distinguish between sexual excitation (the gas pedal) and sexual inhibition (the brake). This is also known as the dual control model of sexual response. Sexual partners need to be aware of what makes their desire (and their partner's) speed up and what makes it screech to a halt. For example, an unclean body might be a hard brake for one, but neutral for the other; a basket of unfolded laundry in the bedroom might be benign for one partner, but for the other it's a quick slam on the brake.

It's also important to acknowledge that for women, the desire system is nonlinear and cyclical, which is in contrast to Masters and Johnson's initial research on the linear model of sex: desire, arousal, orgasm, and refractory period. When sex is a positive experience that is followed by ongoing emotional closeness, support with domestic labor, and non-sexual physical connection, desire is more likely to increase. In the absence of these factors, desire is lowered.

Given all this, it makes sense that Karine is experiencing a lack of desire. But before I can dig into what is happening between them sexually, Karine's focus jumps elsewhere. She clears her throat before saying, "I think I'd feel closer to Peter, more sure of his feelings, if we were married."

I look to Peter who is shaking his head. "How can I marry someone who doesn't trust me? Who doesn't want to have sex with me?"

I nod at my rare agreement with Peter and say to Karine, "He's asking a valid question. A proposal does not erase the day-to-day challenges of a relationship. In fact, a ring can provide a false sense of security. Marriage in and of itself doesn't bring a sense of emotional safety, and I don't believe it would fix your lack of desire."

Not wanting Karine to think this is all on her, I turn to Peter and ask, "What do you think you could do to build up Karine's trust? What can you start doing to protect the relationship against Charlotte's attacks, for instance?"

Peter is unmoved. I'm feeling what it must be like for Karine to interact with him. "Karine should trust me. She knows that I love and value her. That should be enough."

I sit back, feeling stalemated once again. It's plain to me that neither one of these partners is solely at fault for what is happening between them. But they cannot see this yet. As much as they clearly love each other, both are vilifying the other while making themselves out to have no agency in their problem. This is keeping them trapped in an infinite loop of conflict fed by unresolved attachment issues with their parents and reinforced by their previous relationships. What makes it all the more frustrating (there's that word again) is my knowledge that once they start to buy into the power of boundary setting and emotional vulnerability for rebuilding trust, the entire relationship can shift toward a healthy intimate connection.

Acknowledge

Exploring Your Attachment Styles

Use the following questions to explore the ways in which you try to seek closeness with your partner.

◈ When you are in distress or something good happens, do you turn to the other person, or do you shut down your feelings and desire to share?

◈ For you, what do comfort, support, and encouragement look like?

◈ What tells you that your partner is responding and listening to you?

◈ What are the things your partner does that tell you that you are important and that you matter to them?

◈ Do you trust that your partner will hold your vulnerability with love and attention? Or do you believe they will use it against you or reject you?

CHAPTER 11

Lydia and Sam

Boundaries are often thought of as a means of creating individuality. I challenge you to instead consider boundaries as part of building healthy interdependence. Just as personal boundaries are an integral part of protecting your individual autonomy, shared boundaries in a relationship are an important part of protecting the couple's dyadic unit.

◇◇◇◇◇

Lydia drops her briefcase beside the couch with a heavy thud. *What*, I wonder, *could be inside this bag that she has to lug it up the stairs and into the office every time?* I may be reading too much into it, but I can't help seeing it as a sack filled with emotional baggage that she isn't yet ready to let go of.

Lydia begins the session with her customary power move. "Why don't we start with your mother, Sam?" Her words are laced with anger. Obligingly, Sam shares that his parents are coming to stay with them for several days. There is a long-standing conflict between Sam's parents and Lydia. While they were initially cordial back when they thought Lydia was a fling, the relationship took a negative turn when Sam proposed. They wanted him to marry someone of their cultural background, someone who would uphold their values and customs, someone who would give their family of origin equal priority in their marriage.

Lydia's strong love for Sam helped her forge through the discomfort, but she has still not found a good connection with his parents. Her interactions with Sam's mother in particular are filled with tension and toxicity. Understandably, Lydia finds their extended visits intrusive and would prefer the protection of separate living spaces when they visit. But Sam never feels comfortable asking his parents to stay in a hotel. After all, he says, "They are family." Sam is planning to prepare an elaborate meal for them during their visit, expressing his love for them through food. While he sees this as tapping into what he finds meaningful, I can't help but wonder if it's an unconscious play to get their approval.

It's interesting to note the contrast in their dynamic today against the last several sessions they've attended. I had just started to see a shift for Lydia and Sam thanks to their commitment to doing fun things together over the past few months. They've been trying new recipes together, listening to their favorite music, and feeling the heat that arises between their bodies as they dance in each other's arms. Simply put, they've been making time for play. What is play? Although it looks different for everyone, play is any activity where you find yourself in a state of flow, described by psychologist Dr. Mihaly Csikszentmihalyi as the optimal experience of being completely absorbed in an activity. For some, play can come from witty banter; for others, it can involve putting on a nineties playlist and guessing the songs. Other couples enjoy movement, via dancing or working out, or exploring new places together.

Play is what keeps a relationship alive. It allows us to get to know different parts of each other, make new memories, and rekindle intimacy that can get lost in the daily routine. With play, there is a renewed connection where evaluation and judgment are gone. However, this isn't easy for couples in relationship distress. After all, having fun with a partner requires trust and ease. And true to form, Lydia's feelings about her in-laws' visit are putting the brakes on their reconnection. She mentions that during the last visit from Sam's parents, Sam's mother admonished Lydia for her long hours at work, wanting to know why Lydia wasn't more focused on looking after her son. Put off by this perspective, Lydia told her that Sam was a grown man and could look after himself. (It didn't escape her that Sam's mother chose to bring this up right after Sam and his father went outside to look at the garden.)

The interference didn't end there. Sam's mother made comments on Lydia's appearance, questioning why she had "let herself go," and asked if they were ever going to make her a grandmother. Lydia finally reached her tipping point and called out Sam's mother at the dinner table. Her mother-in-law slipped seamlessly into the victim role, asking why Lydia would be so vengeful, refusing to acknowledge her negative comments or behavior. Lydia left the dinner table and didn't engage with her in-laws for the rest of the visit. Meanwhile Sam, rather than take Lydia's side, tried to persuade her that his mother didn't have ill intentions.

Obviously, Lydia feels quite differently than Sam does about his mother's behavior. After a lifetime of deflecting his feelings when his mother guilt-trips him ("I guess you're too busy for a visit from your own mother"), it's easy for Sam to do the same when she approaches him with a backhanded critique of Lydia ("Are you eating enough? Is she feeding you well?"). Sam doesn't see the boundaries that Lydia craves as protection against his mother's actions. Rather, he labels her logical arguments for why his mother's behavior is toxic as going into "lawyer mode." Even though it creates conflict in his marriage, it's ultimately easier for Sam to characterize Lydia's complaints as argumentative than to really listen to them. Listening would force him to confront his mother.

I am not surprised by this. Men typically take longer than women to separate from their families, particularly their mothers. As the primary caretaker, the mother is their first example for developing physical and emotional connection. But if the bond with the mother is an unhealthy one (e.g., Mom withholds affection or uses guilt to manipulate her son), he will struggle more to communicate boundaries with his family of origin once he commits to a new relationship. This aligns with research showing that more men compared to women have avoidant attachment styles, which includes the tendency to keep their emotions and needs to themselves.

One of the most fascinating elements about relationships is how the thing that drew us together can be the very thing that drives us apart. Lydia was drawn to Sam's creativity back when he channeled it into cooking. But with his gradual loss of confidence, his creativity has warped into the attention-seeking behavior at the crux of their relationship distress. Seeking validation from his parents is just another form of this behavior.

Seeing Sam put aside his own selfhood to please his parents dims Lydia's attraction still further. But Sam is oblivious to how his response to his mother plays a role in their marital breakdown. I wait for Lydia to finish listing all the reasons she refuses to participate in Sam's family visit before I speak.

"I see your anger, Lydia. You have good reason to be upset. I get the sense that you create distance with Sam when he doesn't take your side in this. No one deserves to be treated that way, and I can only imagine how hurtful this must be for you."

"Of course, I'm hurt!" she agrees loudly.

Looking for deeper feelings, I press her, "Can you talk from this place of pain? This will allow Sam to understand more of what it's like for you." Lydia's affair hovers like the proverbial elephant in the room, waiting to be acknowledged. I'm frankly amazed at how Lydia continues to plow forward as if this secret doesn't exist for her (or for me). *Will this secret continue to be part of their dynamic?* I wonder. *How will she feel if she's still holding it twenty years from now?*

Lydia goes on to share that Sam's refusal to take her side makes her feel unimportant, like she could just be discarded for anyone else. *Discarded*—an interesting choice of words. Remembering the experiences with her father that she has shared, I invite her to use that word to connect this time in her life with her past. Exploring this feeling with Sam would give him a chance to disprove her notion that he doesn't value her (or, as therapists describe it, give her a *corrective emotional experience*) and build compassion for her inner experience.

But Lydia just rolls her eyes and shakes her head. Pushing away emotion is her strength as a lawyer who deals with traumatic cases every day; it protects her from becoming consumed by emotion. On a personal level, though, it prevents her from restoring the connection she desires. I decide to take the direct approach. After all, you don't go to therapy to stay comfortable.

"Lydia, I wonder if there is a piece here with your dad . . ." I stop short as she takes a tight breath at the word.

"My dad. . ." Her voice trails off.

"Where did you just go in your mind?" I ask.

She's silent for a few moments. I wait patiently. Silence is our entry into internal experience.

"I was remembering when he left," she murmurs. "The emptiness in the house. His bedside table untouched. His chair tucked in at the kitchen island. Even though my parents fought all the time, his presence was soothing. But he didn't fight to stay with me. He just left and chose a different life." A single tear runs down Lydia's face. She quickly wipes it away, as though flicking a leftover crumb from the table.

It wasn't just her father leaving that made Lydia feel discarded. It started with the repeated fights she witnessed and ended with her discovery through Facebook that her father had another family. Lydia tells me that she felt like a piece of clothing no longer in style, a feeling that only intensified when she was teased during adolescence for her freckles and burning-red hair. No one else in her class had her hair color. No one else's father had left them to start a new family.

"How can anyone love me?" she whispers, her gaze on the floor.

It seems to me that engaging in an affair had an additional advantage for Lydia: It was a defense. Instead of being discarded again, this time by Sam, she chose to do something that provided a perfectly good reason for someone to leave her. While her father's abandonment left her wondering what terrible flaw made him leave her behind, an affair meant that this time she would be left because of something she did. It would hurt, but at least she'd understand it.

I see this moment as an opportunity for inner child work, allowing us to shift between the couple's relationship dynamics and individual healing—both of which are key in the process of couples therapy. Healing our inner child is a process of acknowledging our own wounds and hurts, things that we needed and didn't get, and learning to give that to ourselves today. If clients are open and willing, this can be powerful work.

I ask Lydia to imagine an earlier time when she felt discarded. She tells me that she can see herself in her bedroom on the day her father left, crying into her purple quilt while her mother was in her own room with the door closed. With tears streaming down her face, Lydia admits she longed to have her father wrap his arms around her and tell her she was still loved.

Then I ask her to imagine sitting in front of this younger part of herself. "What does that thirteen-year-old child need?" I ask, using the word *child* intentionally in hopes of bringing a more compassionate view to herself. Sometimes we tell ourselves that we should have been able to handle hard things in our teen years, forgetting that being a teenager requires no less connection and support from our parents.

Lydia's chest rises and falls. Her voice shakes. "She needs to be held. She needs someone to tell her that she is okay and that she will be okay."

"Can you tell her that?" I ask.

Lydia squeezes her arms around herself more tightly and nods her head. She whispers, "You're okay . . . I'm okay."

Sam, witnessing Lydia's inner processing, has a sunken look on his face, his eyes glassy. "I wasn't trying to hurt you, Lydia. It's my mother. She's just like this. I love *you*, Lyds," he says. His voice rough, he adds, "But you don't believe me. It puts my character into question when you think I'm not going to love you."

I recognize Sam is caught between trying to be present with his wife and personalizing her experience to protect his ego. When we see a loved one struggle, we often take it to mean something about us. I ask Sam to put his feelings aside for a minute to stay focused on seeing the softer parts of Lydia that get hurt when he chooses his mother. Sam presses his lips together and clears his throat. If he is upset with me for interrupting him, I can tolerate it. After all, this is what he needs to practice.

"I just want to tell her that I choose her," he says, rubbing his hands up and down his thighs.

"Tell her that," I encourage him.

Sam puts his hand over Lydia's. "Lyds, I get it . . ." His voice trails off for a minute. "You feel like I chose my mother over you. I think I can understand that. There are things that we can do during this visit to make sure that you and I are on the same team. I'm sorry. I'm sorry this happened and that my actions caused this for you. I want us to be different."

I'm encouraged by his willingness to do this work. We can't change our past; we can only gain insight into the parts of ourselves that are not yet whole. The ego wants to protect our more vulnerable parts from the unbearable feeling that even a well-meaning action (a behavior, word, or boundary) has hurt the person we love. I see many relationships get stuck in self-protection mode against the shame spiral that says, *You did something bad, therefore you are bad.* But healthy interdependence considers the impact of our behavior on others, regardless of our intention.

Sam needs to look outside the insecurities created by his upbringing to see the courage it takes from Lydia to let Sam know her fears of losing him, the one person she clings to, the person who knows and understands her best. Since we didn't get to return to Sam's feeling that his wife's vulnerability questions his character, I let him know that in the sessions that follow, we'll continue to work on him sharing his need for attention and love.

Acknowledge

What Type of Boundary Setter Are You?

There are three types of boundary setters outlined in the chart below.

A Person with Rigid Boundaries	A Person with Healthy Boundaries	A Person with Porous Boundaries
• Avoids intimacy and close relationships • Prefers to not ask for help • Withholds internal thoughts and feelings • May be detached from others • Reacts to others by cutting ties with them • Keeps others at a distance to avoid potential rejection	• Values their thoughts and feelings • Communicates their thoughts and feelings in an assertive way • Remains firm on their values • Doesn't let rejection stop them from taking care of themselves • Accepts no from others	• Becomes over-involved with others' problems • Tends to overshare their internal experiences • May accept abuse or disrespect from others • Fears rejection if they assert their needs or say no • Self-sacrifices or people-pleases

Take a moment to reflect on the type of boundary setter you are.

◈ As a child, what did others do when you would express what you wanted (e.g., "I don't want to hug Grandma," "I don't like broccoli," "I need time alone")? Did they listen to you, or did they enforce their wishes or rules? Did they dismiss what you needed, tell you to stop being silly, or use guilt?

◈ Thinking of these earlier experiences, what beliefs do you have about sharing your needs and setting boundaries with loved ones today?

◈ Are there relationships where expressing your boundaries is easier? Harder? What makes them easier or harder?

◈ Write out one boundary you wish to set and find a time when you can practice it with someone who would be able to acknowledge it.

CHAPTER 12

Tracy

The ways you show up in relationships today stem from both implicit and explicit messages you received in childhood. Behaviors such as people-pleasing, caregiving, and playing the victim are often rooted in unconscious memories—in the internalized messages you received from caregivers, significant others, and the world.

◇◇◇◇◇

My mother likes to tell the story of my first big tantrum in the grocery store, an event that I barely remember since it happened when I was two years old. As she tells it, I was sitting in the front of the shopping cart and really wanted the red cereal box on the shelf. Since it wasn't on the grocery list and not in the budget, my mother said no. As I wailed for the breakfast item, she told me to stop. When I didn't, she picked me up, left the full cart in the middle of the aisle, and walked out of the store with me screaming and kicking in her arms. (I still don't know when she had time to go back for the groceries.) She finishes the story with a proud assertion that I never had a tantrum in public again.

Like most parents of that time, my mother's parenting style didn't allow much space for emotions. Sad or frustrated kids were simply told to stop crying. The closest thing to sympathy we received was a cliché like "No sense crying over spilled milk." Even positive values were instilled with a heaping helping of shame: "If you don't share, others will not like you" or "Be good and give Grandma a hug." Even though I don't remember it perfectly, my cereal box experience is one of the moments that taught me I had to be a "good girl," and I have been driven by pleasing and perfection ever since.

Many of my clients have similar stories from childhood. Their big feelings and deep needs were minimized or ignored. They were told to be quiet or criticized for being too sensitive. Something happened to them or around them but no one said anything. These "felt" experiences form the unconscious narratives behind our triggers and reactions, sometimes even more than the things we can remember happening. It's like being given a pair of sunglasses as a child and viewing the world through these lenses.

While I believe that most parents, my mother included, did the best they could with the information they had, it's important for us to acknowledge that they didn't always give us what we needed, that sometimes they even gave us information that has created more problems than it solved. Until we develop new ways of giving ourselves what we need, the unmet longings of our inner child keep us grasping for a solution—usually one that reflects a "script" we learned from the same dubious source.

It's these implicitly held scripts, rather than our explicit memories, that give rise to many of our relationship behaviors and beliefs. Psychiatrist and author Dr. Dan Siegel describes the difference using the example of a bicycle. An *explicit* memory is one you can call to mind, like the first time you learned how to ride a bike without training wheels. You can remember what it felt like to engage the pedals and grip the handlebars, how your tongue hung out of your mouth with fierce concentration, the leap in your stomach when your parent released their hold on the back of your seat, and the sudden steadiness you felt when everything clicked and you took off down the block. But when you get on a bicycle today, you are using *implicit* memory. You don't have to think back to the first time you rode a bike to tap into that ability today. The movements and technique are embedded in your mind and your muscles; in fact, you'd have to try extra hard to do it any differently.

Now imagine realizing as an adult that you were taught to ride a bicycle the wrong way. You might spend years avoiding bicycles because riding them is just too difficult, or maybe even dangerous. But then you see someone riding correctly, and it looks graceful, effortless, fun—so much so that you feel like giving bikes another try. You hop on and try to do it like them, but your body's instincts get in your way, and you take a spill onto the pavement. You could ask an experienced cyclist for pointers, even watch bicycle tutorials on YouTube, but even the best information isn't enough to change your patterns overnight. It's not easy to work against implicit memory.

In the same way, our relationship patterns are formed when explicit experience comes together with the implicit meaning we take from it to form specific neural connections in the brain. As the famous saying goes, "The neurons that fire together, wire together." If we experience repeated emotional or physical harm or neglect from people we trust or are close to, we may form neural connections that tell us (at an unconscious level) that trust and closeness are not safe. If our emotions were repeatedly ignored by our caregivers or we received negative consequences for speaking up about our needs (e.g., being hit, ridiculed, or ignored), we may form neural connections that say emotions are not safe to share. These connections are why we continue to respond according to the same "script" over and over, even when we know better, even when we desperately want to change.

Learning about these neural connections can make us feel like we're destined to keep repeating the same behaviors forever. But research shows that the brain can, in fact, make new neural connections by simply doing new and different things. Think about which leg you use to get on a bike. Next time, try using the opposite leg. Getting that leg over the bar will be awkward the first few times, but the more you repeat it, the less awkward it will feel. The same goes for trying new patterns of communication, sharing your feelings and needs, setting boundaries, and stepping out of old cycles to choose *us* over you or me. Choose a different path and you can create a new connection—literally!

While I don't remember the event in the grocery store, as a therapist and an adult, I know that my need as a two-year-old wasn't to be swiftly removed. I needed help learning how to ride the wave of emotions, for my mother to tell me how she could see it was hard that I couldn't have the cereal and for her to stay by me as I had these big feelings. This is what I have needed to unlearn—being good and pleasing, choosing others over myself. These patterns were created to keep me safe back then, but all they're doing now is fostering the resentment clouding my marriage.

Safety in our relationships as adults looks different from how it looks when we're young. As children, we are dependent on the help and support of our parents. When we grow up without the protection we needed, we may long for a partner who will always catch us when we fall, always give us what we want. But just as I discussed with Ashley, it is not possible for one person to do all of this. Moreover, the reality is that, as adults, we no longer require protection in the same way that we did as children. Healing requires us to first recognize that we can both nurture our own needs *and* risk seeking comfort and soothing from our partner—and, second, to take that risk.

As we saw with the bicycle example, having the right information isn't enough to change our behaviors in relationships. Real change comes from putting ourselves out there—facing the risk, taking the spill, getting up, soothing ourselves, and trying again.

It's easy to sugarcoat this process with another cliché like "Practice makes perfect." But as I know all too well, there's no practice harder and no stakes higher than the kind required in our intimate relationships. A skinned knee is a lot easier to recover from than a conflict that triggers our fears of shame, abandonment, or neglect. Rebuilding relational intimacy asks us to face those fears without expecting our partner or ourselves to get it right the first time (or the hundredth time). The real practice lies in trusting in ourselves, in our partner, and in the love that brought us together in the first place. Only when we get past those fears can we find each other again.

As couples therapist Terrence Real describes in his book *Us: Getting Past You and Me to Build a More Loving Relationship*, each moment between you and your partner can answer the question "What path do I want to choose today?" Learning to choose *us* over the individual you and me is what interdependence is all about. Integrating our individual autonomy with the closeness that comes from intimately being known and seen by another person is how we live meaningful and rich lives.

Acknowledge

Accessing Internalized Beliefs

Use the following questions to explore the internalized beliefs and unconscious messaging you hold from your past experiences. Your answers to these questions can help you access your negative *core beliefs*. One of the first things you can do with these beliefs is start telling yourself that everyone is worthy, good, and enough, including you.

◈ What were you told about being a "good" partner or person? What did you watch your parents do or not do that formed your beliefs about what it means to be a good partner?

◈ What happens today when you make a mistake?

◈ When something hard happens, what thoughts follow for you? When did you develop this way of thinking?

◈ Think about a recent moment when you struggled or didn't feel good about yourself. What kinds of thoughts did you have? What did you think about yourself as a person for having this difficult experience? You can try answering the question "When ___ happened, I felt ___ about myself. Struggling in that moment means that I am ___."

◈ What does it mean about you if you ___ [*insert hard thought here*]? Examples of hard thoughts might be saying no to someone, getting in a bad mood, or doing something that upsets your partner.

CHAPTER 13

Tracy

A strong relationship entails building a united front. This involves, among other things, a willingness to set loving boundaries with other loved ones. The goal of these boundaries is not to exclude family members from your life, but rather to include them in a way that works for your relationship.

Greg and I are sitting on the living room couch, staring out the front window as the sky changes from blue to pink behind the houses across the street. Neighbors walk by with their dogs and baby strollers, waving to us through the window. We wave back, united in an unspoken resolve not to reveal the tension crackling between us.

Our night started like any other night. Better, actually, since Greg has been taking a greater share of the daily parenting responsibilities. He did bath time with Anderson and then read him a story while I gave him his bedtime bottle. I see efforts like these as proof that he's listening to issues I've raised and working to prioritize intentional time with us as a family. His efforts mean all the more to me when, after kissing Anderson good night (and crossing my fingers that he'll sleep through the night), I look down at his sleepy smile and try to etch the look of his baby face into my mind. I want us to help each other preserve these precious memories as our son grows into a boy in front of us.

But now, with the soothing sounds of Anderson's sleep machine in the background, Greg and I are revisiting a conversation we've been trying to resolve for weeks. Greg's entire family—his parents, his sister and brother-in-law, and our two nieces who live in Western Canada—is planning a get-together in his hometown to celebrate his younger brother's wedding. I'm all for showing up to support his brother; I still remember how amazing it was on our own wedding day to look out on the guests and feel a loving connection with every one of them. However, the family is pressuring us for an extended visit outside of the actual wedding—five days, to be exact. (It's been hinted strongly that his sister and her family will be staying for two weeks.)

I understand his parents' desire to see all their kids together. We don't get to see them often, so this is a rare and memorable event. But . . . what can I say? Trips like these are hard for me, especially since I've graduated from being an anxious person to an anxious mother. Scratch that—an anxious, sleep-deprived mother. With our fifteen-month-old child's sleep schedule barely established at this stage, even two nights at a hotel feels like a stretch for me right now. Greg's family has offered for us to stay with them for the remainder of the trip, but a house packed full of family (including three kids under the age of three) without private sleeping space for us isn't within my realm of possibility. Add in the idea of moving around to two different locations, and my anxiety is already through the roof. I wonder how many times I will have to explain all this to my husband, who is supposed to be on my side.

Apparently, at least one more time.

"Can't we just stay?" Greg rubs his forehead restlessly. While on the one hand, he says he hears me and understands my reasoning for wanting to return home after the two nights for the wedding festivities, he continues to push for what his family wants. This is the crux of our issue.

"No, I can't," I tell him. Confident in the soundness of my reasoning, I proceed to restate all my points to Greg: the five nights of disrupted sleep, the resulting surge of postpartum anxiety, and (it occurs to me just then) the inevitable microscope I'll be under as the primary caregiver. I'll be the one fielding judgmental comments if Anderson only wants to be held by me or isn't eating his food. Furthermore, I point out, the exhaustion and sleep deprivation would then bleed into *my* vacation time after the wedding. I've been looking forward to this time off for weeks, desperate to unwind and do things that fill me up. All people require time to rest, I remind him, with the implied addendum *especially therapists*.

Rather than end my catastrophizing spree by telling him how this trip will almost definitely end with even greater rage toward my husband, I finish by pleading that I just can't do it. I'm about to underscore my points with some clinical wisdom about the importance of boundaries around mental health, but he interrupts.

"Okay, okay, I get it," he says. "It's just frustrating that you're always so flexible when it comes to your family and not with mine. But I get it—you don't want to."

I'm stung by the injustice of this comment, which we both know is inaccurate. I hold far many more boundaries with my family than Greg does with his. "It's not that I don't want to," I insist. "It's that I *can't* go that many nights with disrupted sleep. You're trying to push me, and I'm telling you that I'm not able to."

Even as the words emerge, I hear myself exercising "tough love" with my clients who struggle to apply themselves to their work in a relationship, reminding them that we all have times when we must acknowledge our discomfort but still do the hard thing in front of us. But this isn't one of those times for me. This is a time when I need to honor myself. Stepping out of the "good wife, mother, daughter-in-law" role is incredibly hard for me, but I can't keep dismissing my wishes. Motherhood has already required me to give up so much of myself. What I want now is for my husband to support me in doing my best.

Trying to recalibrate my approach before the conversation gets combative, I ask, "What's stopping you from calling your mom?" Inwardly, I cringe at how therapist-y I sound, but I have a genuine wish to support Greg in this moment. I have compassion for what gets in his way: fear of letting others down, difficulties setting boundaries, a desire to avoid others' negative emotions. He's so human in all these struggles, something I try not to forget amid my desire that he would do this work himself.

"Nothing," he replies, a little too quickly. I know it's not nothing. Greg sits at the tipping point of what I see many men experience: *Do I displease my mother to protect my wife, or choose my partner and upset my mother?* Lydia and Sam naturally come to mind. Like Sam, boundaries are not Greg's strength. Despite the conversations we've had about this trip since it came up, he still hasn't communicated our limits to his family.

I can't deny that having this experience in my personal life benefits my professional life by helping me build greater empathy for my clients' difficulties. While my experience will be different from theirs, the similarity grounds me in the struggles that they present with and guides me to the questions and possible roads to explore further with clients. I don't want to remove my humanness from the work that I do with my clients.

Now, with the wedding just two weeks away, Greg has painted himself into a corner. Since we haven't said any differently yet, it stands to reason that his family is expecting us to show up. His sister looking forward to catching up one-on-one with Greg, and his mother eager to have all the children and grandchildren gathered around the table for meals together. In all honesty, I've wondered if I should concede to make it all easier. But then I think of what my friend Lindsey said just this week, when I called her to talk about the friction surrounding our trip: "You get to choose you, too." Hearing it in her voice helped me find that same softer voice in myself, amid the self-criticism and expectations to care for others before myself. If I were advising a client on this matter, the right words would roll off my tongue: *Your wife has a reasonable need here, and while this may not be what your mother wants, your focus must shift to protecting your chosen family.* But when I decide to put myself first, there's always a voice that says I shouldn't.

Even before we got engaged, I found myself carrying the burden of coordinating visits with our loved ones for vacations, holidays, and special events, even while finishing my doctoral degree and balancing clinical work. Greg's mother would text an invitation, and he'd leave it unanswered, tacitly putting the ball in my court to respond and set it up. Having seen far too many women cornered into being the "schedule keeper" in the relationship, I told Greg that it was too much for me to play this role for both of our extended families. We agreed that he would handle communication and planning with his family and I'd look after the same things with my family.

But despite our agreement, it remained an uphill battle the first year of our son's life. It seemed like every conversation around family events came back to Greg's desire to accommodate his family of origin. While his parents remained blissfully unaware of the wishes he had (or we had) as a new family, I routinely found myself in tears of frustration at not being able to get through to him that making a commitment to a partner means separating from one's family of origin to create a new bond, a new set of obligations and priorities. This doesn't mean that someone's extended family no longer plays an important role in their life but that each person in the partnership openly says, "I will put my partner first and choose us." (I want to note that there is a cultural component here, which means this idea may not resonate with everyone. In some cultures, families of origin come before the partner. This is okay if both partners agree to it and find a way to get on the same page.)

Here again, being a couples therapist is a mixed blessing. I understand that Greg's reluctance to set boundaries goes beyond just wanting to keep his family happy. Many men struggle to express themselves, which leads them to create distance with their loved ones at any sign of conflict. It's like pulling teeth to try to understand where Greg is coming from, especially with topics like these where we have a long history of disagreement. What makes it worse is that knowing what he thinks would give me so much insight into how to support him. At the very least, it would help me be less angry. As it is, I feel endlessly frustrated by his inability to do something that seems so simple for me: State the boundary, hold it, and if others are upset, that is not your responsibility. While I have plenty of empathy for my clients who struggle to express themselves and set boundaries, when it comes to my husband, my cup is empty. *Knowing a better way to approach a situation doesn't always translate to doing it that way, does it?* my brain whispers.

"Well?" Hearing the impatience in my voice, I raise my glass to my lips, willing the Sauvignon Blanc to lull me back to calmness.

"What if we just did one more night?" he asks.

I look out the window in disbelief, my insides boiling. I know I shouldn't say what I'm about to say next, but here it comes.

"You go to bed with *me*. You wake up beside *me*. You live your life with *me*." My rage builds with each repeated *me*. "Why are you protecting everyone else's feelings except the people that you live with?" I see Greg's overwhelm growing right in front of me, but I'm too outraged to care at this point. I feel like a kid again, trying to get my parents to understand me, fighting to be right. My desperation to be seen has made it impossible for me to see *us* anymore.

My mind swirling, I put on my sneakers and grab my phone, signifying that I am done with the conversation, though we both know I'm not really done. I'm just doing what I do when I don't feel seen and heard. Even as I escape, my therapist brain calls me out; this is the same move my dad used to pull on my mother when his frustrations boiled over. It's a bad look as a therapist to repeat what I saw my parents do to each other. Still, walking out on someone is a great way to protect myself from being walked out on.

I speed-walk several blocks, my heart rate increasing and my breath short, outrage and anguish nipping at my heels. I break into a jog, then a run, faster and faster, until I can't catch my breath and my vision starts to blur. Stopping, I bend over, unsure whether I'm going to throw up or pass out. At last, I collapse on a nearby bench at the park.

It doesn't take the feelings long to catch up with me, though. I start texting Greg, anger surging through my fingers and onto the screen. One text after another, charging him with his failure to stand up for me, demanding he be a better role model for his son. Even though I know it never ends well, text-bombing is a release for my trigger of not being heard or seen. Each word I bitterly stab into the message field brings a spike of vindication: "Choose me, or your family."

The satisfaction it brings is short-lived, as I always know it will be. My thumb hovering over the "send" button, I hear my therapist training doing its best to talk me through it, as if I'm my own client, sitting on my office couch: *Ask yourself, does this urge align with what is meaningful to you? With where you want to go? Remember, ultimatums are like throwing a grenade into the relationship—it's not appropriate to use them unless you are truly ready to leave.*

I squeeze my fist tight as if to make my body stronger than my urge. With another rise and fall of my chest, my fingers tap the delete button, replacing the ultimatum with one last text: "I need you to choose us."

I get back from my walk to find Greg standing on the porch in the dark. His voice shaking, he tells me he's ready to get on the phone with his mother. My angry texts worked. But I do not feel any better.

Greg asks me to stay with him during the call to help him navigate the communication with his mother. Under different circumstances, this could be an opportunity for us to draw close to each other. As it is, I feel another wave of resentment, even as I sit down beside him and silently pledge to keep quiet and let him do the work that belongs to him.

My resolve lasts about five minutes, maybe less. Greg's confession of our plans to attend just the wedding elicits a piteous reproach from his mother: Why doesn't he want to spend more time with his own family? Seeing Greg stumble for what to say, I step in, uninvited and unannounced, to emphasize that we are trying to focus on our family and our health too, that we need time for ourselves.

In response, my mother-in-law's tone grows concerned. "Is everything okay?"

I'm not surprised by this question. Greg never says no to her requests—of course she senses something amiss. For whatever reason, hearing this tone in her voice softens my anger toward Greg. I know it's not easy for him to let his mother down, and I appreciate him for risking her disappointment to stand with me.

We end the call, wash the wine glasses, and say goodnight. I got the result I was after—Greg standing up to protect my needs—but I don't have the felt sense of safety I was looking for. Instead, my stomach is churning with shame at how our pattern keeps cementing itself with every conflict we endure.

Should we seek couples therapy for ourselves?

It's not the first time I've wondered this. But like all the times before, I'm resistant to it—stubborn, actually. My impostor syndrome isn't having it. I believe I can (or should be able to) work through this on my own. *Besides,* I think, *what therapist would we see? I'm connected to most couples therapists I trust in the city. We would have to travel out of town for an intensive retreat. And what about childcare?*

I can't be the only therapist who struggles in their marriage. Surely I'm not the only therapist trying to reparent myself, to heal my own old wounds within my new family. Little by little, the steps in our dance could change if I could just translate what I do in the office to what I do at home.

Acknowledge

Become a United Front

A united front means that you and your partner are a *we*, a team that works together and not against each other. But even the best teams sometimes have internal conflicts. In a moment of conflict, it's important to recognize that neither one of you is right or wrong. You simply have different experiences and you are both okay. Identify some ways that you struggle to feel like you are a *we*. Does it have to do with your family of origin? Parenting? Navigating the household tasks? Here are some ideas to practice being a united front.

◈ Ask your partner about their opinions and wishes without interrupting. Listen with the intent to understand them.

◈ Have clear boundaries with family members. Before attending family events or sharing decisions with extended family, ensure that you and your partner have discussed each other's wishes together. Share your boundaries with your extended family in terms of *we*, *our*, and *us*. This ensures that you avoid *scapegoating* or blaming your partner.

◈ Keep your parenting differences between the two of you. In front of your children, practice letting them see you on the same page and giving positive feedback to each other.

◈ Celebrate each other's wins, even if you would have done it differently.

CHAPTER 14

Ashley

There are events early on in a romantic relationship that can confirm old beliefs about yourself. The big question is whether what you heard was the intended message from your partner, or if there was a different intention that was not initially explored and resolved. Going back to these events can be a way of healing old wounds in your relationship.

◇◇◇◇◇

Ashley shows up to our appointment despite being on sick leave from work, her appearance a stark contrast to our previous sessions: track pants, oily hair, face ashen. She's the type of mother that I worry about the most: highly conscientious with a tendency to juggle all the things. Our bodies know our experience of stress well before our minds become conscious of it. If we don't listen, they will, at some point, stop responding to the high demands we put on them and collapse into physical ailments, like a cold that turns to pneumonia, digestive issues, or chronic pain. For Ashley, it's a loss of energy and severe fatigue. But even though she's on a break from work, she's still going nonstop.

"I just feel so guilty that I should be doing more," Ashley tells me, crossing and uncrossing her legs. "I started organizing Liam's clothes and shifting the seasonal stuff out of the kids' closets. My boss needed a document, so I took a few minutes to send that to him. And Daniel . . . well, he just doesn't understand my anxiety."

I'm not surprised guilt is showing up for her. Ashley is so used to high functioning that, for her, sick leave feels like she has abandoned her boss. Instead of prioritizing her healing (and sitting with her guilt), she's adding more to her household to-do list. When she starts listing off the projects she plans to complete, I stop to remind her that a leave from work is a time for recovery, similar to if someone broke a bone. Reluctantly, she agrees to hold off on organizing her pantry.

Brené Brown talks about the three P's that women get stuck in: performing, pleasing, and perfecting. I particularly see this with people who experience anxiety, like Ashley. These P's stop women from tapping into their authentic selves and living a life connected to what they find meaningful. Rather than asking themselves, *What do I need to be well in this moment?* they are consumed by a drive to fulfill accomplishments and meet others' needs.

What do these P strategies offer us in return for their constant demands? Ultimately, they help us avoid feeling that there is something fundamentally wrong with us. If we can just get everything "right," if we can just keep others "happy," we'll feel like we measure up to something. But if we need to be perfect in order to have worth, we're coming from a place of shame—the secret inner place that says we are bad, unworthy, not enough.

Ashley's acknowledgment of her burnout is a good step for her. Her husband, however, continues to be unaware of many things about his wife, not the least of which is the unexpressed anger that our last few sessions have identified.

"Maybe this break is a good time to talk to Daniel about what you're actually experiencing," I suggest, taking a sip of my hot coffee. It's not only because Ashley is one of my first sessions today—I need a kickstart after being up in the middle of the night with my toddler.

"Interesting you should say that." Ashley tucks her hair behind her ears. "Daniel discovered my pile of new clothes hidden in the guest closet last week. He never goes into the guest room, but he was looking for a book he had tucked away."

Yelling out to Ashley, his voice penetrating, Daniel demanded to know where the clothes were from. He picked up each piece of clothing, his face turning redder with every price tag he inspected. Ashley, wringing her hands, told Daniel that they weren't hers. She claimed they belonged to Alexis, the mom down the street whom they always see yelling at her husband in the front yard. Ashley's lies accumulated. "I'm just holding onto them. They got into a big fight last week," she said with a shrug, then turned her back to Daniel so he couldn't see her cheeks burning red. Even in the moment, Ashley says, she understood how her lie about her friend mirrored how she feels in her own marriage. Daniel shoved the pile of clothes back into the bag and mumbled something about women not being able to manage money.

In retaliation for Daniel's harsh commentary on women and finances, Ashley started to transfer money in small amounts from their joint account to pay off her debt.

I see Ashley's choices as an adaptation of the same unhelpful coping patterns she has used her entire life. In every challenge, the ever-present specter of her unpleasable mother hovers over her with something, always something, that she isn't doing right. Today, with her husband, kids, and boss, she agrees with everyone and to do everything—not even carving out ten minutes for herself to have a coffee. She instead self-soothes by secretly shopping and then hides it with lies and illicit transfers from her family's joint account to pay off her debt. These are all behaviors where Ashley attempts to deal with the distress that comes with not asserting herself as an autonomous person with her own independent needs.

If something doesn't change for her, these lies could spiral into something else, like an affair or the need to remortgage her house should her spending continue to amount to large sums. Ashley isn't having an affair, but her behavior around money is a form of infidelity. I know she values her marriage—she wouldn't have started therapy at her husband's request if she didn't—but she continues to focus on Daniel's actions rather than her role in cocreating a stronger relationship for both of them. This outward focus is often where people start therapy: "If my husband weren't so defensive . . ." or "If my partner helped more . . ." This makes sense, as looking inward at how we contribute to issues can trigger shame and fear of being unworthy or unlovable. But to change your relationship, you need to first be willing to change yourself.

Good people make mistakes. This is often the conversation I have when it comes to any kind of infidelity—emotional, sexual, or financial. We use powerful coping mechanisms inside of our mind to manage our actions and behaviors, particularly those that create pain, anxiety, and sadness. This justification is called *cognitive dissonance*, which is the uncomfortable feelings and tension that someone has when they experience conflicting beliefs, attitudes, thoughts, or opinions. One study found that in order to make the choice of infidelity seem okay, people were able to change both their view of self (how they understand themselves) and their view of infidelity (their belief that it is wrong or hurtful). Cognitive dissonance comes on fast—often we aren't able to catch it at a conscious level. This means that we need to be curious and open to getting uncomfortable in exploring our beliefs and the choices we make.

We do the hurtful things we do for good reasons: to protect ourselves from criticism or denigrating comments, to keep others from rejecting us, to remain included with loved ones. There is something deeper going on for Ashley, a deeper pattern she needs to shift. To get out of the blaming pattern that keeps her relationship stuck in codependency, I invite Ashley to be curious with me about her pattern of secrecy. I point out that while she consistently blames Daniel for their lack of connection, in the actual relationship she backs down and takes all the blame for their problems on herself. What she shares with me in therapy makes Daniel come off as a jerk, but in reality, he has no idea how she feels. If we remain closed off to understanding the thoughts and feelings that precede our behavior, it is impossible to change. If Ashley continues to stick to her narrative that Daniel's lack of support is the only reason she has anxiety, she'll never understand how she participates in their dynamic.

"When Daniel discovered the clothes you'd hidden, what stopped you from being open with him? It seems like this could have been a window to share something—anything—about what has been going on." My hope is that Ashley can identify why she wanted these items enough to keep them a secret. But she avoids my question.

"But Dr. Tracy, you don't understand. Your relationship is amazing. You're a perfect couple."

I shift in my seat and look down at my notepad as my marriage—me as human—is showing up in our session. I know what Ashley is referring to. Last week, Ashley walked past me and Greg while we were on one of our "day dates" at the local market. Out of respect for my clients' privacy, I typically don't address them when we cross paths in public. Clients know they can say hello to me but that I will allow *them* to initiate it. Greg also knows that if someone says hi to me and I don't introduce him, that it is someone that I may have interacted with in a work context (therapy, corporate presentations, group sessions).

I feel flattered—even slightly validated—that she thinks we have that kind of marriage. At the same time, what Ashley saw was a snapshot of ease in our relationship, holding hands, laughing over some inside joke. The irony is that it's an increasingly rare occurrence in the thick of our disconnection. Ashley didn't see me looking at myself in the mirror earlier that morning, wondering why I'd even chosen to spend the day with Greg. She didn't see me walk away from him when I asked him why he hadn't taken out the lawn chairs yet and his reply was that he'd been busy.

I refocus on Ashley and sidestep her comment. "We caught each other in public, didn't we?" I'll make a note to address this at another time. Self-disclosures can be powerful interventions in therapy, which could sound like "All marriages struggle, including mine" with Ashley. But any kind of self-disclosure has to be carefully timed in therapy so that it is beneficial for the client and not just a "me too" experience. This is a clinical decision that a therapist must make, which is dependent on the client, the stage of therapy, and the therapist's processing and understanding of their own experience. And I know that sharing the authentic parts of my marriage with Ashley today will prevent her from reflecting inward.

"But there's something that creates distance in *your* relationship. Was there a time where your trust was broken in some way? Or something happened to change your connection?"

Ashley glances down at the faux marble coffee table and starts twisting her hand over her opposite wrist (a nervous twitch I've noticed in other sessions). I watch her face change from relaxed to pained. She swallows once before she speaks.

"Daniel once told me that I wasn't the right person for him." Tears begin to well in her eyes.

Back during their pre-married days in France, Ashley was visiting family in Ontario for a month before attending a family member's wedding. Daniel would be joining her for the last week of her trip to be present for the wedding and they would fly back home together. Ashley also secretly hoped Daniel would propose. However, she didn't hear from Daniel during the first three weeks of her trip. Knowing his social personality and tendency to live "in the moment," Ashley didn't think much of it and kept herself busy connecting with her friends and family. When she finally met up with Daniel, just days before the family wedding, his face was pale with dark circles under his eyes. Chalking his demeanor up to jet lag, Ashley chatted about the wedding and their own future plans to get engaged and married. In response, Daniel grumbled, "We need to talk."

Still remembering the look on his face, Ashley shares that Daniel expressed doubts about their relationship. Blindsided, she searched for a rationale for the change of heart—there must have been someone else that he was seeing or talking to. He denied this. Going into panic, Ashley pressed for more information. In return, Daniel asked for space. He skipped the wedding, spent a few days in Ontario visiting extended family, then flew back to France alone, leaving Ashley gutted and bewildered.

Ashley received no communication from Daniel when she returned to France until, a few weeks later, he reached out to her to meet at a café to talk about getting back together. He told her that he needed her to be more flexible and agreeable, and Ashley was so relieved that he still wanted to be with her that she quickly obliged. But in doing so, she also agreed to tuck away the other parts of her, like her need for one-on-one time or her wish for him to validate the stress she experienced as a result of work and family. Perhaps Daniel thought this feedback would help strengthen their relationship, but it backfired. His focus on Ashley only increased her feelings of self-consciousness.

What was left unexplored at that time? Ashley's repeated experience of abandonment. As her desired future husband was breaking up with her, she was brought back to the moment in her childhood home where her father held his suitcase in his hand, stood at the front door, and told her he would see her later. Still, she didn't make that connection in the moment of their breakup. Instead, driven by self-doubt, she committed to hiding herself behind the person she thought Daniel wanted her to be. Just as she now hides the overspending that both soothes and increases her sense of guilt in the relationship. Just as she is hiding from my questions in session today. She does this to stay safe, and it works to some degree—by agreeing to Daniel's terms, she has kept their relationship. But at what cost?

I encourage Ashley to acknowledge her painful pattern, to consider that her people-pleasing is a false way of establishing self-worth and that perhaps she is playing her own version of the victim (like her mother would do) by not standing up for herself. She agrees that she is striving to find her lovability, looking for others to tell her that she is worthy. I ask her what she likes about herself beyond her caregiving skills. She needs to start paying attention to other internal aspects that make her lovable in many other ways. I also invite her, as part of her return-to-work plan, to write a list of situations where she self-sacrifices at home and at work. By identifying moments like these, she can start to assert her desires.

Ashley agrees to stop taking over bath time and bedtime when she sees Daniel struggling with these tasks. "I'll try stepping back," she concedes. "Maybe I'll go out for a walk."

It's more than just stepping back, I think, nodding my head to prepare myself for where we need to go next.

"I could be wrong," I start, allowing myself the possibility of not always getting it right, "but it's almost like you now see Daniel doing what he likes, doing what he wants, and you resent it, when in fact this is a projection of yours. You tucked away your wants and needs when Daniel came back to you and asked you to change. It's not that you and Daniel are so fundamentally different. It's that he chooses to be vocal about what he wants; he doesn't carry the baggage of thinking that you will leave him. You, on the other hand, fear that he will leave if you decide to show up as the authentic you."

Ashley sits in silence, her fingers tracing her raised eyebrows. I meet her in this silence, letting my interpretation hang between us. Outside, a siren blares in the distance. Ashley blinks a few times and takes a slow, deep breath. Something is shifting.

"I have never thought of this . . ." she murmurs. "I used to be that person. I used to go with the flow and laugh and have fun. Now I have panic attacks whenever I'm solo parenting or have to meet Daniel at a work event." She takes another breath. "When I look back at my life, I think I was always looking for someone to tell me that I was okay. To tell me I was good and that I mattered in the world."

"What if you started letting yourself act this way?" I suggest. "Tapping back into this old part of you that you've pushed away for so long out of fear?"

"I don't want to inconvenience him. What if he leaves?"

I interrupt her before she can retell the theoretical story. Our brain is built to act on repeat so that we cement the hardwiring that this narrative is a reality, when in fact it is not the truth. This is what our minds do. They retell stories over and over, making those stories inherently true inside our minds. They replay what is familiar even when the story no longer works for us.

"He *could*." I lean toward her. "Ashley, any of us could lose our partners. We don't have any control over other people. We can only choose our intentions and how we want to act in our most precious relationships." Even as I'm saying this, my choice to pour Greg's coffee this morning flashes before my eyes. I was tired from being up with Anderson during the night, but I wanted to show Greg that I cared about him. He thanked me for the coffee, and I felt his sense of appreciation for me. It's so small and inconsequential—and yet it is meaningful when he sees that I thought of him, that he crossed my inner world and I considered him.

Just as we change, we also have to allow our perceptions of our partner to change. I press further, looking for a new narrative that Ashley can adopt. "What is different with Daniel today compared to back then?"

Ashley lists several ways that she and Daniel have deepened their bond over the years: going through a miscarriage together, buying and selling homes until landing on their dream house, raising two young boys. In spite of their difficult day-to-day life, these shared experiences have forged their commitment to each other. Ashley needs to believe that this kind of intimacy doesn't evaporate just because you share something that's hard for your partner to hear.

"Given all of this, maybe now you can share with Daniel," I suggest, being direct to finish our session. I challenge Ashley to write a letter to her husband that expresses her feelings and deep desires, lets him in on her difficulties, and yes, confesses her spending. This kind of homework is risky, as it puts power into the hands of people not in the therapy room. But her vulnerability with Daniel could also bring closeness and healing, ultimately allowing her to offload the weight of her resentment.

Acknowledge

What Thought Patterns Do You Get Stuck In?

There are several faulty thought patterns that can interfere with relationships and lead to increased distress. Here are just a few.

◇ *All-or-nothing thinking*: The tendency to think in black-or-white terms without nuance, to only see two extremes of a situation while missing other possibilities.

◇ *Confirmation bias*: The tendency to only observe information that confirms your own beliefs. In relationships, these beliefs are often negative views of your partner.

◇ *Jumping to conclusions*: Making assumptions about your partner's thoughts, emotions, and actions based on limited information to support your belief.

◇ *Labeling*: Narrowly defining your partner or categorizing them based on limited information.

◇ *Mind reading*: Assuming what your partner is thinking or feeling without concrete information to support your assumptions.

◇ *Personalization*: Believing that your partner's thoughts, feelings, and actions are about you.

Take a moment to reflect on the above misperceptions.

◇ Which faulty thought patterns do you tend to get stuck in?

◇ Are there past experiences that are impacting the beliefs you hold about your partner today? (For example, if an ex-lover was unfaithful, do you now question whether your partner is telling the truth? If your mother complained about your father in a certain way in front of you as a child, do you now only see the negatives of your partner?)

◇ To practice letting go of these unhelpful beliefs, write out five things that you are grateful for about your partner. Over the next week, intentionally notice something positive about them.

CHAPTER 15

Emily and Matt

You need to acknowledge two truths: Your parents did the best they could, and your family of origin impacted your beliefs related to yourself and what it means to have a healthy relationship. Old patterns of interaction, stemming from the way your parents interacted with each other or with you, become central to your relationship conflicts. However, these unhealthy patterns can stop with you.

◇◇◇◇◇

Here's the thing about therapy: We spend fifty minutes together, once a week or every other week, trying to tease out the root causes of the issues that create pain in our relationships. At best, those fifty minutes can show us what we're dealing with. The real work—taking risks, trying something different, doing hard things—happens between sessions. This is one of the reasons therapists give homework assignments: to nudge clients into doing the real work.

It's a little-known fact that these assignments usually involve a leap, not just for the client but also for the therapist. While my homework assignments are based on what I have learned about a client and their world, I can never fully know how they will go when put into practice. For example, when I instruct a client to challenge the thought that they aren't liked by asking their friends what they appreciate about the client, I am hoping that the friends show up the way friends should. When I recommend that a client go home and ask their spouse for the reassurance they need in their relationship, I cross my fingers that their partner will rise to the occasion.

Alas, in the case of Emily and Matt, the leap did not land.

Matt invested in the homework. He felt relief when he wrote a letter to the little boy who just wanted to be liked by his father, the boy whose attachment figure had his own traumatic upbringing and couldn't offer the kind of support and care that Matt needed. He decided to also write a letter to his father, expressing how he just wanted his love and attention. Matt didn't send the letter—often this type of homework is not meant to be shared—but he felt like writing it enabled him to start putting aside his fear of not getting things right.

Emily, on the other hand, went from writing a letter to her child self to a "things Matt doesn't do" list. Her anger grew as the items accumulated: buying groceries, purchasing Alice's next size of clothing, booking doctor's appointments and oil changes, paying household bills . . . It went on for quite a while.

This wasn't all. While visiting her parents with Alice, Emily showed the list to her mother. Naturally, her mother weighed in with her characteristic blame, reiterating her belief that Emily is wasting her time with Matt and would be better off with someone else. Worrying that her mother was right, Emily closed herself off further from Matt instead of bringing her concerns to him, locking away her true feelings and fears in a protective shell of anger.

I learn all this at the start of our next session. Matt's pained face expresses his feelings of fury and betrayal, and I can't deny that I feel some of this too. Emily pulling this bad-faith stunt just as Matt is finally engaging in the work to build a better connection makes me doubt that she will do the work on her end.

"What did you hope to get out of showing the list to your mother?" I ask.

"I just want someone to see it. I'm exhausted. I'm doing everything. And since Matt doesn't acknowledge all that I do for our family, I'm going to bring it to someone who gets it, who will say that my feelings are real." The high pitch of righteous indignation in Emily's voice is a thin cover for the primary emotion behind her words: sadness, not just at the *mental load* she carries but also at Matt's continued failure to propose marriage.

"So Mom offers you empathy and validation?" She nods. However, from what I have learned so far, that narrative doesn't hold up. *Empathy* is a willingness to be in someone's experience without judgment or problem-solving, while *validation* is the act of letting the other person know that you see and understand their experience. What I hear from Emily is that her mother vilifies Matt and tells Emily to break the relationship off. This isn't empathy or validation; it's projection.

Emily continues rehearsing the same story I've heard countless times already: If Matt just did more, their arguments wouldn't keep happening. Therapists are supposed to be neutral, but watching Emily grow dysregulated despite my efforts to bring her back to the present moment triggers my own frustration. *How can he help her when she keeps railing against him this way? How will he see her vulnerability when she won't share it?* In a flash of irritation, I raise my voice slightly and tell her to stop, that I can't let her continue to speak to Matt in this way. She narrows her eyes at me with a look that could pierce glass.

I take a breath. "Emily, let's consider . . ."

"I've had enough," she snaps. In a blink, she leaps off the couch, opens the door, and leaves my office.

Matt gazes at the open door for a moment, his face blank, then his head falls into his hands. Equally shocked, I validate his efforts toward healing and remind him that what just happened is the result of Emily's "stuff" preventing her from turning to him for what she really needs.

Working with clients like Emily—critical blamers who are highly sensitive to shame—requires me to proceed with caution. Even though I see Matt's contribution to their difficulties, as the quieter one he naturally attracts more empathy. To be blunt, it's easier to like him.

I have to work harder to like Emily, to remember that somewhere behind her fierce defenses hides a scared and lonely little girl. I can't call her out like I would a less fragile client; I have to keep a balance between letting Emily know that I see her reality and reminding her that holding impossible standards for her partner and turning to her mother for emotional "support" is working against the close connection she ultimately wants in her relationship. Sometimes that balance eludes me, though. A familiar feeling of powerlessness presses in my gut, as it always does when I'm reminded that I have no control over what happens for a couple I'm trying to help.

I leave Matt in my office to bring Emily back and, I hope, repair the situation. The elevator ride is restorative; with each floor down, I descend back into my calmer self. But I find the foyer and front steps empty. It's a long journey back to my office. I take the stairs this time, one heavy step after the other, contemplating what I could have done differently to stop Emily from leaving the room while equally not allowing her to continue to rail her partner. Matt and I spend the remainder of the session sitting across from each other in silence. At ten to the hour, we stand.

"I'll see you next session," I say.

He nods.

It turns out our next appointment won't be for a while. Like many clients, there is no announcement that they aren't coming back; instead, two months go by before I hear from either of them again. I learn later that during our break in therapy, Emily and Matt got into another fight, this time over the texture of certain foods for Alice. As usual, Emily's belittling tone touched on Matt's feelings of unworthiness, which just happened to be heightened at that time by some difficult feedback from his boss. Instead of seeing that Emily craves acknowledgment, Matt snapped at her to stop. Emily then spent the weekend stewing over her catalog of Matt's failures until, enraged and dysregulated, she announced that she wanted a separation. Shocked (and, frankly, exhausted), Matt retreated. He didn't want the separation but agreed to it, moving to the basement (as he's not able to afford rent on his own), and the couple began to live parallel lives, only talking when it concerns caring for Alice.

When couples feel like they have tried everything, they often want to know if a separation will be helpful. The answer? It depends. Factors that contribute to an effective break include having a set time frame and boundaries around contact. Both partners need to be willing to change to make the relationship work. If you separate and keep pointing fingers, nothing will be different. It's important that you understand the behaviors that led to the separation and what each person needs in order to come back together (such as more connection, less criticism or defensiveness, a commitment to attend therapy to improve communication, more intimacy or emotional support). I have seen couples come back together after a break, willing to make things better, while some make short-term changes only to fall back into familiar patterns. Some choose to not get back together at all.

Matt's absence meant that Emily could no longer hold him responsible for her feelings. To get away from the tension stewing in her own home, she took Alice to her parents' house several times over the past two months for help and distraction. But something unexpected developed during this time: Emily began to see her parents' marriage in a new light. Had she never noticed that her father starts drinking at 2 p.m., getting louder and louder, eventually going to his study, slamming the door behind him? Had she never heard her mother put her father down in front of her with frequent criticisms and passive-aggressive remarks? Emily had been exhausted from carrying the weight of household labor, but now she was exhausted by the tension in her parents' home. Emily imagined talking to her daughter about Matt in the same way Emily's mother speaks to her about her father, and she realized how she'd hate to imprint such toxic patterns into her child's brain. For perhaps the first time, Emily was beginning to genuinely wrestle with the choices she has made.

Equipped with these new insights, Emily and Matt return to therapy. I start things off by asking if their separation acted as a reset, whether they were able to reflect on their own needs, and how they want to change. When Emily expresses fear that she is just like her family, I offer her my favorite analogy: The things we learn from our parents are like gifts, some of which we like and others we don't. The model of a romantic relationship that Emily acquired from her parents is like a wool coat—it fits great and keeps her warm, but it itches. Emily can choose to keep wearing the itchy coat and carry it with her everywhere, or she can choose not to wear it while recognizing that her parents offered her the best they had.

Emily declares that she is ready to burn the hand-me-down. "I think I need space from my mother." Matt's surprise is palpable—this is the same woman who previously stated that her mother was the only person who understood her. But Emily is beginning to see that her mother's toxicity is impacting her way forward in this relationship. It's becoming clearer to Emily that repeatedly turning to her mother to confirm her feeling that Matt is the problem in their partnership is keeping her fused to old family dynamics. This new awareness is key for Emily to build her individual autonomy as well as intimacy with Matt. She can start to see him as a separate individual with his own experiences—and a partner who isn't perfect but is trying his best. These are essential steps toward healthy interdependence.

Faithful to his work to continue reaching for her instead of dismissing her experience and expounding on all the things he does in the house, Matt asks Emily if he can hug her. Emily responds with a passive nod. Given that their main point of connection for the past year has been fights, it's not surprising that she's still awkward in the new connection they've begun to form. I see her eyes close and her throat move up and down as she swallows back tears. I'm pleased to see that

Matt continues to hold her until she relaxes into his arms and, finally, wraps her arms around him. He says, "I want you to open up with me. We can do this together." Emily squeezes her eyes tight.

If Emily continues to step out of her hostility and make her invisible mental load visible, she will start to see a different connection with Matt. Having seen many couples do this work, I know that as Matt continues to step into the relational arena, it will invite Emily to step into it with him. The physical and emotional connection they have had in session today is only the beginning.

Acknowledge

Your Unmet Needs and Repeating Patterns

When our parents are unable to meet our core attachment needs (e.g., need for soothing, comfort, unconditional acceptance), we find ways to continue holding our parents in a positive light (a natural protective impulse for a child) and instead build internal schemas, or belief systems, about ourselves. These belief systems lead us to act in repetitive ways with significant others that stop us from getting our needs met. These repeating old patterns may be seen in one of the following ways.

◈ You internally respond to yourself in the same way your parents did (e.g., rejecting, dismissing, criticizing).

◈ You treat your partner in the same rejecting, dismissive, or critical way that your parents treated you.

◈ You choose a partner who treats you in the same hurtful ways that you experienced from your caregivers.

Take a moment to reflect on these three patterns. Which of these resonate the most with you? When you feel yourself not getting your needs met, do you try to move closer to your partner (e.g., pleasing, caring, giving), further away from them (e.g., avoiding, shutting down), or against them (e.g., attacking or intimidating them)?

Spend some time acknowledging your unmet attachment needs from childhood and allow yourself to hold two things as true: Your parents did their best *and* your needs were valid and real. Call to mind a younger version of yourself and offer a statement of compassion to the child who didn't get their needs met. With a hand over your heart, try saying, *I am lovable and I am enough.*

CHAPTER 16

Karine and Peter

Contrary to popular belief, your partner isn't supposed to be able to give you everything you need. This simply isn't possible for human beings to do for each other. If your partner is unable to change in the ways you want, you may need to shift out of judgment and criticism and learn to accept them for who they are.

◇◇◇◇◇

Karine leaves me a voicemail, saying that she urgently needs an individual session. My gut sinks; I wonder what has unfolded between her and Peter. Memories of how Emily's homework assignment derailed are still fresh in my mind.

I don't normally see couples separately after their initial one-on-one assessment. I can't have one partner feeling favored or the other feeling ganged up on. However, the urgency in Karine's voice tells me that this is different. A quick email to Peter confirms that he gives permission for Karine to see me alone. He also refuses an individual session for himself and reminds me, as he did in our first session, that it is Karine who needs the help. My hands thus tied, intuiting that this is therapeutically important, I proceed with caution.

Karine comes straight from her shift at the hospital, dressed in scrubs, hair pulled tight in a ponytail. Wide-eyed, she hurries to tell me of the recent events: Earlier this week, sensing that Peter was struggling with stress at work, she tried to support him by asking questions but kept hitting the brick wall around his emotions. Finally, Karine spoke up, telling Peter that she needed him to see how unbearable it felt for her to have him lock her out.

I let Karine know that I'm proud of her for doing the self-other piece—that's therapist-speak for considering your own thoughts and feelings while also exploring what the other person might be thinking and feeling. Asking, "Can you see me here and step into my world for a minute?" is a task that many people struggle with, but it is important for building empathy and understanding in our relationships.

Karine smiles sadly, pleading to me that she's done everything they've been working on in therapy. But that evening, exhausted by yet another dead-end argument, Karine sought the wisdom of her circle of friends. Unfortunately, because Karine frequently goes to them with her distress, they have only heard negative things about her relationship and thus weren't able to properly support her. Instead, they did what friends tend to do: They told her that Peter was gaslighting her. Far from soothed by this layman's diagnosis, Karine spent the next several days analyzing her interactions with Peter until she finally decided to consult me about it.

I notice that clinical labels such as *gaslighting* and *narcissist* are entering everyday conversations and being thrown out in escalated disagreements. While labels can be helpful and validating, it can also be incredibly harmful when terms like these are misused—it can easily stand in for name-calling and denigrating the other person. Labels for people and their behavior need to be explored carefully and with proper guidance, or they can implode a relationship.

I see Karine's real distress when she asks me whether I agree that Peter is gaslighting her, if I think he might be a narcissist. Her fear of making the same mistake as in her last marriage is heightened by her friends' one-sided perspective of their relationship. She is scared of being duped, of replaying out the same old pattern, of even being emotionally abused again. I must admit that I, too, had wondered about Peter's personality orientation in our initial appointments: His recurrent difficulties in being able to see her emotions, his insistence on telling his story over her story, his frequent dismissal of her experience. But I don't need to let Karine know this. As a therapist, my words hold weight. It's important that I don't get this wrong.

"I see how difficult it must have been to have your most trusted supporters question Peter, to put this big term out," I say. "And more, I see how much you long to connect with Peter and just how hard this work is." I take a breath. "I don't believe that Peter is gaslighting you. There is a difference between someone gaslighting you and someone dismissing or disagreeing with you." As Karine exhales a sigh of relief, I continue to explain the difference between gaslighting and dismissiveness. Gaslighting, I explain, occurs when someone manipulates you into questioning your reality, all for the purpose of gaining power and control. It leads you to doubt yourself and your sanity. Dismissiveness, in contrast, occurs when someone invalidates, minimizes, or belittles your experience. It doesn't carry a malicious intent or a desire to manipulate. I let Karine know that I believe that Peter dismisses her to protect a fragile part of him, a part that was never acknowledged in his history. Peter is not intentionally leading Karine to doubt herself in order to get his own way; rather, invalidating her perspective is a coping mechanism for relational stress.

We go on to talk about the ways she can show up differently in conversation with Peter, ways that may help him understand her. I offer her the idea of prefacing the conversation. Instead of prompting a big discussion without warning, starting with something like "I really need you to just listen to what I'm about to say" can radically change the outcome. This clear statement sends a message that disarms any reflexive defense in the other person's brain, letting them know that they don't have to *do* anything with the information right away except be open to it. Simply acknowledging that what you're saying may take some time to process, and that you're allowing for that time, lets your partner know the impact you have on them. It says, "I see you outside of the context of me." This is interdependence.

We also talk about turning down her emotional dial. Her ease with expressing her feelings is a good quality, but it's overwhelming for Peter's shutdown brain. Instead of eliciting his compassion, it only triggers his shame. While I hope that Peter can develop his emotional receptivity in our sessions, Karine would benefit from practicing more grounding breaths while communicating with Peter instead of upping the ante through her tears.

Karine leaves the session visibly relieved, but that doesn't stop her shame spiral in the weeks that follow. When Karine and Peter arrive for their next session, I can sense the uneasiness between them. They sit farther apart on the couch than ever before. Something big has happened, but neither one of them is eager to tell me what it is.

Finally, Karine fills me in. Despite her fears of overstepping, she continued trying to bond with Peter's daughter by taking her to a soccer game. At the game, Brielle began to have an allergic reaction. Responding quickly, Karine rushed the girl to the emergency department at the hospital where she works. Peter's ex-wife arrived before he did, storming into the exam room, demanding to know what happened, then blaming Karine before she could even explain. When Peter finally arrived, Charlotte started yelling at Karine, making a scene in front of the other patients and staff. Karine shrank away, resentful of being treated like a delinquent babysitter and ashamed that her colleagues were witnessing this outburst. Peter, meanwhile, was forced into a dilemma that many blended families face: Whom would he stand up for? The mother of his child, or his partner?

It seems Peter chose neither. He froze and asked his ex-wife to keep quiet until their daughter's treatment was finished.

In the days that followed this event, Peter attempted to apologize to Karine and even to prove his commitment to her by getting home early from work, being physically affectionate, and tuning into her every word. But Karine, in a rare move, shut down. Not only did she stop sharing with Peter, but she began going to bed alone, skipping their typical evening rituals of connection. During the day, she started keeping herself busy with work and going out to see her friends. Whether out of self-preservation or sheer exhaustion, she started doing to Peter what he does to her.

These are hard moments to witness as a therapist. Still, I know that sometimes a relationship has to get worse before it can get better. Now that I can see Peter's more vulnerable parts, I'm eager to get to work with them so Karine and Peter can start to feel close again.

"I just hate when he does this tiptoeing around me," Karine laments. "He knows he should have stood up for me, but now he's doing all these nice things for me instead of owning his mistake." She sighs heavily. "These are the times that I think I didn't sign up for this. I didn't sign up for an ex-wife to rail at me. I didn't sign up for my partner to shut me down."

When I ask Peter to tell me what happens for him in these moments of conflict, he rebuffs me as usual, saying that this is just how he is. But despite his tough shell, he looks like someone stranded in a dark forest without a map. I think he knows that if he doesn't change, he is going to lose Karine, and he's afraid. I can use that.

Once again, I ask Peter about different events involving his parents that occurred throughout his childhood, trying to help him connect what he does today to his earlier experiences. Peter looks down and then, for the first time, opens up.

"I think my divorce from my ex really impacted me. It was first love for both of us. I remember trying to prove my devotion to her." His face scrunches up, expressing the pain of the memory replaying in his mind. Charlotte wasn't just Peter's first true love; she was his exit from an emotionally neglectful home. There were hopes and dreams attached to that relationship that have never fully healed.

Karine starts to jump in, but I put my hand up as if to signal for her to pause. She obliges.

"I remember making mistakes with Charlotte," he goes on, sharing how he would be late between classes to pick up Charlotte, or withhold information about his friends or family, or tell his friends about a fight they had—normal missteps in any relationship, especially a young one. Charlotte was enraged by Peter's behavior, also arguably normal for young people learning love through trial and error. But instead of offering compassion and healthy communication, Charlotte would guilt-trip him, telling him to prove his love for her. For days afterward, he would serve as her chauffeur, purchase her meals, and buy her new clothes.

"You had to earn her love back," I reflect back to him.

"Yeah, I guess so. I never thought of it that way." Peter ponders this further.

"Go back to that eighteen-year-old Peter in his first relationship, learning about love. What would you say to him?" I ask.

"I don't know . . ." he says. Karine puts her arm on Peter's leg, an offering of companionship that seems to soothe his discomfort in opening up to this degree. "I guess I would tell him that he didn't need to prove his love so much. It's just . . . I've just let myself down. I'm just so stupid. I should know better." His eyes start to well up but just as quickly, he pushes the tears and the feelings away.

This is the first time we've tapped into this highly self-critical part of Peter. I want to explore this more, to use this window into his world to inform what he can do differently with Karine. The question (or choice point, as we say in therapy) is which type of intervention will meet him where he is. If I use an emotionally focused approach to process his feelings of inadequacy and shame, I could lose him. I also don't think challenging his cognitions (his thoughts and beliefs about his life) would be particularly helpful. I decide to work from an Internal Family Systems (IFS) approach and ask Peter to imagine a big boardroom. All of the "board members" at the table represent different parts of him, while his *Self* (his ways of thinking that are aligned or awakened to whom he truly is) sits at the head of the table. I ask him to stand at the top of the room and look at the part of himself that just showed up here in this session and give him a name.

He responds quickly. "Oh. This is Critical Peter. Yes, definitely Critical Peter."

"What role does he play for you?" I ask.

With surprising ease, Peter shares that this part keeps him thriving and maintains his success in his professional life. In IFS language, we'd call this a "manager part" of Peter—a part that acts to protect him from bad things that could happen.

"What does Critical Peter fear?" I ask.

Peter thinks for a minute. I can tell he hasn't asked himself this type of question before.

"Failing," he says. "Like I'm never going to be enough,"

I'm inwardly elated. For the first time, Peter is opening up in a meaningful way. My next move is to help him find a different way to respond to this part.

"I get it," I say. "Critical Peter helps you get things done and helps you thrive. This part plays an important role at the table. He stays sharp and harsh to keep you vigilant. He supports you in your successes at work. He led you to leave a really difficult marriage. He got you to move away from a tumultuous upbringing with your father. He helped you build a home, a career, and now, a relationship with Karine and her kids." In highlighting all the ways that Peter's critical part has helped him, I am honoring a core assumption of IFS: that there are no bad parts within our makeup. They all play a role and hold an important function. By working to understand the parts of ourselves that show up at different times in our relationships, we can begin to act and respond in a more conscious and aligned way.

Next, I speak directly to the critical part of him. "Critical Peter, I see you, and I understand what you're doing here. You're trying to protect

Peter. You want him to always be on edge because deep down inside, you fear failing, never being enough." As I speak, I see Peter's wheels turning. He visibly lightens as he begins to engage with this therapeutic process. I'm excited too, but I can't get ahead of myself—if I go too deep into his emotions, his avoidance will click in. I need to keep him talking about the parts.

"Yet sometimes Critical Peter gets in the way. Like when Karine just needs you to be present and to admit that you made a mistake." I take a breath as I watch Peter absorb this, hoping he feels the empathy I have for him as a victim of my own inner critic. "Can you ask this part of you what he needs?"

Like many people, Peter has little practice connecting to his needs. After a long pause, he says, "He needs safety."

Hearing this, I decide on an audacious next step: I take on a role for him, one that I know Peter doesn't hear from many people, certainly never from his ex or his parents. Karine watches intently, entranced by these parts of Peter that she doesn't usually get to see.

"Hey, Critical Peter," my voice just above a whisper, "I see you. I hear you." After a pause, I add, "It's going to be okay." I choose these words instinctively, having the sense that no one has ever told him this before.

What I'd hoped would happen, happens: Peter softens. In fact, he starts to cry. Karine gazes at him softly and wordlessly passes him a tissue.

"What are you offering him, Karine?" I ask.

"Acceptance. I want him to know he is okay," she says to me, her cheeks flushed.

"Can you tell him that?" I nudge.

Without hesitation, she goes in to hug him, whispering her acceptance in his ear. It's a moving thing to witness, a simple moment that represents so much progress. I'm reminded for the millionth time what a privilege it is to do this work with people.

Looking into ourselves and acknowledging the damage we are doing must be followed with making space to forgive our mistakes—and, in Peter's case, seeing that he doesn't need to earn his love back from Karine. I tell him that he must acknowledge his ex's toxic behavior and the impact of his silence on his relationship with Karine. He expresses regret for how the event unfolded and lets Karine know that he wants to change, that he will do better next time.

However, despite seeing Peter's part and hearing his remorse for the event, Karine expresses reservations. I get it—how many times can one be hurt? Afraid of being duped, she wants a tangible time frame for how long it will take for him to begin standing up for her.

Neither Peter nor I are surprised by Karine's fears. Rather than dwell on them, together we develop a plan for the next confrontation with Charlotte. Before reacting to Charlotte's texts and emails, Peter will take a pause, then share these things with Karine, and they will draft responses together. This approach will allow both of them time to process their emotions, think about how they want to respond to each other, then deal with Charlotte as a united front. When we can learn to respond in a slower, more thoughtful way, we are more likely to connect to our conscious mind and discover what we feel and need.

Peter was able to express himself in session today, to shift out of frustration and own his behavior. This allowed Karine to see a different part of Peter, a part that assures her of his underlying emotional vulnerability. Seeing that part made her feel more connected to him, easing her toward acceptance of the fact that she and her partner are very different people who will always emote differently. They are building interdependence, untethering their dynamic from Peter's ex-wife and Karine's history of an abusive marriage. It's hard, but it's finally working. I'm happy for Karine and Peter, and it's a relief to know that what I'm doing as a therapist is part of their progress. Today my inner critic can take a break.

Acknowledge

What Is Within Your Control in Your Relationship?

There are three choices in your relationship when it comes to moving toward something being different:

1. You commit to changing together and each do your fair share to grow.

2. If your partner is not willing to change, then you must shift from focusing on them to focusing on yourself. This involves practicing acceptance for your needs not being met, changing the way that you communicate, and committing to setting boundaries for yourself.

3. You end the relationship, acknowledging that you have needs and desires that you want to be met.

Here are some questions to explore when it comes to choosing to stay in your relationship when your partner isn't yet able or willing to change with you.

◈ On a scale of 0 to 10 (where 0 is *not important* and 10 is *very important*), how important is this need for you? How did you learn about the importance of this need?

◈ What are the ways that your partner tries to show up for you or to connect with you? Is this in the same way you need or in a different way?

◈ What characteristics does your partner have, or what experiences have they endured, that contribute to their inability to change with you or give you what you need?

◈ Where else can you try to get this need met? (For example, a member in my Be Connected community shared with me that her husband was coping with posttraumatic stress disorder and could not provide her with the physical touch that she needed. She ended up scheduling monthly massages to fulfill her need for more frequent physical touch.)

◈ How can you make yourself responsible for getting this need met? (For example, if you have a bottomless bucket for validation, can you practice daily self-validation?)

CHAPTER 17

Tracy

The anger you experience in your relationship may arise from your attempts to create closeness and connection through an over-functioning-underfunctioning dynamic. It's important to recognize that both partners contribute to this tricky cycle. However, when one partner shifts their role, it can sometimes spark a change that eventually stops the cycle altogether.

◇◇◇◇◇

I attempt to walk the dog with a crying newborn strapped against my chest and a toddler who refuses to move off the side of the road. Sweat pools on my chest in the late summer heat, wilting the messy bun holding my past-wash-day hair. I'm awkward in my postpartum body and even more uncomfortable navigating the needs of three dependent beings—Anderson; my newborn, Eloise; and a twenty-pound West Highland terrier—up the neighborhood hill and around one block. Still, it's better than being at home right now.

My life has become a drastic contrast to my well-ordered clinical days. Now a mother of two, I spend my days switching from nursing and nap times to filling up plastic buckets for a car wash game that (I hope) will occupy Anderson while I am tending to Eloise, all while battling the societal imperative for a clean house and a full-body "bounce back" within the first six weeks of giving birth. While Eloise is a decent sleeper, Greg and I aren't sleeping much between night feedings and Anderson's new habit of waking multiple times in the middle of the night. I lean heavily on that first cup of coffee every morning. My only respite comes each night when I breathe in the sweet smell of milk and embrace the familiar rhythm of the rocking chair that cradles me and our last baby through middle-of-the-night nursing sessions.

Just as with my first child, the process of wrapping up with clients before maternity leave was bittersweet. Many clients pressed pause on our work together, while others were referred to trusted colleagues. It was hard to pause my career and say goodbye to clients, yet I was excited for this next chapter in our family, and I welcomed the break with great relief. Contrary to the "glowing mama who cherishes her growing belly" fallacy that society promotes, I was throwing up multiple times a day throughout my pregnancy, trying to balance my hormonal shifts and accommodate my protruding abdomen while also being an attentive mother to Anderson. I felt Greg's weekend absence more than ever during this time—I spent Saturday and Sunday mornings begging Anderson to sit quietly and watch *Paw Patrol* on the couch with me while I tried to calm my morning sickness, not to mention the new set of worries that accompanied my gratitude for being pregnant again: *How can I love another child as deeply as my first? How will I be able to manage it all? What will happen to my relationship?*

The first two weeks after Eloise's birth were magical—all of us home with no overnight visitors, no schedule to follow or demands from the outside world to meet, just the sweetness of getting to know our new baby girl. But then the honeymoon stage wore off and postpartum despair set in. Now all I feel is alone and desperate to be recognized for just how tough it is to be a mother. As I feared, my already strained connection with Greg has grown even more distant while we tend to the needs of our children. It doesn't help that we are engaging in the same dynamic I saw unfold between Karine and Peter. I am overfunctioning by continuing to make the bulk of the decisions for our family while handling my despair in silence in order to protect Greg from experiencing difficult emotions. I pack the diaper bag and toys for Anderson before we leave the home, arrange doctor's appointments and playdates, plan and prepare all the meals, send pictures and organize visits with our extended family. Meanwhile Greg, in the underfunctioning role, allows me to do all this without a word (much less a move) of support, cedes all decisions to me without speaking up for his own desires and wishes, and avoids addressing the fact that we are barely more than roommates at this point—and not very friendly ones, at that.

I tell my clients that changing a relationship pattern starts with becoming aware of what led them to it. With that understanding, they can more easily notice when the pattern shows up, which then empowers them to change it by taking responsibility for their own feelings and needs. To get them started, I use the analogy of two balloons in a small box: Both balloons start at relatively equal size, but if you add air to one of them, it will take up more space. It won't be long before the only way to keep both the balloons together in the box is for the other balloon to let out some air and get smaller. In the same way, both partners may have an equal share of responsibility at the start of a relationship, but as one partner takes on more tasks, the other partner (if they aren't aware of the pattern) is likely to allow their task load to get smaller. Over time, the underfunctioning partner may (consciously or not) decrease their already low level of responsibility, which creates more "space" for the overfunctioning partner to fill.

I've repeated this analogy so many times that I don't even have to think about how it applies to my situation. If Greg leaves his clothes on the floor, rather than yelling at him to put his dirty socks in the hamper, I need to let him feel the consequence of not having clean clothes on laundry day. Instead of me planning our weekends ahead, I need to create space for him to share his wishes for what to do in his spare time. Rather than packing the diaper bag to ensure he has everything on a trip to the park, I need to let him gather the items himself and feel the consequence at the park should he forget something. In general, I need to allow him the space to work through things on his own while sitting in my own anxiety about not controlling the outcome. After all, he is competent—most people are, despite what high performers and control appreciators (like me) tend to think. When we witness a partner not rising to the occasion, it's almost irresistible to jump in and fix things. But despite what we often believe, the majority of people actually *are* able to do hard things. They may not do it the way we would do it— they may even stumble a bit more through the process—but failing at tasks is exactly what helps them learn and grow. The problem is that they rarely get a chance to practice this because we have a solution ready for them.

Both overfunctioners and underfunctioners gravitate to their roles, in part, because of their childhood experiences. Many overfunctioners were tasked with attending to everyone else's needs before their own, while underfunctioners likely had parents who always jumped in to fix things for them. That's why, in parenting my own children, I'm learning to be more curious about how they want to solve an issue, rather than just telling them how to do it. I'm having a hard time doing this with Greg, though. I'm waiting for him to step forward into initiating before I lean back to allow him to do this. It takes both partners to be aware of this in order to change, and neither of us seems ready to make the move.

Anderson's voice pierces my ears, demanding a ride in the stroller as we make our way around the block. I validate his wish, then remind him that he chose to walk, so we'll have to keep going the way we are. It's easy to offer him validation, compassion, and loving boundaries because I can see him for who he is: a two-year-old desperate for one-on-one time that I can't give him right now. Watching my child melt down in moments of big feelings has helped me see that my parents likely didn't know what to do with all my outward expressions of emotion as a child. I didn't discover until after the birth of my second child that I'm a *highly sensitive person (HSP)*, which meant that as a child, I felt my emotions deeply. The personality type of an HSP, as articulated by psychologists Drs. Elaine and Arthur Aron, includes a high degree of sensory-processing sensitivity, which brings increased emotional sensitivity and a strong reaction to stimuli, both internal (e.g., pain, hunger) and external (e.g., noise, light).

Still, I can see clearly how giving in to Anderson's demands in this moment will only make it harder for him to develop healthy strategies for dealing with big emotions. The tremor of mom guilt that comes with lovingly holding limits and boundaries for my son is soothed by my knowledge that learning this now is a key skill for Anderson's future relationships.

So why, my training asks me, *can't I do the same thing with Greg?*

Part of it is that it is easier to maintain the status quo. Our dysfunctional roles have at least the virtue of feeling familiar. The bigger issue, however, is fear. *What if I try to change my pattern but he doesn't change? Or worse, what if he rejects my changes, dismisses my desires, and then I have to decide if this is still the relationship I want to be in?* My stomach drops when I sit in this uncertainty. The core of my struggle, I'm realizing, is less about the share of roles and responsibilities than it is about my longing to know that I matter to Greg, my fear that maybe I don't anymore. But I can't bring myself to step into the vulnerability it would take to share this fear. As hard as it is to shoulder this burden, it's easier than asking him for what I really need.

All of this flashes through my head as I wait for Anderson's big feelings to taper into something more manageable, a few minutes that feel like an eternity as cars and neighbors pass by. Eventually, I reach down for Anderson's hand and stand him up.

"I will hold your hand," I say begrudgingly—that small gesture feels barely within my capacity right now. Slowly, we climb the neighborhood street toward home, Anderson repeating, "Stroller, stroller, stroller," for the entire twenty minutes it takes to get home. I grit my teeth and will myself to not lose my cool at my child.

By the time we reach home, all I want is to text-bomb Greg about his schedule, his ignorance of what I'm going through, his leaving all the domestic work to me. This time, however, I don't. The instinct now brings a recent memory into sharp clarity: the moment last week when Greg said to me (while doing dishes, no less!), "I just feel so helpless when you send me all of those angry texts. I'm at work. I can't do anything for you in those moments."

I can still feel the impact of those words and the forlorn look on his face that he tried to hide with intense concentration on the soapy sink. For the first time, I understood not only his feelings of helplessness but also the vulnerability he risked in sharing those feelings with me. After all, my anger is only a cover for my own feelings of helplessness in our relationship. This realization didn't solve our issues, but it did resolve me against launching any more text bombs.

Greg arrives home that night and effortlessly shifts into dad mode, taking Eloise from my arms and sitting on the floor with Anderson, leaving me with the quick peck on the cheek that has taken the place of our deep kisses. As much as I try to focus on the "isn't he a good dad?" narrative, I can't fully ignore my desire to have an equal share of his attention.

I typically give Greg a play-by-play of my day when he comes home, letting him in on my ups and downs just as I wish he'd do with me. But today, I decide not to say anything. I'm too tired to muster the courage to share my fears and needs, too worn down to face his quick solution that feels more like a dismissal of my feelings. My loneliness, my longing for connection, can't bear the idea of another unconvincing answer to the question of whether I truly matter to him.

Do you even see me? My inner voice quivers. *Where did we go?*

Acknowledge

Which Role Do You Take in Your Relationship?

Looking at the chart below, identify which role you tend to take in your relationship.

Overfunctioner	Underfunctioner
• Initiates uncomfortable conversations	• Allows others to make decisions
• Overtakes responsibility for others	• Is often disorganized
• Tends to make difficult decisions	• Has difficulties taking initiative
• Avoids sharing their own vulnerability	• Struggles to perform under stress
• Frequently problem solves for others	• Rarely shows that they are competent
• Rescues others in their distress	• Avoids bringing up emotionally difficult topics
• Identifies as a caregiver	• Feels inadequate and like a failure
• Feels angry and resentful with loved ones	

After identifying which role you tend to take, ask yourself these questions.

◈ For the overfunctioner: What are things that you do or take over so your partner doesn't have to do them? What feelings do you have inside when these things show up?

◈ For the underfunctioner: What are the things that you allow your partner to do so you don't have to do them? What feelings do you have inside when your partner does these things?

Write out a recent example where you stepped into the overfunctioning or underfunctioning role and describe what you would do differently next time. Then commit to doing one thing this week that you would normally take over or allow your partner to do (e.g., initiating a hard conversation, planning or preparing dinner, helping the kids with homework).

CHAPTER 18

Lydia and Sam

You can't change the past, but you can meet the needs of your own inner child. Acknowledging these younger parts of yourself can also help you build greater differentiation.

◇◇◇◇◇

My sessions with Lydia and Sam continue while I am on maternity leave. I welcome the respite from mom mode, the calm and quiet of my office in stark contrast to the crying at home. I know it will get better eventually, that creating change within a family system doesn't happen overnight. In fact, I'm sharing this very insight with Lydia and Sam as they focus on setting boundaries with Sam's mother. Sam has recently said no to daily phone calls with his mother, which has freed up his time to focus on himself and Lydia. Lydia is learning to recognize her triggered feelings as a sign that her inner child needs soothing and to use her *wise mind* to respond to Sam. Instead of following the pattern of emotional fusion by making the other person's experience about themselves and spiraling into shame, Lydia and Sam are practicing interdependence by hearing the other person's feelings and identifying their own.

Amid all these signs of growth, however, Lydia and Sam's problems with his mother have reached a new low. One sunny Saturday, the couple had planned to spend time in their garden, make a charcuterie board, and play a new board game, when their doorbell rang. When Lydia opened the door, she found Sam's mother standing on the front step. Caught off guard, Sam defaulted to being a "good son" and invited his mother in for lunch. Sam would later justify that his mother made the long drive on her own, so how could he not invite her in? Lydia, shocked and frustrated, couldn't believe how easily her husband discarded their weekend plans. Equally caught off guard by the situation, Lydia lashed out at her mother-in-law over lunch, which only led Sam to get more upset with his wife.

As they share this story, I hide my disappointment with Sam. I know he wants his marriage to work, and I just wish he could have slowed down, turned to his wife, and made a decision *with* her. Had Sam said something like, "Mother, what a surprise. Lydia and I need to talk for a minute as we've already made plans for the day," Lydia might have felt seen and understood enough to respond with something like, "She can stay but let her know this can't happen again." I also know that my feelings aren't just about Sam. They're also about my own experience with a husband who struggles to set and hold boundaries with his family.

Lydia is stuck in lawyer mode, which isn't helping us move forward. "All you had to do was tell her to leave. Tell her it wasn't a good time. That's not very hard, Sam, yet you couldn't just say that." Her voice rises. "She's so manipulative! She always finds ways to come into our relationship and stir the pot. Of course I lashed out—I was so angry at her!" My sense is that she is, in fact, angrier at her husband for not holding their boundary than at her mother-in-law for showing up unannounced.

Sam remains quiet as Lydia continues, a common resort for partners when they don't feel heard. "What will happen when we have a baby? Is she just going to visit without asking us? There will be no room in our house for her. You just need to start saying these things to her and it will start to sink in." Lydia is in full fix-it mode, her go-to strategy when she feels a loss of control. Her repeated use of *just* is a giveaway that she feels defensive of her core feelings and needs. But trying to protect herself only makes it harder for Sam to understand her emotions and needs.

"Maybe you don't understand why I did that, Lyds," Sam says.

"So tell me. I want to know," Lydia huffs, her attitude clearly indicating the opposite.

Seeing that we're not getting anywhere, I redirect the conversation by challenging Lydia to consider her own behavior. The lashing out doesn't work with her mother-in-law and only deepens the rupture between her and her husband. Lydia insists it's not her fault that she acts this way, that if her mother-in-law wouldn't have shown up unannounced, she wouldn't have gotten angry. *Fair enough*, I think, even as I remind her that we can't control outside factors and nudge her again to take responsibility for her actions. Identifying the triggers from her past, I add, will help her step back and respond differently when her security with Sam feels threatened.

Lydia turns the tables, telling me that she feels like I'm blaming her. This is another go-to strategy for Lydia to protect her ego and avoid seeing her trigger, one that I'm well acquainted with by now. Looking her straight in the eye, I tell her that I get why she did what she did— that I, too, have spoken out in ways that are not helpful. There was a time I'd never have shown up as "human" to this degree in my practice, but this is something I am more willing to do as my career evolves. When shame shows up, we need to know that we are not alone in our bad feelings or behavior. Calibrating my voice to resemble a security blanket that Lydia can wrap up in, I add that two things can be true at once: She can take responsibility for her behavior *and* know that she isn't bad to want her husband to stand up for her.

I then shift my focus to learning more about the core emotions and needs that make Sam so quick to bend his boundaries with his mother. "It's like I see this younger boy in front of me," I say, letting the image hang in the air in hopes of pointing him in the direction I want to go. "What leads you to quickly say yes? Is there a cultural piece of not wanting to upset your mother?"

"I think that's part of it," Sam says, going on to explain that South Asian culture often dictates putting one's family of origin before a spouse. However, I believe there is more going on for him than just following cultural norms or being considerate of his mother's long drive. I again reflect to Sam that he still seems to be looking for some kind of approval from his parents and ask what he feels in the moments before he does this.

Sam recalls how, at the age of eight, he was already experimenting in the kitchen and trying to get his parents to try his recipes, only to have his parents tell him they didn't have time for random daytime meals. Sometimes they would even say, "Shoo, fly!" to make him go away. Instead of seeing their child's talent and passion, they told Sam that he should be more like his straightlaced brothers. These feelings of exclusion and unbelonging continued when his family moved from South Asia to Canada when Sam was thirteen. Removed from everything that was familiar, Sam struggled to fit in with a predominantly White school in a small town north of Toronto. He had to change his friends, his culture, the way he viewed the world, and ultimately himself. Blinking back tears, Sam says he's always felt "othered." To this day, he questions where he fits in.

At our core, we all want to know that we belong, that we can be loved just as we are by those we love. Many of us leave our families of origin to seek the sense of belonging we are looking for in a partner. But while we may feel at first like they complete us, we inevitably start playing out old narratives and reverting to familiar coping mechanisms in the face of stress, to the point that we risk losing the relationship that gave us what we wanted. Sam fears feeling that old sense of unbelonging with Lydia so much that it became a self-fulfilling prophecy.

I invite Lydia to see the little boy inside Sam who was constantly compared to his brothers and never acknowledged for his own individuality. Of course his ability to differentiate was stunted; becoming fused with others helped him feel some sense of safety in his new environment. For the first time, Lydia understands what happens to Sam when his mother shows up—or, for that matter, when Lydia enters problem-solving mode. But Sam still needs to see his fear of being "othered" in how he appeases his mother.

I decide to call this out. "Perhaps, Sam, your work is about finding your self-worth within you. Maybe you stop seeking the attention from your mother, who doesn't seem to be able to truly give it to you, and start giving yourself that reassurance instead." We can't change our parents, but we can *reparent* ourselves—that is, we can offer ourselves the compassion, validation, or acknowledgment that our attachment figures couldn't give us.

Sam runs his fingers through his thick dark hair and looks out the window. An uneasiness rises in my gut. *Have I gone too far?* I wonder. I rationalize that it's often the things we don't want to hear that we need to hear the most. I look at Lydia. She knows I'm right, but she's not jumping in. It seems she has learned that making space through silence can be more powerful than hammering home a point. I'm proud of her growth.

After a few seconds, Sam says, "You might be right." But I don't sense that he is fully engaged with this interpretation or that it will lead to a change in his behavior. Instead, I sense that he has shut down. I glance at the clock and see that our time is up. It's not ideal to end a session in this space, but I resist pressing my interpretation. That impulse feels more about my desire to be seen as a good therapist than what would actually be therapeutic for Sam. The best I can hope is that my words will percolate until our next session.

Acknowledge

Healing Your Inner Child

Reparenting means learning to give yourself what your parents were not able to give you. To do this work, you need to learn to identify your needs (emotional, physical, spiritual), notice when you are pushing away what you desire (and recognize the inner critic that stops you from listening to yourself), and offer yourself what you need in the here and now. You don't get to go back and change the past, but you can bring awareness to what you didn't get and learn to offer this to yourself today. Here are some ideas that you may use to reparent yourself.

◈ Ask yourself, "What do I need to be well in this moment?" Pause frequently during the day to ask yourself this question. Do you need to use the washroom? To get a glass of water? To say no to replying to one more email? Pausing to listen and act on your needs is an essential act of self-care.

◈ Practice self-compassion. When your critical voice shows up, acknowledge that this voice was never yours to begin with. It might sound like "Do more" or "That's not enough" or "Why would you ____?" Bring awareness to this critical part of yourself and practice saying something kind instead. Ask yourself what you would say to a dear friend. Place a hand over your heart as a physical gesture of compassion. Here are some go-to statements of compassion that you can say to yourself:

◇ I'm allowed to struggle with this.
◇ This is hard and I'm not alone in this struggle.
◇ I am learning to be kind to myself in hard moments.
◇ I am accepting that I am okay where I am.
◇ I am doing my best.

◈ Tap into play and fun. Playfulness, laughter, and fun are great ways to access your inner child and soothe your nervous system. Here are some go-tos:

◇ Put on your favorite music list.
◇ Get creative with paint or pick up some modeling clay.

◇ Dance or sing in your kitchen.
◇ Ask your partner to play a game with you (e.g., cards, a board game, a video game).
◇ Try something new that you have always wanted to do.

◈ Recall a difficult moment from childhood and, using a pen and paper, write a letter to that child, describing the event and what your child self felt from one moment to the next. Acknowledge their struggle and offer them words of love, compassion, and understanding.

CHAPTER 19

Tracy

We all make multiple bids for connection to our partner each day. When you see your partner struggling or looking for connection, do you turn toward them? Or do you find yourself turning away from them? These bids for connection can tell you a lot about your partner's need to be seen, to be acknowledged, and to receive affection. The way you respond to these bids for connection can tell you a lot about your own needs too.

◇◇◇◇◇

The hot water runs over my body as I sob silently in the white-tiled shower. Steam floats around me, and I wish I could disappear along with it. I can't tell the shower water from the tears.

It's okay to feel angry, I say on repeat, trying to catch my breath. *It's okay to feel angry. It's* not *okay to rage at your partner. It's okay to feel angry. It's* not *okay to threaten to leave your partner.*

Then comes the self-recrimination: *How can you complain? You wanted children.* The tightness in my chest intensifies. *Who am I? I don't even recognize this person, this body, this part of me.*

I place a hand on my chest, over my heart, an act of kindness to myself that I've repeatedly modeled for clients in therapy sessions. This shower is the only moment when I will be alone today. My inner critic is not what I need to hear right now.

It's a sunny but cool fall Saturday. Like every weekend, I'll watch Greg leave for work, seemingly carefree. Meanwhile, I'll be at home with both kids, sporting a stained shirt and dark circles under my eyes, saying a small mantra to calm my gag reflex while wiping my children's bums. Now that Anderson is two and a half and Eloise is three months, I'm confronting the hard truth that I'm not the mother who thrives being at home with her kids all day. There are moments when the urge to run away grips my stomach like a vise. This isn't the mother I want to be, this isn't the relationship I want to have with my husband, but this is the place my mind goes to when I feel disconnected and insecure.

I know I am not the only mother who feels their identity has been swept away in the undertow of parenthood. I know I'm not the only one who puts bandages over deep emotional wounds because I don't have time or energy to do the real work to heal them, or who turns to fantasies of running away to escape from my current difficulties. In my clinical work, I have sat with many women for whom intrusive thoughts like these create temporary relief and deep distress at the same time. I've reminded them that these thoughts don't mean they really want to leave their children, husband, or life; they're a sign of unmet needs that require fulfillment. But knowing all this doesn't make it easier to practice, for them or for me. For an exhausted mother, the overstimulation that comes from meeting everyone else's needs all day creates an overwhelm that makes it nearly impossible to ask for our own to be met as well.

Amid all the needs and feelings that I don't share, there's another truth about our marriage that I keep even quieter: It's easier for me when Greg isn't around.

I know how counterintuitive this seems—how can I resent solo parenting yet feel more resentful toward him when he's around? Here's how: When Greg's with us, he doesn't show up the way I'd like him to. While Greg is more than capable of looking after the kids on his own when I'm not present, if we're both home, he'll ask for direction and reassurance on a million little issues like meals or nap schedules. Sometimes he says he will do something but doesn't take ownership of the task and I end up doing it myself. Instead of taking ownership the way I want him to, his presence adds to my mental load and sometimes even my physical load. I often end up doing things myself rather than ask him one more time. Knowing that this is what our brains do when we are in distress—build narratives of other people's thoughts and intentions that confirm our fears and resentment—I'm working extra hard to see the things he does to support me. But inevitably, my unmet needs find new fodder for irritability and loneliness around every cluttered corner.

I could, of course, do exactly what he's asked me a million times before: hand him a list of what I do and don't want him to do throughout the day. But playing taskmaster is hardly the type of connection I dreamed of when I committed to this man. Support with household tasks is only part of what I want from him. The other part is much harder to ask for directly.

When I ask him to take the kids, I'm wanting him to see my overwhelming reality.

When I ask him to sit with me on the couch, I'm wanting him to pay attention to me.

When I ask him to tell me about his day, I'm wanting him to show that I matter to him.

Instead of hearing my asks as bids for connection, Greg hears problems and wants to fix them. Our society has trained men to seek solutions, rather than understanding, for hard and painful feelings. But this only leaves the emotion unprocessed, which causes it to grow bigger. For example, when I share how I'm lonely and missing my friends, he tells me to "just send a text" to Lindsey or call my mother. He tries his best, I know, but it doesn't work to tell me it's not that bad or that this won't be forever. Not only does this leave me feeling even more alone, but it also contributes to the emotional fusion within our relationship.

What makes it all the more distressing is that I remember how well our dynamic worked before we had kids. We effortlessly met each other's needs and navigated stressors as a team. There was a sense of security, connection, and closeness. We were interdependent. But our attunement to each other faded when parenthood pulled us apart to attend to the needs of our children. He no longer senses my entry into deep feelings that threaten to take over our relationship. I no longer see his need to feel like he is enough. And so I cry, by myself, in the shower.

I didn't sign up to be the default parent.

I didn't sign up to feel distant and unimportant.

I didn't sign up for any of this.

Hearing Eloise stir, I step out of the shower. Being the keeper of the baby monitor means never being truly alone. Through the video screen, I see Eloise turn her head and her chest rise and fall with a contented sigh; then she slips back into a deep sleep. Relieved to have a little more time to myself, I get out a piece of paper and start writing, my hand moving quickly, the tears freely flowing down my cheeks. I notice the difference of this feeling compared to my explosive sobs in the shower—I am connected to myself again, processing my emotions through the movement of my hands. I imagine sitting with my younger self, the small Tracy who was constantly told that she was being "too sensitive." I see her curled up in the corner of the stairs in her childhood home, having left the dinner table at a harsh remark from her sister. I see her flinch when her mother, hands on hips, tells her to stop feeling sorry for herself and come back to the table, then walks away. I see the tears rolling down her face as she longs for her mother to sit on the step, wrap her arms around her, and tell her that she sees her hurt. Little Tracy doesn't need a solution. She just needs to be held, comforted, seen.

I imagine my adult self crouching down in front of little Tracy, the light from the kitchen casting shadows down the hall where so many of my early memories were formed: the nights I snuck downstairs for one more hug or another glass of water, the dolls my sister and I lined up on every step, the Christmas tree lights glowing from the living room as the scent of cinnamon and apples filled the air. Little Tracy had a good childhood, I know, yet she needed things that weren't given to her. I imagine reaching out for her, placing my hand on her shoulder and whispering, "I see you."

The tears traveling down my cheeks carve a gentle path through the anger and resentment. This exercise really works; the younger part of me feels held and soothed by the adult me. I know I can't change my past. I know my parents did the best they could. I know I can heal this part of me if I choose to. *I can continue to retreat inward and stay on the destructive path of resentment,* I think, *or I can keep working to heal what is inside me so the space between us is clear for us to connect again.* I want Greg to know what I am struggling with, to understand what I need from him, to show me that he wants to find our way back together as much as I do. Do I want this badly enough to release my anger and let myself be seen by my husband? I make my choice: *Yes, I do.*

Later that night, when the kids are tucked into bed and Greg has returned home from work, I take my familiar seat beside him on the couch. I fold my legs under our shared blanket and pass him the folded piece of paper from my post-shower journaling session. With a heavy breath, I ask him to read it without his problem-solving "hat" on. He agrees and reads it, tucking away his defensiveness or problem-solving mode. When he's done, he holds me.

Acknowledge

What Are Your Bids for Connection?

Bids for connection are your attempts to connect with your partner. They are ways you try to be seen, to be acknowledged, and to receive affection. They can be big (e.g., asking for help or sharing difficult feelings) or small (e.g., making eye contact, asking about the weather, touching your partner's hand). In his study of newlyweds, Dr. John Gottman found that couples who were still married six years later turned toward each other 86 percent of the time, while couples who ended up divorced turned toward each other only 33 percent of the time.

What would your partner say their bids for connection are? Have you shared your bids with them? Consider how you and your partner respond to each other's bids.

PART THREE

◇◇◇◇◇

Align

Newly conscious of old patterns and equipped with strategies to change, my clients are empowered to make choices in their relationships that align with what is truly important to them. This is known as consolidation, the final stage of therapy. In these chapters, we see individual partners shifting from an outward focus into the inward reflection that paves the way for authentic and meaningful connection. They are doing the work, both within themselves and within their relationships.

CHAPTER 20

Ashley

A healthy relationship means letting go of the need to be right. In each moment, you get to choose: Do you want to be right, or do you want to be connected? You can defuse moments of conflict by practicing differentiation: I have a different reality than you, and we are both okay.

◇◇◇◇◇

"He hasn't replied to the letter." Ashley's sleek brown hair is neatly combed in a side bun, and I notice she is wearing designer shoes that match her bag. She shares that during her kids' nap time one Saturday afternoon, she sat down at her laptop and wrote a detailed email expressing how she feels disconnected from Daniel, how she feels a pit in her stomach every day worrying that he will leave her. She ended by stating her desire to feel closer, then clicked send.

However, Daniel has never mentioned the email, let alone responded to it. Not wanting to disrupt their daily flow, Ashley pressed on with the status quo. With the letter now hanging silently between them, their relationship problems feel more unresolved than ever.

Once again, Ashley is stuck. On the one hand, I'm sympathetic; whenever we make a significant change, our loved ones are bound to have a reaction to it. It's quite possible that Daniel could respond unfavorably, and I understand why her fear of that would lead her to remain quiet. On the other hand, I'm slightly exasperated at seeing the progress of our work stalled. We need to trust ourselves to withstand other people's negative response, and today, I'm determined to ignite Ashley's resilience.

Two weeks ago, during my regular Friday consultation meeting with my colleagues, we spent some time analyzing the behavior of people-pleasing. The idea was sparked by a popular social media post that claimed "people-pleasing is a form of manipulation." Since this definition was the furthest thing from how I understand people-pleasing, I wanted to check in with my colleagues for their reaction to it. Truthfully, my interest in examining this definition was more than clinical—I was fired up. Not only was I fearful of having all my clients who struggle with people-pleasing ask me if they are manipulators, but I also felt personally defensive, remembering all the times I have pleased others. There were plenty of reasons behind my instinct to agree and placate—to avoid rejection, to restore peace—but manipulating others was never one of them.

As I explained to Meagan and Melissa, I look at people-pleasing from an attachment perspective. When a parent or authority figure is emotionally aggressive or neglectful of our needs, we learn to do things that make them happy. This creates a false sense of security in times of distress by making us feel safe, soothed, and seen—but only seen for our people-pleasing behaviors and not for our attachment needs for true security. If this approach is successful (the yelling stops or we get paid some attention), it reinforces the pleasing tactic. In other words, it's an adaptive approach, meaning that it evolves in response to a painful situation or traumatic incident. It's a survival mechanism, not a strategy to gain power. I asked my colleagues if I was wrong in my understanding of this.

"It depends," Meagan said. "We have to look at intention and the function of the people-pleasing behavior. If the intention of pleasing people is to get them to do what we want, then we're looking at manipulation. But the intention has to be conscious for it to really be manipulation."

"Right, that's how martyrdom shows up," Melissa added. We all nod, having experienced clients (and even some personal relationships) where someone took on the caregiver role and tried to keep everyone happy, even if no one asked for it, but proved to require constant recognition for their efforts, particularly when those efforts involved sacrificing their own wants and needs. Tending to find comfort in tension as a way to feel like they matter, the martyr uses passive-aggressive communication to trigger guilt or even push others' buttons, only to say, "Look at all I've done for you!" if the other person responds negatively. This was the tactic used by Ashley's mother, I recall, waiting at the front door for Ashley to arrive home, only to object to Ashley's request for space and list out all that she sacrificed for her daughter.

When I share more examples of people-pleasing from my work with Ashley, Meagan and Melissa both suggest that it sounds like she is *subjugating*, a behavior pattern where a person allows others to control and dominate them. Believing that they must please others to gain any validation of their own needs, thoughts, or feelings (and to avoid punishment or abandonment), the subjugated person puts on a façade or mask of happiness as they give up their own needs to focus on the wishes of others. In short, it's the opposite of interdependence.

Of course, anybody who sacrifices their desires all day long needs to have some kind of outlet, a brief respite of time and space where they feel in control. For subjugated people-pleasers, this usually comes in the form of secrets and subterfuge. They might cope by staying up late after everyone else is asleep to get some time to themselves (rather than asking for alone time during the day). They might hide food and eat in secret because they fear someone's judgment (instead of eating what they want when they want to). Ashley's outlet is secret shopping. At the core of her spending—her subjugation—is a deep sense of shame, and instead of believing that she is lovable the way she is, with all of her own thoughts and feelings, she continues to keep her wants and needs from Daniel, whether it be a nice pair of boots or ten minutes to herself.

This past week, Ashley seamlessly executed her son's fourth birthday party with ten kids and their parents in attendance—a feat that would leave anyone exhausted. As usual, she pulled it off without assistance from Daniel. He was more interested in the football score on his phone. Ashley's frenzy of activity went completely unnoticed.

I'm sympathetic, but not surprised. Yes, acknowledgment should be a basic part of our relationships, especially when we notice our partner making significant efforts or putting aside their needs for our own, but Daniel isn't even aware of Ashley's needs. Ever since the early days of their relationship, Ashley continues to search for validation from him by *not* asking for anything and instead making sacrifices he didn't necessarily require of her. If Daniel never saw recognition, gratitude, or appreciation modeled in his formative years, and Ashley hasn't requested these things from him, how could he know? No wonder they have spent years in this dynamic.

I'm not going to use the word *subjugation* with Ashley—sometimes therapist jargon can end up functioning as a label that keeps people looped in their drama—but I scratch it on my notepad as she speaks. I'm going to push for something to shift in today's session, and this word provides a road map for my interventions.

"I wonder if there is something about Daniel's history that leads him to not validate you?" I ask. She desperately wants him to see her, but I think her healing will be served by validation coming from within. This is such a hard thing for people to acknowledge: Our partners are not going to be able to fill up all of our buckets.

"His family wasn't very available," she offers. "They grew up in a small town and barely scraped by. There were five other siblings and he was in the middle."

"So Daniel never received validation from his own family." I wait for her to nod in confirmation. "It's almost like maybe he doesn't know what this kind of connection looks like. If so, this is something that we need to accept about him."

She raises her eyebrows, struck by this possible insight into her partner's history and the limitations it might create. Encouraged by her reaction, I continue.

"Let's say we can accept this about him, we don't have to like that Daniel's formative years didn't teach him how to show up in this way, but it is what it is. What would that free up for you?"

She thinks for a moment. "I guess I could release the idea that he's going to have some kind of aha moment and say to me that I'm okay. Give the validation that I really want." She looks to the ceiling and a corner of her lip pulls up. "It's not like he doesn't see anything. He's obviously noticed how triggering bedtime is for me, because he has taken the initiative in putting the kids to bed. I do see that as an act of caring for me."

I nod. "So there you are, trying to pull off the perfect birthday party—for what? For yourself? For your son? Or for Daniel? Whom are you really performing for?" I pause, letting that word *performing* hang between us. "I wonder if this is connected with your need to be loved and your belief that you will be loved if you can make everyone else happy."

Her eyes begin to well.

I continue, "Daniel doesn't see any of this, and maybe he wouldn't be able to give you exactly what you need even if you told him how you felt. That limitation on his part doesn't make you unlovable. And it doesn't make what you have to say any less valid."

Ashley casts her eyes up to the ceiling in an attempt to hold back the overflow of tears. "I'm scared," she whispers. "I'm scared that Daniel will do the same thing as my mother. That he'll take away something— his love. Or worse, he'll leave the family. My father left me. I saw my mother play the victim, play the martyr." She takes another disjointed breath, trying to hold back a sob.

"I know you're afraid," I say gently, leaning in. "But Daniel is not your father. This is an old wound from childhood." I sit back and take a slow breath to model using the flow of air to help steady emotions. "That little girl, little Ashley, needs something. Let's acknowledge her. Imagine she's standing in the middle of the living room, trying to hold her parents together. Can you imagine sitting beside her? What would you say to her?"

Ashley's tears stream one by one down her cheek. "I would . . ." Her voice wobbles. "I would tell her . . . that she is loved. That she doesn't need to change any part of her. I would tell her . . . that she is good enough." She places her right hand over her heart, just as I taught her in a past session, and squeezes her eyes against the tears. No one told that little girl that her father leaving wasn't about her, that it wasn't her job to please her mother, and that her wishes were still important.

My eyes begin to well and my throat tightens. This is a truth that I struggle with in my own life—in saying "yes" to a friend when I really don't want to, in making the decision to visit family when I'm exhausted, in navigating the pressure to always be "good." I too have spent so long seeking validation from others, even though I know it needs to come from me.

Ashley keeps going. "I'm so lonely," she says. "I have to hold it all together."

"Maybe to change what is happening between you two, you can challenge yourself to try one new thing," I suggest. "Can you tell him that you need to know that you are enough for him? Or that when he is on his phone during a birthday party, you feel invisible?"

"I did!" she quickly responds. "I told him I needed help. But he's just so busy with work, so I don't think he can make space for it." I want to validate her for trying, but I wish her request for "help" had come from a more emotional place. It's one thing to say from a practical perspective, "I need help with this party" and quite another to open up from a gut-level emotional experience and say, "Love, I feel so deeply alone in this world, and I frequently question whether I'm enough. I need your support and to know you're in this with me."

I nudge Ashley forward. "I get that you have tried. But this is where the emotional fusion shows up—do you see how you put away your own feelings to take on his stress?" She slowly nods, permitting me to continue. "But what if you could practice being interdependent? Interdependence is about making space for both of your experiences, followed by cocreating what you both need and desire. Yes, Daniel is stressed with work *and* you have anxiety and need support around the house and with the kids. Can he cross the bridge to see your experience? Can you ask him to?"

I often get asked the question, "Why does my partner's mood impact me so much?" When we first enter into relationships, being together is an experience of happiness and lightness. But over time, this changes. Our partner comes home after work and they are in a bad mood, instantly deflating our excitement to see them. Our partner is frustrated with the kids' big feelings on Saturday, so we also start to feel frustrated with the kids. We stop asking for things that we need or expressing our thoughts to our loved one out of fear of what they might do. But a key skill in healthy relationships is learning to separate ourselves from our partner's emotions—in knowing that they can be upset *and* we are still lovable.

Which is what I am trying to do with Ashley. I want her to find the *I* in her relationship, because she has been so focused on the *other*. Part of the work around healing subjugation and people-pleasing is practicing being an individual person with healthy people. It might sound like: *My partner doesn't feel like doing bedtime* and *I am deserving of my husband stepping up.* Instead of looking at things from an either/ or perspective, we must look at things in terms of both/and. We must learn to accept that two opposing views can be true: Our actions affect the other person *and* we can't control others' experiences.

Ashley looks out the window. The hum of passing traffic fills the quietness. At length, Ashley swallows and rubs her neck.

"I just want to feel . . . like I'm the person he wants to be with," she confesses. "I don't want to be just a warm body in the house. I need him to pay attention to what I have to share."

"So go do that!" I say. "Go tell him that you want him to listen to you." *Stop digging in your heels*, is what I want to say. But perhaps in this moment, I'm also recognizing that I'm digging in my own feet and standing still.

Ashley is a client who ends sessions before I can, indicating her great discomfort in having to be vulnerable with me. I see her glance at the clock—even though we have five minutes left, she is ready to end. We agree that Ashley's goal is to get Daniel's attention by opening up: about her doubts whether he loves her, about needing him to connect with her.

Ashley returns several weeks later, reporting that she has been working to set boundaries since she went back to work: logging off at the end of her shift (and not checking emails after), taking credit for the work she does, asking her colleagues for help, and most importantly, separating herself from her boss and his mood.

These are all good developments, but it doesn't escape my notice that she starts with what is happening at work. Frankly, I'm much more interested in what is happening in the harder parts of her life. "And Daniel?" I ask. "Have you brought up the letter?"

"I thought you might ask." A slight smile plays across her face. "Well, I asked him to respond to the letter. And you know what he said? You probably won't be surprised. He said he simply didn't know that there was a response needed. Like, he was waiting for me to start the conversation."

She's right. I'm not surprised. I congratulate her for taking this risk with her partner. It isn't insignificant. After weeks of avoiding the letter, she is learning to challenge her belief that her partner's admittedly low levels of emotional intelligence and attunement amount to him rejecting her or wanting to leave. As Ashley accepts Daniel for who he is, she becomes more able to vocalize her needs while also telling herself that her feelings matter, and her experience is real.

I remind Ashley of how one person's change impacts the whole family system, that her communication shifts create potential for Daniel to start learning what emotional attunement looks like. With this in mind, I raise the possibility that she might invite Daniel to our sessions to help him learn about her fears of him leaving and assist Ashley in fully expressing herself. Sometimes having an objective person participate in this process can open the door for understanding. I also suggest that he might seek therapy on his own to address his early childhood experiences of emotional neglect and his use of alcohol to numb. However, she's not ready to bring this up with him just yet. While I have compassion for her hesitancy given her history, I also see her as measuring her requests with her husband.

I ask what she feels is front and center for her in our work today.

"Well, I think I need to return to the seeking-approval piece that we talked about last time," Ashley says. "My mother came to visit recently, and I noticed for the first time how this theme kept showing up." Prior to the visit, she shares that she felt uncontrollable anxiety, to the point that she stopped sleeping through the night. She found herself worrying constantly about all the things that her mother could possibly criticize her about. "Before her visit, I made sure we had organic everything. That's her thing these days: Everything has to be grain-free and grass-fed. We were also going to my son's dance recital—don't even get me started on her view of boys taking ballet. I tried to tell my mom all the reasons dance is good for any person and how it doesn't matter what sex the child is." She rolls her eyes. "But still, I wanted her to *approve* of my parenting decisions and the attention I gave to her dietary needs, Dr. Tracy, like I'm a child again!" Ashley shakes her head at the choices she made. Again, I'm encouraged by her progress. Even if the people-pleasing behavior hasn't been "solved" yet, it's a big step for her to see it now, instead of operating on autopilot as she used to. She has peeled back the layers of stress and anxiety and now sees her actions for what they are, and how they are impacted by whom she is with.

It's never been clearer to me that Ashley's efforts at performing and people-pleasing are not about manipulation. Deep down, she fears the loss of connection. On some level, she believes that if she pleases everyone else, she'll be safe from rejection. I want to help Ashley build tolerance for the moments of disconnection that sometimes happen between people and know that this doesn't have to mean that she is rejected. Having a healthy sense of separate selfhood will allow her to shift into healthy interdependence, which will foster the connection she longs for.

I also think Ashley needs to feel her anger toward her mother for always putting her needs and wishes down. Anger is an important emotion to explore when we feel wronged or hurt by others. But Ashley never lets herself feel this. Instead, it seeps out in worry and anxiety. Tapping into her primary emotion of anger and making sense of it will help her let go of the pain she feels for not being acknowledged for her feelings as a kid. But I don't think expressing this to her mother will be part of her healing—her mother wouldn't be able to respond to her in the way she needs. Instead, we'll keep processing this in session, and she can work toward setting healthy boundaries with her mom.

"What would it mean about you if something really wasn't good enough? If your mother was upset with you?" I ask.

"Well . . ." She pauses. "That I am judged and rejected." She takes a short breath in, her eyes widening. "Oh! There it is. I see it. It would mean I'm not enough . . . Ooh, I get it. I'm seeking my mother's approval so that she can tell me that I'm enough. I just want her to tell me I'm good, so I do all these things perfectly for her." Another beat. "And I'm doing this with Daniel."

Ashley recalls a story from the time in France that followed their breakup and reunion, a time when she was working hard to tuck away her true self and be the "good girlfriend." After spending all evening at a vineyard while away on vacation, Ashley wanted to get back to the hotel and rest before traveling the next day. She asked Daniel to take her, but he wanted to stay. When he told her that she would be fine getting back to the hotel on her own, she didn't press further. She *was* fine—she navigated her way through the streets and got home safely—but it didn't feel safe to her. However, she didn't say anything to Daniel about how vulnerable she had felt. She wanted his approval, fearing that if she shared how she'd really needed him—if she asked him to step into the relational space with her—he would grow frustrated and say, "See? This is why we don't work well together."

I highlight to Ashley how, by not telling Daniel about her feelings getting home alone, her brain was, in fact, scanning for threat—for the moment when she could be rejected. Her brain can't tell the difference between confronting a bear in her path and asking her partner to support her. In the face of that panic, she did what her old beliefs and narratives told her she had to do to stay safe: subjugate. Now that she's becoming aware of how powerful her internalized scripts are, I challenge her to find ways that she feels safe with Daniel today. We are going to keep repeating this process—coming up with examples of how Daniel is committed to their marriage—to help her brain create new neural connections of safety and connection with her husband.

We also make a plan for the next time her mother comes to visit, which just so happens to be scheduled for two weeks after today's session. When I suggest that she respond to her mother with a boundary, she scrunches her face but says she is willing to try. We agree that if her mother says something critical or steps into a martyr role, Ashley can either ignore it or say, "That's not helpful. I'm going to end the conversation." She also agrees to not buy all organic food before the visit and plans to ask her mother to bring a meal to help out.

Finally, Ashley shares how expressing her needs—telling Daniel that she wants ten minutes alone, asking him to stop slamming cupboards when he's in a bad mood, and leaving him to do bath time while she goes for a walk—has quenched her thirst for shopping. She's truly feeling the anger that emerges at herself when she gets stuck wanting to put aside her own feelings and longings.

When she acknowledges the discomfort she feels from this anger, she can use that as a cue to make a different choice. She goes to the bathroom and splashes cold water on her face, or she goes outside for a brisk walk. Finding new ways of managing her anger is allowing her to process all of the times that she didn't speak up for herself.

"I'm trying, Dr. Tracy," Ashley beams. "I'm trying to make my marriage like yours."

The corners of my mouth pull slightly upward. Having only seen the external image of my relationship, Ashley is projecting what she wants to see: her therapist's life as perfect, something for her to strive for. Sometimes this is how we give ourselves hope that we, too, can experience deep connection, safe vulnerability, authenticity—all the things that we are missing in our relationship.

"I wonder if I can share something with you, Ashley," I begin. "Afterward, you can tell me what it's like to hear this from me." The progress we have made to date will allow her to see a different side of me.

"You saw a snapshot of my marriage that day," I continue. "The reality is that I, too, get stuck in cycles and have seasons of disconnection with my husband. Perhaps our goal in our relationships isn't to find a state of perfection, but rather to continue to make conscious choices *toward* connection."

This disclosure isn't just an intervention for Ashley. It's also a chance for me to grow by showing up in session as a therapist *and* human. The hope is that when I am human with my clients, they will be encouraged to show their own humanness with others.

We are all motivated to find belonging. Belonging is key to our overall sense of well-being. Without it, we struggle to feel worthy, to feel whole. But belonging isn't just about what happens with another person. It is also about what happens with *ourselves*. Having had a father who abandoned her and a mother who tried to make her into someone else, it's no wonder that Ashley was willing to forfeit her true self to feel connected with Daniel. But she could only tuck her own needs away for some time before anxiety began to show up. In the end, she could no longer continue to sacrifice herself without a cost to her own functioning.

"I guess I just really needed someone to tell me I'm okay," Ashley shares. "For so long, I haven't been happy with myself. So many things have gone awry in my life, and I was in survival mode, waiting for someone who would sit with me through those hard moments." She pauses again. "But I think what you're saying is that we all struggle at times, and healing is about me trusting that I am okay." Twisting her watch, she looks down at the time but, for once, doesn't jump up to leave. "I think I'm realizing that there are these parts about me that are good and that even though I struggle with anxiety, I am okay at my core," she says. "Maybe I don't need others to validate me as much."

Ashley does what many clients end up doing in therapy: She changes herself, and this, in turn, shifts the relational dynamic. She learns that even though there are characteristics of Daniel that are similar to her mother's, she is an adult and no longer needs to find safety in her mother's love. She doesn't get the full validation she needs from her husband, but she learns to validate herself and express her needs, which in turn eases her anxiety and guilt. This is Ashley moving toward differentiation and toward building interdependence with her partner.

We talk about how normal it is to find that others are not able to give us everything we need, and how important it is to be able to sit with the grief of our imperfect relationships. This grief, though painful, is part of the human experience. I challenge Ashley to envision herself as a good person, a kind and whole person, even if others are upset with her.

Even as I say it, I think about Daniel. Without having ever met him, my sense is that he has unhealed wounds of his own that he isn't ready to address. As Ashley continues to grow in her journey of self-acceptance, her anxiety will diminish. Without having Ashley as a focus of concern, Daniel may find the space to look at himself. There are no guarantees, but a shift in one partner often instigates a change in the other.

In the meantime, Ashley can only continue to choose actions that make her more empowered in her relationship. I feel proud of how Ashley is changing but keep this to myself. Her own pride in the changes she has made is more important than mine in her journey of healing.

Align

Mantras to Help with Individuation and Self-Validation

To help you move toward differentiation and interdependence, here are some scripts for practicing self-validation.

◈ "We are each allowed to have our own thoughts, feelings, opinions, desires, and wishes. Neither one of us is wrong."

◈ "I have a different reality from you, and we are both okay."

◈ "We learn different ways of dealing with hard feelings. My partner may not be able to express them in the same way that I can."

◈ "My partner is allowed to have difficult feelings. Their feelings may not be about me."

◈ "I am going to practice doing what feels good for me. This is going to look different for me than it does for my partner."

CHAPTER 21

Emily and Matt

Taking risks with your partner is an act of moving toward connection. You always have two choices: You can share your deepest fears and give your partner a chance to support you, or you can keep to yourself and shut down.

◇◇◇◇◇

"We're engaged!" Emily beams, leaning on Matt's arm as they sit close together on the couch. Matt looks at Emily and back at me, a big smile spreading over his face. Several months have passed since their separation and there is a noticeable lightness as we start our session today. It's abundantly clear that something is different for them, something deeper than just their relationship status, and I'm eager to learn what it is.

The first thing I learn is that Emily has softened her high expectations of Matt. Instead of looping on her old "Why do I have to do all the things?" narrative, Emily is giving Matt permission to not see the household to-do list in the same way that she does. Focusing on interdependence has helped her recognize that she can feel overwhelmed at everything on her to-do list *and* communicate her desire for Matt to take ownership of various household and childcare tasks *while* approaching him with curiosity and a willingness to understand what is going on in his internal world.

I point out to Emily that she has finally broken out of her *confirmation bias*, a common unhelpful thinking pattern that only lets us see things that support the stories we carry in our minds—in Emily's case, the story that Matt can't do anything when it comes to caring for their child or the home. This belief prevented her from seeing the times that Matt made a meal or cleaned the house—or, for that matter, the joy and laughter between Matt and Alice when they're playing. These stories, often constructed in relationships from our past, are the reason why committed people have the same fight over their five, ten, twenty-five years together. We continue to reenact them in the here and now, whether or not they are based in any truth about our partner. For example, one of my stories is that Greg doesn't help out. Despite knowing that this story originally comes from hearing my mother lament "I have to do it all myself," I have found myself repeating similar words about my own marriage. The thing is, the more I tell myself this story, the less likely I am to ask for help. Until I update this negative perspective of Greg, I will continue to manifest the very problem I want to correct.

The recent shifts in our relationship—his choice to share how my angry text bombs make him feel, my choice to refrain from it when I feel enraged—haven't changed the fact that I still carry more than half the domestic load. However, we know from behavioral studies that positive reinforcement, rather than punishment (e.g., criticism, anger, hostility), leads to increased engagement in the actions that we want. If I want more active participation from Greg in running our family, I have to acknowledge when he does try to do his fair share.

I see the same effect with Emily and Matt. Her positive feedback gives him the opportunity to feel like an appreciated and valued partner, rather than being put down for choosing sausages. Leaning into that feeling has helped heal his old wounds that tell him that he is not enough, which in turn helps him be less defensive when Emily slips into "Why can't you ____?" mode. Rather than protect his ego by listing off the ten things he has done that day, Matt goes to hug her and asks her what she needs.

With all these positive changes to report, it comes as an abrupt shift in the air between them when Emily pulls her arm away from Matt, clears her throat, and straightens up on the couch. The office space seems to darken as if the sun went behind the clouds.

"So . . . I wanted to bring this up here so that we can talk about it together." Emily glances over at Matt. His eyebrows rise, but he tilts his head, indicating for her to go on. Not many things surprise me anymore, but I'm still curious what this is about.

"I have been thinking about our wedding, I mean, about our marriage." She pauses again, takes a big breath in, looks at Matt, and says, "I want a prenup."

I watch Matt's face contort through a range of emotions, starting with surprise and ending with an angry narrowing of his brows. The prenup issue is a hard conversation for couples to navigate; I understand why Emily wanted to have it here. Given Matt's facial response, I jump in quickly to explore the significance of the prenup for each partner.

"It sounds like this is something that you've been thinking about and—" I start.

Emily interrupts me. "Yes. And, Matt, I can only imagine what it's like for you to hear that right now. I'm not trying to hurt you by bringing this up. It's just something that I need, and I really want you to understand that." I'm impressed—this is a good first step from Emily. She isn't jumping into hostile justifications at Matt's facial expression. Instead, she is acknowledging how it might be perceived by him in light of his experience. It seems she was listening during our sessions, after all.

"Okay, but I don't understand." Matt's voice has an undeniable edge. "I don't get why you would need a prenup. You trust me or you don't trust me? And why bring it up here? Why couldn't we talk about it in the past few weeks that we've been engaged?"

"See, this is why I didn't want to talk about it," she says. "It's not about you, Matt. It's that I need to be protected."

"Protected from what? From me?" Disbelief comes through Matt's voice. He crosses his arms and looks away from Emily.

"Let's slow down," I suggest. "I think there is more to explore for Emily, Matt. Let's do this together." He reluctantly nods with me. I can tell the possibility of a prenup is hard for him. For many couples, it can feel like a separation of the union before it even starts, but for Matt in particular, it feels like it's about his adequacy to provide for his partner. But the word that Emily used—*protected*—tells me that it is less about Matt than about a desire for safety, something we all crave from our loved ones.

Suspecting that this could, at last, be our opening into Emily's early experiences, I decide to shift into emotionally focused interventions that will lead to what is known as a *blamer-softening*, a key event that helps a critical partner access their core emotions and attachment needs, enabling them to turn to their partner from a place of vulnerability and emotional attunement. I ask, "Emily, what is 'protected' about? From whom? From what?"

She lets out a deep sigh. "From my family."

"You've seen that your parents' marriage is not one that you want to model yours after," I offer, "and somehow you have also not felt protected emotionally. Help us understand. When you go into that mode, what are you seeking protection from?" I intentionally repeat her word *protected* several times to help her stay in this space.

Emily goes on to describe her father, an alcoholic who was almost never available either by physical comfort or emotional connection. When he was around, she tried to make herself invisible so he wouldn't get angry. His expressions of anger—throwing things against the wall, pounding his fists on the table, slamming cupboards and doors—kept Emily afraid that if she got in his way, she might be the next thing to suffer his wrath. Even a threat of violence is a loss of safety, sending a constant danger cue to a child's brain that can result in anxiety, hypervigilance, insecure attachment, and enmeshment.

What made it worse was that Emily's mother wasn't a safe place to land. Quite the contrary—instead of seeing how Emily was feeling, teaching her resilience, or standing up to her husband, her mother leaned on Emily for emotional support. It isn't a child's job to navigate their parents' feelings and outbursts, but children can and will learn to do anything that's asked of them by those they depend on in order to feel okay.

Left by her parents to figure out her feelings on her own, Emily learned to keep to herself and hold her heart tight. Today, she is deeply guarded against giving her heart to others, fearing that they will be unsupportive, be neglectful, and ask too much of her, just like her parents did.

"If I give my heart to him, I'm scared he will just drop it," she confesses. "Everyone else did; they just left me. I fell out of a tree as a kid once and no one came to me. No one held me while I cried. I'm afraid Matt will just let me fall too." Emily's tears are streaming down her face. I know now why she has avoided this hard place for so much of our work together.

"So here with Matt, it's so scary to lean on him, to give your heart to him. You stay in that critical space, but underneath, you're longing for him to hold your heart. Is that right?" I say. "This is a risk for you: to let Matt see that you are scared to lean on him, scared to pass your heart to him, to let him hold it." Intentionally repeating myself to stay in her emotional experience, I lean into Emily as I speak, a nonverbal demonstration that I am here with her too.

"Yes. It's too much to let him in," Emily says, her voice cracking as the tears course down her cheeks.

"What do you need in the moments when you feel scared to lean on him?" I ask. "What could make it easier to offer Matt your heart and let him hold it?"

She looks at Matt with an openness that is light-years away from the woman who walked out of our session months ago. Instead of puffing her chest out in protection mode, her shoulders slump forward in surrender. People often think vulnerability looks ugly; I think it looks magical.

"I need him to hold me. I need him to tell me that I'm okay and that he's got me. Like he's holding my heart and he won't let it drop."

Seeing her emotional wall dismantled, I line up the pieces for her, telling her that it makes sense that she'd be afraid to lean on Matt in their relationship. She hasn't felt protected her entire life, not even when she fell out of a tree. Why would Matt be any different from what she has known? She wants a prenup to keep her safe, but what she really needs is to know that Matt will hold her and that he won't leave her. I ask if that sounds right and she agrees, her attitude touchingly soft—hopeful and fearful at the same time.

"Turn to Matt and share this with him," I tell her. "He needs to hear it from you."

Emily wipes her eyes and looks at Matt. "Okay . . . what she said." She points to me and lets out a light laugh. Her response is not original. It's amazing to see how people will process something so deep with me but then struggle to say the same thing directly to their partners. I'm about to give her a nudge when Matt speaks up instead.

"Em." He reaches for her hand. "I'm here."

Emily isn't the only one who has made a dramatic turnaround compared to when we started. Despite being full of shame and anger just minutes ago, Matt lets me help him respond to Emily's fears. I encourage him to see the scared part of Emily and ask him to tell her what he feels when he sees this part.

"I'm sad when I see this part of you. I see how much pain you feel and that you need to feel protected. You need someone to hold your heart. I'm not going to drop your heart." Matt says, his empathy underscored by his use of Emily's own language.

Then, without my instruction, he holds her hands in his and says, "I will catch you. I will hold you and not let your heart fall."

I let them savor their moment for a few beats before saying, "*Now* we're in a good place to talk about this prenup." It feels like a record-scratch in this tender moment, but in fact, all the emotional progress we've just made has finally created the right environment for this conversation. When we can understand the deeper emotions at work inside of us, we can make sense of why we need the things we need and where our reactions come from—and find ways to move forward. This process opens roads that we can journey together rather than walking alone.

I reframe the prenup as something that offers the protection Emily was never able to give herself as a child. Seeing this fragile part of Emily helps Matt no longer see the prenup as an attack on him or an insult to his trustworthiness. Building interdependence asks us at times to give things to our partner that we ourselves don't need or wouldn't request. It's not relinquishing power—it's using your power to honor the *we*.

Matt responds, "I will sign the prenup. Not because I am afraid of our relationship ending, but because I see how much you need this."

I can never predict what will happen when a couple first enters my office. Some reject therapy if things are not moving fast enough for them or their partner isn't changing in the way they had hoped. Others stop attending after their fights de-escalate and there has been some improvement in their dynamic, and still others continue their search for the "right" therapist rather than looking inward at the work they need to do. Even those who stay the course can remain stuck in de-escalating conflict or sometimes even resume their old cycles. A few have left me shaking my head, questioning how they found each other in the first place and wondering what they really think can be different in a relationship when neither individual is willing to change.

Then there are those who surprise me, who show up (sooner or later) ready to allow me access to their deepest parts, who choose to look at themselves and the narratives they hold. These are the couples who come out of therapy different than they were before. I come out different too. Couples like these leave me with a feeling of great hope that two people can learn to build a close and secure attachment.

In the following weeks, Matt signs the prenup, Emily creates some healthy space between herself and her mother, and the couple takes off on a spontaneous family trip with Alice. They leave town with a secret kept even from their families: They've packed wedding attire in their bags. Unsurprisingly, Emily's mother is displeased with their elopement and tries to blame Matt, but Emily stands up for both Matt and their relationship. The couple also starts attending extended family events together. Although Matt previously used work as an excuse to avoid any interaction with Emily's mother, he can now face her with confidence, knowing that Emily will not denigrate him in front of her. Meanwhile, Matt creates strategies that help him be a fair partner in household and childcare tasks. While he still tends to get in a rut regarding meals and isn't able to predict Emily's ongoing to-do list (nobody can mindread, right?), Emily feels supported by his efforts and continues to dismantle her wall, letting Matt hold his fair share as well as her heart.

I find myself thinking of Emily and Matt often in the days that follow (particularly while driving to the grocery store to pick up sausages). I know our stories are different, yet our steps in the relational dance are so familiar. If I'm honest, I feel deeply validated by seeing them finally experience vulnerability together in therapy. Vulnerability is something all couples need. It offers the love and belonging we need to feel less alone and isolated in the world, the reassurance that our efforts are seen and our internal experiences are understood. It challenges our view of our partner and of ourselves by giving us the real, in-the-moment experience of them becoming a safe place to land, someone whom we can securely ask for what we need.

The late afternoon sun is blazing in my eyes, the radio is off, and there are no kids in the backseat with me. As I enjoy the moment of silence alone in my car, their choice to risk vulnerability with each other hits something inside me. Could I make different choices too?

Align

Sharing Difficult Experiences
from a Place of Vulnerability

When you decide to open up to your partner, consider exploring these questions first.

◇ What feelings are you experiencing in this moment? Listen to your body first, instead of your thoughts. Where do you feel the emotion in your body? What does it feel like? Are there any images or colors attached to the feeling? What is the sensation associated with this feeling (e.g., nausea, stiff shoulders, constricted throat)?

◇ Now let the feeling come over you and try to name the emotion you are experiencing. Is it sadness? Pain? Loneliness? Fear?

◇ Continue to listen inward to the feeling you're having. Ask yourself what it needs. Does it need connection? Something physical? Something emotional? Something to do with your values? Try not to judge what comes up. Write out the need.

◇ Share your experience with your partner. Start the conversation by asking them to just listen. Use "I feel ____" statements and avoid criticizing or name-calling. Simply connect your experience to your thoughts and emotions.

◇ Identify and share your needs. What do you need to help you with this hard experience? How can your partner support you? Be specific and clear so they know what it means. For example, your ask for support needs to come with a tangible act your partner can do to support you (e.g., "Can you give me a hug in these moments?").

CHAPTER 22

Lydia and Sam

You can create security in your relationship by learning how to reach for each other in moments of difficulty and deep emotion. Choosing to lean on your partner and helping them understand what you need is key to creating a strong connection.

◇◇◇◇◇

Lydia is pregnant. They conceived the month before they were scheduled to start IVF, and now they are just two weeks shy of her due date. This new season in their marriage is evident in how close they sit together, their knees touching as they face me. Nevertheless, we are still focusing on how they can navigate the difficult presence of Sam's mother in their lives. They continue to set boundaries together; Sam has limited the number of visits to his family's house and has asked his parents to get a hotel when they come to Ottawa.

His mother, naturally, is not happy about any of this. I remind them that the goal of boundaries is neither to please others nor estrange them; it's to include people in your life in a way that works for you. This is difficult for people like Sam's mother, I add, who subscribe to the narrative that a person's family of origin should remain the most important to their child.

"I just wish she would change," Lydia laments. Her desire is a common experience. We want healthy relationships with the people in our lives, and it's hard to be the only one doing the work to get there. But Lydia needs to work to separate herself from her mother-in-law's behavior and reactions. As Lydia laments about Sam's mother, I remind her that her mother-in-law's "stuff" isn't hers to fix. We can spend time by picking away at every comment from a victim or a martyr, I tell her, or we can choose to let it go and focus on what truly matters to us. Lydia seems relieved at being reminded of what isn't her responsibility. For someone who took on all the responsibility for the well-being of her family when her father left, it's encouraging to see her accepting the limits of her control.

Where Sam used to shut down, he is now engaged in our conversation. He sees that Lydia's core fears of losing him are not an attack on his character, but instead come from the painful experiences of her childhood. No longer feeling the need to defend himself to Lydia is freeing. He can trust that he is a good partner, which empowers him to offer the support and security that she needs.

Still, if it were in Lydia's control, she would continue striving to never have moments of disconnection with her partner. I remind her, as I did with Ashley and Emily, that this isn't possible even in the healthiest relationships. We must be willing to share things with our person that could hurt their feelings or threaten our bond. We must set boundaries that are essential to feeling good with our lovers or family members. We must grasp the powerful concept that two things can be true at once: I am lovable *and* I can share hard things that might upset you. I don't like your mother *and* I can still tolerate a visit with her. This ability to hold two truths at once is at the crux of our work around building interdependence and differentiation.

Healthy relationships are constantly changing, moving through seasons, confronting new or old situations that force us to decide whether to stay the same or grow through the discomfort. Sometimes even healthy or normal changes are an occasion for grief. We grieve that we will never again have the first-kiss butterflies, yet our intimate knowledge of each other can deepen the passion in our kisses. We grieve leaving the honeymoon stage even as we find a sense of calm and security with each other. If we can recognize this grief as a natural part of growth, it won't feel so heavy. Resisting it, however, keeps us stuck.

I am pleased to learn that Lydia and Sam have done surprisingly well with accepting the changes that come with pregnancy. Lydia has allowed herself to slow down at work and share with Sam when she feels insecure about her body and their love. Instead of feeling in these moments like his character is being questioned, Sam hears her vulnerability. It's encouraging to see them grow into the tenderness between expectant parents—a soon-to-be father protecting his wife and child, a powerful woman flourishing into motherhood.

Despite all these positive changes, Lydia and Sam still sometimes get into their negative cycle. Today, our session explores Lydia's turndown of Sam's request for them to go out on the boat together. For Sam, this feels like rejection. For Lydia, it simply reflects her recognition of the limits of her growing belly and upcoming due date. She notes that she has been trying to spend time with Sam in the activities that he enjoys but doesn't want to grow resentful of him by agreeing to something she doesn't want to do.

Sam digs in his heels, stating that he feels disappointed that she will not come along with him. Slipping into what's familiar, Lydia starts to argue with logic, but once I've slowed them down and made space for each partner to share, she expresses her real objection: fear. She wants to keep her baby safe, and the boat makes her nervous. Sam hears this, but his own experience is pressing for recognition. He wants to be able to contribute to Lydia's life, and while he isn't achieving at the top of his career, he wants to give something to her. Lydia listens intently, although I see she struggles with his belief that he doesn't contribute. It triggers her feelings that she has to care for him and lift him up, and their cycle is activated by Sam's withdrawal into himself and lack of participation in their relationship. Even though the issue at hand is about how they can spend time together, they end up feeling further apart.

Sensing that this is not a relational issue but a Sam issue, I ask him to again explore the "othered" part of him. He admits that this part has been loud over the past few months. On a recent phone call with his parents, they never once asked him about his work or acknowledged what he does for his wife and his soon-to-be family of three. He says he feels silly to want this validation. *It's the furthest thing from silly*, I think.

Lydia grabs his hand. "Let *me* validate you, Sam. I'm not rejecting you. When I can't get on the boat, it's for other reasons. I don't like boats. I'm majorly pregnant. I wish it were different. I wish I could be the person on the boat, looking over at you and enjoying it together. I'm just not in that space—not right now, anyway," Lydia says.

"Yeah, but Lyds, it's the experience of us being together that I want," Sam pleads.

"I know," Lydia says. "But maybe the boat just isn't my thing. Can that just be okay? Because then I get to be in the other cool places that we are creating together. Like our family." Lydia places her hand over her abdomen as if to remind him of what they are creating together.

I see Lydia trying to create closeness by asking Sam to see things in a different way. However, I want to understand what this means for him so we can correct and move on from old narratives. "What does that mean *about* you, then?" I ask Sam. "If she isn't on the boat, having the same experience along with you?"

Sam considers for a moment, then—no surprise—brings up his mother. She always told him that he was different and that he should try to be more like his brothers. He wants to feel seen and accepted for all the parts of him, including the fun and silly guy on the boat. With Lydia, he longs for the sense of inclusion that comes from doing the same thing together.

"Maybe this is all silly," he says. Again, his inner critic has arrived to shut down his emotional experience. This is what stops us every time from healing our old wounds. Allowing ourselves to fully sit in what is happening for us is precisely what can help us process hard things, make sense of them, and heal them.

Psychologist Dr. Tara Brach uses an acronym that I find incredibly helpful for navigating difficult emotions: *RAIN* (recognize, allow, investigate, nurture). Start by *recognizing* and labeling what is happening. *Allow* the experience (your thoughts, emotions, and bodily sensations) to be there, just as they are, without judgment. Next, *investigate* your experience with curiosity and openness. Finally, offer something *nurturing* to yourself: What would you say to a dear friend from a place of compassion and kindness?

Today with Sam, I am asking him to recognize and label the part of himself that says it's silly for wanting to feel like he belongs. He calls this part "Stupid Sam," which admittedly shocks me. *Stupid* is such a harsh word, one that we might easily say in our minds but rarely let others witness. I'm reminded of the work I did with Peter and the way he identified part of his personality as Critical Peter. These harsh inner parts that so many men bring to session are a real reminder of how we fail to raise our boys to have compassion for themselves in coping with everyday struggles.

Sam adds that this wound of not belonging has been extra sensitive lately, thanks to his fear that he will not be included in things once the baby arrives. However, when I ask him to tell me more about this fear of exclusion, he expresses wanting validation from others: "Like if someone could give me a boost, you know?"

I tilt my head and raise my eyebrows. We're at the same spot again, with Sam looking outward for what he needs. "Other people can't give you this boost, Sam," I tell him, consciously empathetic in my tone. "It has to come from you. So perhaps in this next season, as you raise your son and see yourself reflected back, you start giving yourself the validation you need. Because I know that when you look at your son one day down the road, when he's seven or eight, you hope that he can also internalize the message that he, too, is okay even if others don't approve of what he is doing."

This seems to resonate for Sam. He nods his head and gives me a small smile. I love using *perspective-taking* (perceiving a situation from an alternative point of view) in this way. We hold a great deal of compassion for children, yet fail to hold that for ourselves or our partner. I think of the many times Greg has observed about our son, "He's sensitive, just like I am."

Lydia pipes in, "Well, it's like Dr. Tracy says!" For a moment, I'm on edge. *What did I say? Did I say it correctly? Did she get out of it what I meant?* "We're trying to bring these separate parts of us together and find our way forward. You aren't supposed to be doing this all on your own."

Nailed it. I'm beaming with pride for her.

"Sam, it's time to shed this old part of you," I offer. He nods his head.

From here, the session shifts to Lydia expressing fears about their relationship changing when their baby arrives. Lydia tells us that she fears Sam not wanting to be with her, giving all his love to their son, or no longer being attracted to her. It's a common fear for many women, but knowing that doesn't make it any easier to experience. Lydia's eyes overflow as she tells him that she is afraid of losing him.

"Of course you're scared, Lydia," I say. "This is the younger version of you who worries that Sam will be like your dad."

Sam passes her a tissue. "I choose you, Lyds. I chose you even before you got pregnant. You are my family. It's us together." He reaches for her face and wipes the tears off her cheeks.

"In these moments, Lydia, I wonder if you could try telling yourself something new. Something like 'I am worthy and deserving of love.'" I'm pleased to see Sam stay close to Lydia as I speak. "Your father did not leave because of you. You couldn't have done anything to keep him from leaving. He had a life he was choosing to live, but his choice wasn't about you."

Lydia breaks into a sob and places her tissue over her eyes. I can see the deep longing of a young girl sitting in front of me as her father walked out the door. She continued to take responsibility for her father's leaving all throughout her life, believing that if she had been prettier, more easygoing, or more likable, she could have kept her family together.

Sam, equipped with a new understanding of his own emotions and childhood wounds, takes a slow, deep breath and says to his partner, so softly that I almost can't hear him, "I'm not going anywhere, Lyds." I see her chest rise and fall as if she is relaxing into a warm bath, their newfound sense of security melting away the long-held tension.

In this moment, Lydia and Sam are practicing interdependence by sharing their own needs (autonomy) while remaining accessible and responsive to their partner (intimacy). In relationships, we want to know that our partner is there for us and that they can attune to our experience. As psychologist and relationship expert Dr. Sue Johnson explains it, we want to have an *ARE conversation* with our partner: *Are* you there for me? Will you *respond* to me with warmth and love? Will you be *engaged* with me, holding my vulnerability as sacred and trusting me with your own vulnerability? These conversations help build attachment security and closeness, especially in times of distress.

This is what Lydia and Sam have learned to do. They certainly have come a long way from when we first met. When they entered therapy, their feeling of severe disconnection was fueled by their deep emotional fusion to each other. But underneath this feeling was each partner's inner child, desperate to be seen and cared for. To restore their connection, Lydia had to see that Sam was not the same man as her father and offer her younger self the comfort and soothing she never got from her mother, while Sam had to tame the attention-seeking behavior driven by his need for validation and recognition and learn to set boundaries with his mother that prioritize his wife. Sam needed to step into his power and into his own identity, and by doing this, Lydia was able to feel the spark of whom she chose to marry.

Even as I admire their progress, my mind flashes to Lydia's disclosure of her affair. Ultimately, she decided to not tell Sam about it. She doesn't think this will add any healing to their relationship and would risk creating great separation between them. This is something that, as a therapist, I don't advise on either way—it's something for Lydia to wrestle with in her own life. If she believes the affair was meaningless and commits to changing her behavior for good, she will attribute her error to a blip in judgment and push it from her mind, continuing to build a stronger relationship with her husband. One thing I know for certain is that our brains are capable of justifying and compartmentalizing all kinds of things. Most of the time, I'm equally certain that that's not such a bad thing. It's an uncomfortable truth to sit in, the idea that we will never completely know the inside parts of our partner and they will never fully know ours. But not knowing every little part doesn't discount the real and meaningful parts you *do* know.

No relationship is perfect, even after a successful bout of therapy. The work Lydia and Sam have done hasn't "cured" them, nor will it stop all their fights. It's not supposed to. What their work has done is establish a new understanding for each other, a sense of their inner children having been seen, and a feeling of greater connectivity and security.

Align

Deepening Your Attachment Security

Security between partners is built on two key components: accessibility (*I believe that I can reach you in times of need*) and responsiveness (*I believe that you will show up with me in both good and hard moments*). Here are some questions to help you explore these components in your relationship.

◈ What beliefs do you have about how your partner will respond to your needs? Do you think they will respond positively or negatively?

◈ When you turn to them, do you allow yourself to access your own vulnerable primary emotions (discussed in chapter nine) and needs (discussed in chapter twenty-one)?

◈ How do you feel about the quality of responsiveness from your partner? What ways do they show you that they support you in the areas of your life? What do you need to be different to help you feel more secure?

◈ When your partner is upset, how do you make yourself accessible? What do you do to show them that you care about what they're feeling and thinking? What ways do you respond to them that may not be supportive? Do you jump into problem-solving or some other mode? If you were to ask your partner, what would they say about your level of responsiveness?

◈ To be more accessible and responsive, the key is to practice responding with empathy first—by expressing some kind of understanding of your partner and letting them know you see their emotional experience—and then ask your partner, "How can I support you right now?"

CHAPTER 23

Karine and Peter

Being a collaborative team is important in a relationship. One of the ways you can become collaborative is by recognizing your mistakes and taking responsibility for the times you hurt your partner, no matter how big or small. Don't let shame derail you from seeing your partner's experience and taking ownership over your impact on them.

◇◇◇◇◇

Karine is leaning in, ready to get started. She has been weighing on my mind since our last session. I was holding hope for Peter to dig into his softer emotions and reach for her. I sometimes wish I could dictate what my clients say to each other from one moment to the next. But this won't make them change. Scripts can only help people practice new ways of communicating. For true change to happen, they need to scrape up old injuries, find ways to heal them today, and then start turning to their partner in a more conscious way, like seeing their own thoughts and feelings and how these could be different from their partner's.

In our sessions over the previous weeks, Karine and Peter were sharing their core needs with each other: Karine explored her fears that Peter would leave her, Peter tapped into empathy and validation. The relationship was starting to feel safe, like there was a tiny opening for greater intimacy and trust. But every time ex-wife Charlotte came into the picture, it was like taking ten steps back.

Today, Karine brings a palpable sense of urgency to our session. I hardly have time to wonder what has shown up for them this time when she jumps in: "Peter shut down again."

I hold off responding for a moment, offering an opening for Peter to step in and share with equal openness. To no one's surprise, he remains silent. Even after all our practice, vulnerability doesn't come easily for him.

"When did it begin?" I ask.

"Last week," Peter speaks up. "But in my defense, I told Karine what was happening: that I got some tough messages from Charlotte about the holidays, and I wasn't ready to talk about it." I'm pleasantly shocked—this is significant growth for Peter. Instead of staying walled up, he made a shift toward the relational space and acknowledged that his partner would need to know what was happening for him before he shut down.

Karine makes her displeasure known with a deep sigh. "Charlotte is right in there again, texting Peter and trying to snake her way into everything we do." As the December holidays approach, Karine and Peter are trying, as blended families must, to navigate the days when they have all the kids together. They want to surprise them with a ski trip out of the city. But as might be expected from a difficult co-parent, Charlotte keeps creating roadblocks, stating that important family members had to see their daughter on those dates and that "leaving the city would not be possible."

In the week before this session, Peter kept pushing off talking about the Christmas holidays while Karine repeatedly brought up solutions and ways to approach the conversation with Charlotte. The more she pushed him to do something, the more Peter shut down; the longer he did nothing, the more she pressed. Finally, growing irritated and concerned that no plans would be made, Karine urged Peter to tell her what was going on with him. In the heat of the moment, Peter snapped, "I'm just trying to make everything work."

When they retell me the story in session, I acknowledge Peter's choice to share his need for space and time, and Karine's difficulties accepting it. I remind her that when her partner asks for space, it doesn't work to keep pressing him. Unexpectedly, Peter volunteers something helpful for us to work with.

"Dr. Tracy, I feel shameful when Karine asks, 'Why did you say that?'" he says. "Like I'm some kind of kid that can't make an adult decision."

Isn't this interesting, I think. *He is now conscious that he doesn't feel good in the overfunctioning-underfunctioning dynamic.* Excited by this opening, I ask him to share this with Karine. He tells her that in past scenarios with Charlotte, Karine has questioned his choices. As a result, when he texts Charlotte asking for more time and Karine blurts out, "Why did you say that?" Peter feels like she doubts his ability to handle his ex-wife. Her questioning comes out as interrogative and triggers his past where Charlotte was always blaming him for things going wrong. This is at the core of his shame: his inability to meet the needs of others. Of course, based on their history, Karine has fair reason to question that. But her standing ready to jump in, take over, or question his efforts only reinforces the unwanted behavior, growing their disconnection and resentment.

I ask Karine what she wants to say to Peter in response to the shame and doubt he feels from her. Putting aside her own pressing needs, she apologizes for her comment and acknowledges the impact she has on Peter. I nod encouragingly—her choice to stay with his experience instead of pressing for her own need for him to fill up her emotional bucket is key. She also could have listed all the reasons why she doesn't trust him, and part of me wouldn't blame her for doing that. But a good repair—a follow-up statement or action that helps prevent negativity and conflict from taking over a relationship—involves acknowledging our impact on the other person, and she has made that shift here.

I nudge Karine to consider why it's so hard for her to step back in these moments and give Peter space. She acknowledges that this isn't just a problem with Peter, that her lack of trust is deeply rooted in the years she spent with her narcissistic ex-husband who would browbeat her anytime she didn't do something in the correct way according to his view. (Another therapeutic gain: Instead of running away with her shame, Karine now vocalizes when she is upset.) I ask Peter to see his partner's fear of trust and, in yet another sign of progress, he leans in and holds Karine's hands as he says, "There is room for your feelings too, and I want you to share with me."

All these new choices surprise me in the best possible way. Now that they have each taken the opportunity to see each other's experience, I guide them to take a step back and explore their wishes for the holidays. They agree that they can be flexible on the kids' pickup and drop-off dates, but they come up with three boundaries they need to hold with Charlotte: time of pickup, time of drop-off, and no contact during the time that the kids are with them.

Unfortunately, the work of this session doesn't stick.

Karine comes back in two weeks sharing that she is exhausted from handling all the things—the gift shopping for the kids, the homework check-ins, the task of managing their family calendar, all while trying to support Peter in holding the boundaries with his ex-wife. She adds that she continues to say no when Peter tries to initiate sex, not because she doesn't love him but because she doesn't feel safe and emotionally connected. Peter doesn't understand what he has to keep doing to help her say yes. In his eyes, he is being emotionally open with her by sharing his day with her.

I'm not overly surprised to hear this. Difficulties in a couple's sexual relationship are a common symptom of their greater problem. In this case, it's not hard to see how their fusion, and Peter's problems with boundaries, connect to their lack of sexual intimacy. Peter frequently expects Karine to be ready for sex during the same weeks they've had major stressors with his ex-wife, but Karine has shared many times that she can't just switch gears from being a boundary-keeping tyrant to a lusty sex goddess.

"Karine," I begin, "I could be wrong, but when you tell me that you take on all these things, I hear resentment. I remember you said this earlier in our work together—that you resent having to keep the family parts moving in sync."

"Yes. Yes, that's exactly it," she says. "It's not fair that I'm the one doing all of these things."

Yet Karine doesn't step back and let Peter take on some of the work on his own. Doing so would be the antidote to their overfunctioning-underfunctioning dynamic but, naturally, this can be very difficult for overfunctioners, especially if it means watching the underfunctioner struggle. The overfunctioner must be willing to engage in what psychologist Dr. Harriet Lerner calls *hanging in*: the act of not taking responsibility for the things your partner needs to do while continuing to stay emotionally connected. It's no small feat, but there is the possibility for your relationship to feel better when you make different (and hard) choices.

"Here's the thing about resentment," I tell Karine. "When you keep trying to fix things, you are, by your own choice, doing something that contributes to your anger. And while you are problem-solving and making sure everyone has their needs met, your partner isn't doing that." I know this is a hard truth for Karine to hear. We generally don't like to see how we contribute to our own difficulties and how part of the change in our relationships comes from our own actions and choices. I also think this is hard for Peter to digest because it's forcing him to see that if he doesn't step into the relational arena, nothing changes for him either. "Maybe you need to step out of your master fixing role. Let Peter struggle a little. We can find the way through difficult things if we allow them the space, and emotional support, to do it."

"Charlotte just impacts me so much," she presses. "When these things happen with Brielle or with Peter, I can't get it out of my mind for days. It just sends me spiraling." As if to prove it, Karine begins to spiral into hopelessness as she adds, "And he doesn't emote with me. When I try to connect to him, he is blank. Stonewalled. Like there is nothing there." Karine looks at Peter, eyes filled with both anxiety and longing.

I turn to Peter, hopeful that the work he's done in our previous sessions will help him engage now. "What happens for you?" I ask.

Uncharacteristically, Peter begins to tear up. His lips quiver and he keeps his eyes on the floor. I wait a minute to see where this might go. Then, before my eyes, he pushes his feelings away, looks up, and says in an even tone, "I just keep it inside."

"What happened there, Peter?" I let my eager interest show. "You were feeling something. What were you thinking?" I ask. This rare revelation is an opening into his core beliefs and how they show up in their relationship.

Peter shares that he feels like he has to be a solid rock for his partner, which means he can't bring up his own feelings. I identify this for him, noting it as part of the messaging of toxic masculinity, and connect how his view of what it means to be a man works against his ability to be emotionally close to his partner. But being emotionally close with others is not about having everything figured out. It's about learning to turn toward our partner to nurture connection while not expecting that we will each fix the other. I clearly state what Karine is trying to say to him. She wants him to address these boundaries with his ex. But I also add that perhaps Peter needs to discuss what boundaries he should be setting with someone impartial, like in his own individual therapy. Otherwise, Karine will continue entering into the "doing" role—allowing Peter to continue sidestepping these decisions about boundaries—which exhausts Karine and impacts their sex life. Peter needs his own outlet.

"I just hate that this affects her so much," Peter says. This sounds like more fusion, but his next statement makes me think we're, in fact, dropping out of his frustration and into his shame. "I just wish this didn't have to happen. I wish I had never been with Charlotte." His eyes drop to the floor again.

The experience of shame is marked by going inward, blaming the self, and disconnecting from the other person. While it might seem appropriate in some situations, like a more intense form of remorse or empathy, shame breaks the ability to be together, to cross the bridge to your partner. It's the driving force behind the emotional shutdown that is blocking their connection.

"Does it feel like you're a bad partner in some way?" I ask. He nods. As a therapist, I'm able to offer the emotional experience that clients never got, to say the things that they have long needed to hear from a caregiver.

"Peter," I say gently, "you made the best decision that you could at the time. You couldn't have known that marrying Charlotte at such a young age would land you here. You aren't bad. You are here now. You get to be with Karine now."

"But look—she just spirals and runs away," he says, his chest heaving in spite of himself.

"Yes, and this is the work that Karine has to do." I hope Karine is paying attention. "We're helping her make different choices. Right now, though, you're saying something important and shame is getting in the way." I point behind him. "See that pillow?"

He looks, nodding.

"Hold it for a minute. Can you feel it in your arms?" He nods. "Can you pass the pillow to me?" He obliges, still looking down, a tear rolling down his cheek. "This"—I hold the pillow up—"is your shame. Let me hold your shame here so you can connect with your partner. Without shame weighing you down, what do you want to say to Karine?"

He takes a ragged breath and squeezes his lips together. "I'm so scared of losing her," he says.

"Can you share this with *her*?" I ask.

He looks into Karine's eyes. "I'm so scared of losing you. I don't want to lose you."

Karine wraps her arms around Peter, and he collapses his face into her shoulder. I hope it's clear to him as it is to me that his vulnerability, rather than his "solid rock" of masculinity, brings her closer. This vulnerability is about intimacy, beyond sex and orgasms.

"I'm with you, Peter. We've blended our families. I'm not going anywhere," she whispers.

◇◇◇◇◇

Several weeks pass before Karine and Peter show up in my office again. They're holding hands and sit close to each other on the couch. Once again, there's a palpable feeling between them, but this time it's a feeling of connection. I catch sight of a shiny ring on Karine's finger. I also notice something different about Peter, but it takes me a while to get it: He's stopped dyeing his brown hair. It's perfectly styled as always, but it now has speckles of gray throughout. Something has definitely changed for them.

Karine announces that on their dating anniversary a few weeks ago, Peter proposed to her. "He asked permission from my kids and also asked for a blessing from his daughter."

I congratulate them and ask what changed for them since the last time I saw them, especially knowing how resistant Peter was to marrying again.

"I did this for her." He looks lovingly into his partner's eyes. "I knew it was important to you. It didn't really matter to me either way. I viewed us as a family already." He pauses, swallowing. "And I want us to spend our life together," he squeaks out before clearing his throat.

On the one hand, I'm blown away by Peter's opening. On the other hand, I know that we all have an inner child inside of us, a core need for love and belonging, and a desire to be close with another person that is hidden behind "I'm frustrated" types of responses. (Truthfully, I think Peter, Karine, and I all sat in frustration for many sessions.) We all have a younger part of us that wants to be seen and known. Yet, Peter was never allowed to be a child (a highly sensitive one, at that) with feelings and needs in his formative relationships. He was punished or shamed for any emotional response and made to feel foolish in his life with his ex-wife. His overwhelm by any emotion and inability to self-regulate, combined with his tendency to take on the role of his cold and distant father, led him to shut down in relationships. But with a second chance at love, he's started to do something differently. Peter is not a deep emotional processor and, as his therapist, my job isn't to make him one. Had I pushed him to process his emotions in the same way I had with Ashley or Emily, he likely would have withdrawn more. But because I honored his resistance while nudging him to where he could comfortably go, he found it within himself to start doing things differently. Over the many months of work, he went from realizing that his emotions matter in his relationship, to slowly sharing his feelings, to now, at last, offering Karine the commitment she wants. For him, the proposal is a move toward cocreating his world with Karine.

Karine, meanwhile, has learned to see Peter for who he is and to trust that she matters to him. Unlike the emotionally neglectful and harmful men in her past, Karine needed to intentionally focus on creating new neural pathways of connection and security. Along with looking for the ways that Peter shows his love and rewiring old messages of insecurity into moments of safety, she found ways to repair the hole in her own bucket by identifying the parts of herself that she finds lovable. Knowing for herself what makes her lovable lessens her need for someone else's assurance. For Karine, the proposal is a symbol of their commitment and Peter's love for her.

Karine giggles as she looks down at her hand and back at Peter, showing the lighthearted part of her that I imagine so many of her patients appreciate. "It just feels different. This proposal . . . it's not like my first where I was naive and lost. But it feels like the first time all over again because I'm marrying someone who truly wants *me* to be in his life."

I say goodbye to Karine and Peter, knowing our work isn't completely done. It never is, really. I don't believe therapy fully takes away the painful experiences we've had or the inner stories that the pain has created. What therapy does is help us build a different relationship with those stories. Sometimes we achieve this change by extending kindness to ourselves, by offering ourselves the compassion that we never received as children, or by finally accepting that our truth is not defined in the hurtful words or actions of other people. We get to consciously choose what we do with our old wounds and narratives in the here and now in the hopes of creating a different relationship, one that is closer to what we desire. These choices are also something that I know is within my own reach, and I know I can choose to put down my own armor that protects me.

Align

Learning How to Repair

One of the most powerful things you can do in your relationship is learn how to repair after conflict. A repair means that you take responsibility for any mistakes or negative impact your behavior had on your partner. Repairs focus on feeling close again. If you don't repair, even for something that happened years ago, you are sweeping important issues and opportunities for connection under the rug. The bumpy rug will impact your daily closeness and can become a layering effect to disconnection and resentment. Here are the four A's of a good repair.

◈ *Acknowledge.* Identify what happened. Share what feelings you were having at the time. Take turns identifying your triggers.

◈ *Ask for your needs.* Take turns sharing what you need from each other. In doing this, avoid saying "You need to ____" (e.g., be compassionate, listen better). Instead, start with "*I* need ____" (e.g., compassion, to be heard). Remember, relational needs can be emotional or physical. Try to be as clear and specific as possible.

◈ *Apologize.* A good apology includes the simple words "I'm sorry" along with taking responsibility for your share of what happened without adding in your own experience as an excuse. Simply own your role in the dynamic and the impact that you had on your partner. A good apology also talks about a behavior change. What are you willing to do differently next time?

◈ *Appreciate.* This is a key step to moving forward and creating closeness. Find something that you are grateful for and express this to your partner. Research shows that for every one negative statement, you need five positive ones to counteract it.

CHAPTER 24

Tracy

You get to make conscious choices in your relationship. Each day, you must choose whether you are growing your tree branches together. Intimacy asks you to practice stepping out of you and me and into a "we."

◇◇◇◇◇

Dr. Eleanor's office isn't much different from mine: three light green chairs, floor-to-ceiling walnut bookshelves, white noise machines humming at the door, tissue box within easy reach. The one difference about this office is that I'm sitting in the client chair.

I'm less self-conscious now compared to when I first began seeing Dr. Eleanor in the months leading up to my wedding. I remember crying in our initial appointment as I told her about the parts of me that I didn't like and needed to fix, how I would wall up my emotions only for them to burst out later, how perfectionism drove my life. In my second session, I showed up with a wave of unexpected nervousness—I confessed that I was worried she didn't like me. It took me a moment to figure out that this came from my deep fear of rejection and unlovability. The most powerful thing she did was to respond to me as a human. Rather than offer a classic therapist parry ("What makes you feel that way?"), she reassured me that she did like me.

I feel seen by Dr. Eleanor. She is familiar with the themes I struggle with. She understands the perfectionist parts of me that show up when I'm hiding from fear and shame and the vulnerable parts of me grappling with my self-worth. She's walked beside me through big life events, like my wedding, fights with family, a miscarriage, friendship breakups. These days, she's a faithful witness to my growing feelings of loneliness and resentment, as well as the shame and self-doubt I carry for having these feelings at all.

Today, as I lament about how I continue to be the household CEO, despite the hundreds of conversations Greg and I have had about fine-tuning our roles as parents and partners, a nagging feeling tells me I've heard this somewhere before. Of course—Emily and Matt flash across my mind. And of course, I know the answer isn't only that Greg needs to step up more; as I said so often (and thought even more often) with Emily, I know that I need to change too. Maybe even more than Greg does. But *how?*

The fact is that I feel fulfilled by the work of caring for others—seeing clients during the week, creating content for my social media channel, writing in the early mornings and on weekends for media sites. However, going home from a full day of caring for others to care for my family, often single-handedly, feels overwhelming at times. I dream of cuddling with my children all day, but once I get home and they begin clinging to me, all I can think about is getting a moment alone to catch my breath. This thing called work-life balance? I haven't found it yet. And I can't shake the belief that it's because Greg won't do his part.

"I just want him to recognize everything that I'm doing," I blurt, dabbing my eyes with a tissue.

Dr. Eleanor's eyes, framed by her black-rimmed spectacles, shift from her notepad to me. "Recognition?" she repeats. "Tell me more about that."

Like my clients, shifting from my blame narrative and going inward to examine my core primary emotions isn't easy for me. Truthfully, I'd rather spend the session itemizing my mental load to Dr. Eleanor and have her join me in pointing fingers at Greg. Therapy is hard, even for therapists.

"It just feels like I'm with my family of origin all over again. I don't feel seen for the things that I do. I don't feel seen *for me*." Memories flash before me like an old movie projector bouncing images on the wall: four years old and being scolded for "knowing better" when I kicked my sister, showing off my top marks in calculus only to be asked (jokingly) where the other 5 percent was, being told I was too sensitive or had too-high expectations. These memories from home blend with similar experiences from others, from the time on the playground when my best friends ganged up to tease and exclude me to the time when my honors thesis supervisor, a man in his sixties, told me that I needed to develop a thicker skin. These memories fuel the narrative I return to when I feel like I'm carrying the weight of the world on my shoulders: that no matter how hard I work or how well I perform, no one sees me for who I really am and all that I do.

"Let's look deeper at recognition," Dr. Eleanor continues. "Do you think you are trying to be recognized? Is that it? I'm wondering if *recognition* is more about you creating *connection* with Greg. You don't need him to pat you on the back and tell you that you've done a good job. You need to do that for yourself. But you've just told me you haven't spent much time together and that you're again in a season of high stress. Perhaps you're longing for intimate real time together, the type of time that parents don't typically get in this busy stretch of life."

In the past several months, Greg and I have added another layer to our relationship: We became business partners. Just a few months after I returned to full-time private practice following maternity leave, Greg said, "You should have your own space." I told him I wasn't ready, that it wasn't possible to add anything else onto my plate. But Greg has always had an entrepreneurial spirit and saw this as an opportunity to fulfill that desire while also supporting me in growing my career. He nudged me to release my urge to do it all and lean on him to handle the business side of the clinic. He was invested in making this a success and was ready to step in as a co-owner who would manage all the day-to-day tasks of running a business. Still, I know that one of my biggest weaknesses is control. It's not that I don't trust him to navigate things; it's that "I'll just do it myself" is such a familiar strategy for me. Finally, I said I would consider it, but only if he found a place and ran the numbers first. To my surprise, he did! He found a beautiful office space and navigated all the financials for us to build the next chapter of our work identities. In the spring, we opened Integrated Wellness, a mental health clinic in Ottawa that has flourished to include five other clinicians in just a few months of operation.

Since making that big move, my feelings of appreciation and gratitude for Greg have deepened. He took a risk to become business partners with me and to invest in a clinic that had no guarantee. I admire him for pursuing something outside his comfort zone. More than that, having him want to participate with my work has led me to feel cared for, valued, seen. But opening a business together doesn't equal more intentional intimate time together. When I get home at the end of the day, my "work brain" is already turned off, but Greg often has a few outstanding office items to talk about. When I say I can't address them now, he struggles to accept my no; operational tasks, like schedules and budgets, can feel urgent for him. Once we finally pack up the business files, our two young kids pull us further apart. Our evenings consist of going into one kid's room, reading a book, giving hugs and kisses and back rubs, then going to the other child's room. By the end of the day, we have little left to give each other.

Dr. Eleanor is right. My craving for recognition—the moments I want to scream, "Just see me!"—is really about connection. Perhaps that is what it's always been about. The childhood longing to be seen and recognized and loved for all of my sensitivity and big feelings by those in my life has grown into a desire to feel intimately and openly connected with my husband. But instead of simply saying, "Hey, I miss you! Let's plan a date night," I keep looking for him to recognize all that I am doing outside of our relationship.

Good therapist that she is, Dr. Eleanor doesn't tell me the specifics of what I need to do to restore our connection. I already have the answer inside of me: change how I interact with Greg, reach for him when I'd rather hide, open up from a vulnerable place rather than point fingers. It's an uncomfortable truth, and if I'm honest, I'm already arguing against it in my mind as our session comes to an end.

A lesson I have gleaned from sitting in front of clients for over fifteen years is that change is complex. The hardest part is the piece that you have the most control over: making your own choices. You need to be ready and willing to take in information that you might not want to hear, especially the idea that *you* could be part of the problem that is happening in your life. People regularly come to therapy wanting insight but not ready to make actual shifts in their life.

With all the mental health insight available to us these days, it's easy to forget that being human is filled with doing difficult and challenging things. As author Glennon Doyle reminds us, doing the hard thing is exactly what we need to practice. We need to get uncomfortable, as many times as we can. We need to speak up when everything inside us begs to stay hidden. We need to take risks when it feels like no one will even notice. We need to ride the wave of discomfort or the urges that don't align with what is meaningful to us. Big shifts don't happen because we think about them—they happen when we take a step in a new direction.

For me, something is shifting. I am releasing old wounds of not being seen and heard, learning to step back and not get angry so quickly. I'm also learning to not be afraid of my anger but to use it to understand my inner experience. Instead of venting it in angry texts or blaming comments, I'm growing more curious about this emotion and using it as a guide to explore my unfulfilled wishes and desires.

As I grow, I am watching Greg change too. He's learning to drop his defensiveness and see that my having a need doesn't mean he is a bad partner. He is stopping our negative cycle and calling me out (in a joking-loving way) when I'm being sharp. When he does this, it works *for* us, not against us. His actions say to me, "I'm in this relationship too and we both matter." If you tend to be more defensive or shut down in your relationship, start saying hard things to your partner. They need to hear it. Not in a critical aggressive way. In a way that says, "Hey, I have feelings too." By taking risks to share your difficult thoughts and feelings, you are implicitly letting your partner know that you trust them and that they matter to you.

Several days after my session with Dr. Eleanor, I'm still mulling over my need for more time with Greg but haven't yet put anything into action. I arrive home from work to find the kids—Eloise, now two, and Anderson, four—running up and down the hall. They yell, "Mommy!" and leap into my arms. Before I'm done savoring the tight squeeze of their little limbs around me, they go back to playing their game. I enter the kitchen and Greg and I have our reuniting ritual—a quick kiss and hug and acknowledgment of whatever chaos is going on around us in the house—before he states that he has something important to ask. I immediately wonder if it's another golf trip or dirt bike weekend—or, even better, an upcoming family event—and how long his usual delay in bringing things up will leave me to consider it.

He hesitates, then takes a leap. "Can you . . . stop leaving your banana peels in the kitchen sink? Can you just put them in the composter underneath the sink?"

I hold a blank face while anger starts to bubble in my body, my mind tallying the things that he does (or doesn't do) even after I ask him many times. My eyes land on the kitchen sponge, a perfect foil to his request—why I should do this for him when he can't ever remember to squeeze out the sponge and remove it from the sink to let it dry?

I take a slow breath.

Greg watches my face and laughs. "Okay, just tell me," he says.

"Tell you what?" My voice is even, eyebrows raised.

"Tell me the list that is running through your mind right now."

I smirk, knowing we both know that what I'm about to say isn't the full truth. "There's no list to share, love."

Right now, I choose to let go of my laundry list of things that I wish Greg would change. Right now, I choose to see his request as an important step in our relationship. I long for him to open up, and if I shut him down over banana peels, what else will he keep from me or risk not sharing? I can create change in our relationship by making choices that build connection. I choose *us* over me.

"Yes, I can toss out my banana peels."

Greg folds me into a hug. "Thank you, love."

Held tight in his arms, I take a deep breath. It comes more easily than it has in a long time.

◇◇◇◇◇

We all have our stories that we cannot escape, and we carry these narratives into our present-day relationships. I like to use the analogy of a suitcase that is filled with our early experiences and memories, as well as the beliefs and narratives we tell ourselves. The question is whether we will remain hidden and guarded, ready to fight and remain stuck in repeating old cycles, or open the luggage, make sense of how the contents impact our experiences today, and show up in our relationships willing to learn and grow together. We can't change the past, but we can work to build healthy interdependence by identifying our individual thoughts, feelings, opinions, desires, and wishes, and take responsibility for meeting our unmet needs without feeling guilty or pressured to please others.

I have spent a long time protecting myself with my armor. To fulfill my need to be seen, I have to practice becoming vulnerable with my husband. For Greg to stop questioning his adequacy, he must practice trusting that he is enough, even when my reactions tell him otherwise. To build our connection, we need to risk communicating our internal experiences with each other. Just because someone in our past didn't meet our needs doesn't mean the person in front of us will do the same thing.

Of course, there are times when we've failed to make space for each other's wishes. But committing to a relationship means that we view each moment as a new opportunity to voice the gap between our needs and what is actually happening in our relationship, while at the same time being willing to truly listen to our partner and step into their world, whether the issue is a problematic ex, a feeling of deep loneliness, or something as banal as banana peels in the sink. When we see that our lovability is not in question, we no longer feel the need to react the way we might have as children. We can see ourselves and our partner as human beings seeking answers to the same fundamental questions:

Do I belong?

Do you love me?

Do I matter to you?

Are we still on the same path together?

Back when I started seeing couples in therapy, I felt deep gratitude when I'd go home to my partner. Being childless then, we had more time and space for each other; it was easy to drop everything to meet each other's needs. Our connection made it feel as though all our wounds were healed just by being together. We felt invulnerable in each other's presence. Parenthood brought more than new stresses; it brought back old narratives, subconscious expectations, and powerful emotions that even a PhD in clinical psychology couldn't compete with. Despite knowing so much about how to change relationship patterns, I chose to stay "safe" in my loneliness and resentment and look outward at Greg to make the change I thought I wanted.

Today, though, I'm using my insight to make an important new choice. I lean into not only trusting myself but also trusting that when I put down my weapons and armor, Greg will meet me in this space of vulnerability. I can be upset that we have to work on restoring the connection that used to come so easily, or I can roll up my sleeves and get to work. These choices are in front of us every single day, waiting for us to decide what kind of relationship we want to create.

I call the kids from down the hall to join us for dinner. The noise of plastic wheels against the hardwood floor is drowned out by Eloise's sheer delight as Anderson pushes his little sister on one of their toys. As I scoop up a forkful of green curry chicken in my mouth, I reflect on how this moment is much different from Lydia and Sam's chicken curry story of what led them to therapy.

I smile across the table at Greg. He doesn't know when my clients' stories cross my mind in everyday moments, like at dinnertime. He only sees the outward impact of me wanting to be different with him. His blue eyes gleam back at me.

"Let's practice our gratitude," I say in between bites. I have a desire to teach my children this powerful coping strategy. We each go around the table sharing what we are grateful for.

When it's my turn, I look at the kids and say, "I am grateful for your daddy." Looking at Greg, I feel how much I mean it. It's more than just a desire to model for our kids what it means to be autonomously connected to a partner. It's a moment of true ease in our bond. We'll never be a perfect couple that never struggles. But we have chosen *us* and we are here, growing together.

Align

Consciously Choosing Your Relationship

Use the following questions to reflect on your relationship to make more conscious choices toward connection. Remember that writing the answers out is a powerful exercise for activating your intentions to change.

◈ Today, I am grateful for . . .

◈ In my relationship, I want to be someone who . . .

◈ I will express my appreciation to my partner today by . . .

◈ When something shows up that is hard in my relationship today, instead of reacting, I will . . .

◈ One hard thing I will do for my relationship today is . . .

Conclusion

I believe that our greatest growth as individuals comes from being connected with other people. These bonds help us feel safe and secure in the world, giving us a strong base from which to change and develop. Moreover, whether intentionally or not, other people hold up mirrors for us, presenting reflections that offer us greater opportunity to grow. That is, if we are willing to look at ourselves.

What comes up for me when I am with this person?

When they asked that question, why did I feel defensive?

*If I think they feel a certain way, am I projecting
something about myself onto them?*

*The anger I feel with them, is it really
about them or something else?*

*What is within my control to change
this dynamic in front of us?*

*When I put my head on my pillow tonight,
can I say that I acted in alignment with how
I want to show up in this relationship?*

There is one thing that is inevitable in all relationships: We change, and so does the dynamic in our partnership. We are constantly evolving, growing, and shifting into different versions of ourselves. Therapist and relationship expert Esther Perel has famously said that you can have a thousand different relationships with a single person. Her words only emphasize the fact that a long-term relationship means grieving old parts of who you were as a couple back then, even while deciding how you want to show up with your partner today. Are you willing to create something new with your loved one? Are you willing to explore different parts of yourself so that you can build a love that is not only rewarding but also exciting?

Humans love control and certainty. We want to be able to predict what will happen and know if (or at least when) we will get hurt and feel pain. But when we accept that the only thing certain in life is that things will change, we open ourselves up to experience greater meaning and joy.

Moving Forward: The Four C's

Throughout my work with clients, the research I have done, and the lessons I have learned professionally and personally, I consistently come back to a few key ingredients that we need in our relationship to help us build healthy interdependence. I call them the four C's: compassion, curiosity, connection, and collaboration. I have broken them down in the following paragraphs and offer ways that you can practice them each day in your relationship.

Compassion

Compassion is the act of letting ourselves be touched by the vulnerability and suffering that exists in ourselves and others. When I started reading self-compassion research for my therapy practice, it was a game changer for helping my clients (and myself!) get unstuck. *Self-compassion* is merely giving ourselves the same kindness we would give others. When it comes to our relationships, we must be willing to see our partner as human, acknowledge their struggle, and give them permission to make mistakes. In a healthy relationship, part of our healing is learning to hold a space of understanding and kindness for our loved ones. We might ask, "If this were a friend, rather than my partner, would I say it this way? How would I feel receiving the information that I am about to give?"

I know compassion can be hard to hold when you feel hurt and wronged. Because your partner means so much to you, they have the ability to hurt you most deeply. However, you can choose to take the high road and show up with fierce compassion for the suffering of others and yourself. Make a commitment to implement one of the most impactful things that you can do in your relationship: Be kind, be respectful, and treat your partner as precious.

Curiosity

Curiosity is about expressing interest in our partner's life. It's an experience that we often see in the early honeymoon stage of a relationship—several studies have shown that curiosity helps us build connection and affection with each other. However, once the limerence stage has faded, we start to form more rigid perceptions and beliefs about our partner. We stop viewing them as someone that has an evolving internal experience, with changing thoughts, feelings, opinions, desires, and wishes. Instead, we assume that we "just know" what they will say, do, or think.

Some common curiosity-stoppers are finishing your partner's sentences, agreeing with what they're saying even though you don't understand them, avoiding talking about difficult topics, not asking questions, and not sharing your opinions so they don't share theirs. Do any of these resonate for you in your relationship?

You can reawaken curiosity by stepping outside of your preconceived ideas (or ideals) of others and becoming willing to learn and ask questions. When you show up with curiosity, there is an opportunity to discover, play, and connect. Here are some ideas to practice getting really curious with your partner.

- Each day, try asking, "Tell me more about that."

- If your partner expresses a desire, ask them questions about what makes them long for that desire or what is exciting about the idea for them.

- When your partner makes a decision, ask them how they felt it went (rather than telling them how it went).

Connection

Connection refers to the continuous intersection of our day-to-day lives. I like to use the analogy of tree branches. Each day, we consciously choose to grow our branches together. Without nurturing connection, we live parallel to the other person.

The key to connecting is not waiting for big date nights, large gifts, or getaways. Rather, connection is based on making intentional choices about the small, frequent moments and daily rituals you share. Here are some simple ideas to build daily connection into your relationship.

- When you wake up, reach for each other first before picking up your phone. (Better yet, spend the first thirty minutes of your day without technology.)

- Greet your partner at the door with a hug and a kiss. Make that hug thirty seconds long and the kiss at least six seconds. Let yourself linger a bit longer than your "normal."

- Send a text letting your partner know that you are thinking of them.

- Eat meals together without any distractions.

- Have a parting ritual (even if it's simply a meaningful kiss) before you leave for work or say good night.

Collaboration

Collaboration means that we are on the same team as our partner. We look out for each other and act as a united front. Collaboration requires prioritizing the relational space over the need to be "right." It acknowledges that we don't only live in your world or mine, but instead we will work toward cocreating our worlds together. Here are some ideas for building collaboration.

- Instead of problem-solving for your partner, telling them the mistakes they made, or explaining how you would have done it differently, show your partner you understand them.

- Practice letting go of the need to be right in your conversations. You don't have to change your partner's mind. You are allowed to have your own thoughts, feelings, opinions, desires, wishes, and values without your partner agreeing.

- Find a way toward fairness in your relationship. It will never feel *equal*, but it has to feel *fair*. Are there tasks that you need to offload? Do you hold the majority of the household tasks on your to-do list? Do you need more time for yourself but you worry it's not equal? Teammates are not always fifty-fifty. Involve your partner to help create fairness in your relationship.

- Make decisions together, including decisions involving parenting and extended family.

◇◇◇◇◇

Relationships are hard. They are also necessary for our survival. This is why I see people in my therapy office taking leaps every day to find true love and belonging. To love and be loved is a risk we must be willing to take to live a meaningful life.

At the end of the day, we want to know that when a relationship goes awry, we can find our way through the dark tunnel and back to the light. Oftentimes, it's not the same place where we started. Instead, time and experience bring us to a new destination that offers us something different, something that is perhaps more meaningful. Your relationship today may not look like what you signed up for, but it may be changing into something more fulfilling than you ever thought was possible.

Acknowledgments

Writing a book does not happen in a silo, but instead in relationship with others. I am incredibly grateful to all of those who have been connected with me to help make this book a reality. First and foremost, to my husband, Gregory. This book and the work I do each day wouldn't be possible without you. From the very beginning, you taught me to unmask my perfectionism and sit more gracefully with my mistakes. You have supported me from the first day I said, "I'm going to share something outside of my therapy office." When I doubted my ability to share my words, you reminded me of what I find meaningful and nudged me to keep going even when I felt scared. You continue to lift up my dreams while holding down so much more of the household and childcare labor. Thank you for being my secure base and for always holding my hand. And of course, I loved seeing the relief on your face when this book was written, followed with your heartfelt expression: "Now I can have my wife back."

To my two children, who unbeknownst to them have given me gifts of reparenting myself and becoming a more healed version of me, you are both amazing in different ways, and I am so grateful that you call me Mom. I love the quiet moments of reading beside each other and the silly moments in our games. You are my teachers in present-moment living, letting go of control, and acceptance. May you both always know what it means to create autonomous connection.

I am grateful to all of those with whom I have had the pleasure to work with on the PESI Publishing team. Thank you to Kate Sample for the continued belief in the power of telling my stories and for reminding me that the everyday dilemmas of our lives need to be shown. Thank you to Chelsea Thompson for working so closely with me to edit these pages. Your alignment with my vision and collaboration to edit this book are deeply appreciated. Thank you to Karsyn Morse and Jenny Miller for your marketing support, Jenessa Jackson for your editorial support, and Emily Dyer for the beautiful cover design.

Thank you to Cecilia Lyra, my literary agent at PS Literary, who told me that great writing doesn't need to rely on punctuation and who informed me that I am, indeed, a good writer. You believed in my one goal: to reach more people outside of my office so they, too, could feel seen and normalized in their own pain and suffering. You continuously called out my impostor and guided me out of many dark tunnels. Thank you for your continued confidence in my ability to listen to my gut and write this book.

Thank you to Ceri Marsh for your editorial support and for getting to know my inner critic and shame spiral faster than my own therapist. Your ability to see the end goal of this book, to keep me focused, and to usher me along in the writing process are deeply valued. Thank you also to Nicola Wright for your early contributions to the book proposal and to Choice Media and Communications for your hard work and support in marketing this book to the world.

Thank you to all of my family members for your words of encouragement, excitement for this journey, and extra visits from Greg and the kids so I could have writing weekends. To my parents, thank you for telling me to take risks and follow my dreams. You cheered me on every step of the way, even when it meant moving farther away from home to complete my PhD.

To my therapist, who saw my vulnerability and fear of not being liked and told me that I was likable in our second therapy session, our work together has not only helped me heal old wounds, but it has helped me be a better therapist by truly knowing what it means to sit on the other side of the chair. You have taught me to accept the hole in my heart and to still live a life that is filled with meaning.

To Dr. Melissa Calhoun and Dr. Meagan Gallaghar, you kept me going by offering to open your doors and consult every Friday morning before starting our day. Our consultations together continue to help me be a better therapist. I couldn't have gotten through the pandemic without you two or, moreover, through the process of building a thriving practice that adheres to our values of connection and collaboration. Thank you to my colleagues at Integrated Wellness for your ongoing support.

Thank you to my dear friends who have supported me along the way. You have always seen me for just me but indulge me by allowing me to be your on-call boundary script writer. I am grateful to Ashleigh who reawakened my desire to write a book by planting the seed through a text message that asked if I had written "that couples book yet." Your words—"When will you start believing you, just like we all do?"— echo on repeat in moments when my impostor is loud. Your support and guidance keep me grounded. Lindsey, you have taught me many lessons along the way, and our long walks and shared love for coffee and psychology have taught me that vulnerability with others is possible. I am grateful for our friendship and the weaving together of our lives.

Thank you to Mer Pavlov and Shannon Leyko for all your encouragement and support in my business and the Dr. Tracy D platform. This book is a celebration of the work we are doing, and I am beyond grateful to have you on my team.

To my clients who have sat with me and shared their vulnerabilities in my office, only to leave and keep trying hard things outside of our time together, I am deeply appreciative of your willingness to sit with me and to venture into the places of your internal world that you might not have ever shown to anyone else before. Thank you for trusting me to walk beside you. Your stories and the work that you do shape me to be who I am today. You matter to me. And you stay in my mind more than you will ever know.

And last, to the Be Connected and Dr. Tracy D community—and to all of you who are healing old wounds, uncovering unhelpful patterns, and having aha moments—your comments, DMs, and shares are invaluable, meaningful, and seen. Your support of this community makes all of this possible. You are changing what it means to love and to be attached, and for those who have children, to one day change their own cycles by watching you break old patterns.

Glossary of Terms

All-or-nothing thinking: The tendency to think in black-or-white terms without nuance, to only see two extremes of a situation while missing other possibilities.

Anhedonic behaviors: Actions or engagement in life in which there is a reduced ability to experience pleasure. Anhedonia is the absence of enjoyment, motivation, and interest that is a core feature of depression.

ARE conversations: Psychologist Dr. Sue Johnson created this acronym to represent a conversation that characterizes a secure bond between partners. This conversation includes these three parts: accessibility (*Are* you there for me?), responsiveness (Will you *respond* to me with warmth and love?), and engagement (Will you be *engaged* with me, holding my vulnerability sacredly and trusting me with your own vulnerability?).

Attachment: The propensity to make strong affectional bonds with significant others. Attachment motivates you to seek closeness to significant others, who are deemed attachment figures. This bond includes behaviors that maintain closeness and contact with significant others, especially in times of uncertainty, stress, or anxiety. The quality of your attachment bond depends on the accessibility and responsiveness of your caregiver while you were growing up. Interacting with caregivers (and, later in life, partners) who are available and responsive helps you to develop attachment security. If your attachment figures are not reliably accessible and supportive, you will struggle to develop secure attachment and will find strategies to help regulate your distress in alternative ways.

Attachment injury: When one partner violates the expectation of providing security and caring to the other partner in a time of distress. An attachment injury is characterized by a sense of betrayal or abandonment, and if not healed, will undermine the ability to feel connected and close. If this injury ultimately becomes a recurring theme, it will block any kind of relationship repair.

Autonomy: The ability to identify as an individual "I" and act on your thoughts, feelings, desires, wishes, and needs from a rational perspective.

Bids for connection: Bids are an attempt to connect with your partner in some way. This occurs when you are looking to be seen and acknowledged, to feel soothed, and to receive affection.

Boundaries: An invisible line that separates two people, indicating where you begin and another person ends. Boundaries are about sharing with others what you want and need, and what you do not need.

Codependency: An overreliance, often unconscious, on another individual for emotional, psychological, and physical support such that there is a facilitation of dysfunctional behavior. The individual assumes responsibility for someone else's needs and behaviors to protect the relationship.

Cognitive dissonance: An internal conflict between two opposing beliefs, attitudes, thoughts, or opinions that creates tension.

Compartmentalize: An unconscious strategy, often referred to as a defense mechanism, in which you mentally separate yourself from conflicting or anxiety-producing thoughts, emotions, or experiences to avoid feeling uncomfortable.

Confirmation bias: The tendency to only observe information that confirms your own beliefs. In relationships, these beliefs are often negative views of your partner, which contributes to relationship distress.

Conscious uncoupling: A term created by Katherine Woodward Thomas to indicate that partners are amicably untethering their union, building healthy co-parenting strategies, and gaining self-awareness to avoid repeating negative cycles.

Contempt: One of the "Four Horsemen," contempt involves the use of sarcasm, cynicism, and hostile humor to communicate with your partner.

Coping strategies (adaptive and maladaptive): The acts you engage in as a way to help yourself feel good and navigate difficult experiences. These might be adaptive (healthy), like going for a walk or meditating.

Or they might be maladaptive (unhealthy), such as avoiding conversations or consuming alcohol regularly. To distinguish between adaptive and maladaptive coping mechanisms, ask yourself the function of the strategy and how it aligns with your overall values in life.

Co-regulation: The process of soothing your nervous system to a state of calm by interacting physically with another person and their nervous system. For example, a parent uses their soothing voice and comforting touch to soothe their crying infant. In relationships, partners hold hands, hug, or sit beside each other to help calm their nervous systems.

Core beliefs: Internally held perceptions and assumptions about yourself, others, and the world. Other commonly used words to describe a core belief are narratives and stories.

Corrective emotional experience: An experience of being able to understand an event or relationship in a different or unexpected way, which then allows you to come to terms with it emotionally.

Criticism: One of the "Four Horsemen," criticism involves attacking the character of your partner and placing blame on them—often communicated definitively with statements like "you never" and "you always."

Deactivation: The (often unconscious) act of minimizing your emotions and needs and pushing away from your attachment figure as a way to cope with stress and anxiety. This strategy is used by people who have avoidant attachment styles.

Defensiveness: One of the "Four Horsemen," defensiveness is an automatic response to protect yourself from a perceived or real attack.

Differentiation: The ongoing process of defining yourself and your boundaries, and navigating fears and anxieties that arise from connecting with another person intimately. An acknowledgment that your internal experiences are separate from another person's internal experiences. A recognition that you are responsible only for your own internal experiences and how you communicate to others.

Dorsal vagal state: According to polyvagal theory, the dorsal vagal branch of the vagus nerve is activated in response to cues of overwhelming danger and threat. In a dorsal vagal state, you become immobilized, freeze, and shut down to protect yourself.

Dysregulation: Physiological overwhelm of the nervous system. An experience whereby an individual has difficulties coping with incoming stimulation and their nervous system is saying, "Too much, too fast, too soon."

Emotional fusion: A person's excessive emotional involvement in their significant relationship such that they lose the autonomous "I." A fused individual reacts emotionally without being able to rationally work through conflict. Partners who are emotionally fused struggle with high levels of sensitivity to each other's emotional states and fear rejection. As a result, they experience increases in anxiety in their relationship.

Empathy: The capacity to understand the emotions of another person, to see things from their perspective, and to *feel into* their internal felt experience.

Evocative responding: A therapeutic intervention in which the therapist elicits an internal (and sometimes not yet formulated) aspect of a client's experience in a tentative manner.

Externalization: The process of blaming others and not taking responsibility for your behaviors or for your role in certain events.

Flipping your lid: A term created by Dr. Dan Siegel to explain what happens in the brain when you are overwhelmed, triggered, or in distress. In these moments, the emotional part of the brain (the amygdala) takes control and the rational part of the brain (the prefrontal cortex) goes offline, resulting in difficulty thinking and acting rationally.

Flooded: A term used to indicate that someone is physiologically overwhelmed and they are no longer able to comprehend information that is being shared. When you become flooded, it is best to stop the conversation and practice regulation strategies.

Hanging in: A term described by Dr. Harriet Lerner where you practice *not* taking over responsibility for the things that your partner needs to do while continuing to stay emotionally connected.

Highly sensitive person (HSP): A personality type where an individual has a high degree of sensory-processing sensitivity. They experience increased emotional sensitivity and a strong reaction to stimuli, both internally (e.g., pain, hunger) and externally (e.g., noise, light).

Hyperactivation: The frequent demand for proximity, closeness, and soothing by your caregiver, which is accompanied by a struggle to feel soothed by their closeness. This is a common coping strategy that individuals with insecure attachment use to deal with distress.

Inner critic: Your internal dialogue that is inherently self-critical. This inner voice developed in response to painful experiences in early childhood.

Interdependence: The ability to see the self and other as two separate people, holding the individual "I" while also cocreating your world with intimate others to flexibly meet each other's needs.

Invisible labor: Behind-the-scenes tasks that people typically do not recognize. These tasks are essential to maintaining a household, childcare, and a relationship.

Jumping to conclusions: Making assumptions about your partner's thoughts, emotions, and actions based on limited information to support your belief.

Labeling: Narrowly defining your partner or categorizing them based on limited information.

Mentalization: The ability to see and understand the self, the other, and the self in context of the other. Using mentalization, you acknowledge that other people can have an entirely different experience than what you are perceiving and that, often, a loved one's outward expressions, emotions, or needs are not *necessarily* about you.

Mental load: The cognitive never-ending to-do list involved in managing your work, household, childcare, family, and relationships.

Mind reading: Assuming what your partner is thinking or feeling without concrete information to support your assumptions.

Negative cycle: A difficult relationship dynamic whereby communication between partners consists of negative displays of emotions, unmet needs and longings, and blame and withdrawal. These cycles become entrenched into a repeating, cyclical pattern that is reinforced over time. Negative cycles perpetuate feelings of rejection and abandonment and prevent partners from being able to solve their problems.

Overfunctioning: Part of the overfunctioning-underfunctioning dynamic that occurs in relationships, overfunctioning is characterized by a partner who takes more control over planning, provides care (sometimes too much), and tries to fix things for others.

Parallel play: A form of play in which children play adjacent to each other but do not influence each other's behavior. As applied to adults, parallel play occurs when you are near someone but not otherwise interacting.

Parentified child: A child who ends up bearing the household duties and emotional burdens of their caregivers. A parentified child learns to suppress their own emotions and needs in the service of caring for others.

Personalization: Believing that your partner's thoughts, feelings, and actions are about you.

Perspective-taking: The ability to perceive a situation from an alternative point of view.

Polyvagal theory: Created by psychologist Dr. Stephen Porges, this theory provides a physiological understanding of how the autonomic (meaning, automatic and without control) nervous system responds to cues of safety and danger in your environment. Through a process known as neuroception, your neural circuits are constantly searching for cues of safety and danger and then responding to those cues, leading you to experience different states as a result of that information: a ventral vagal state (connectivity, calm), a sympathetic nervous system state (fight-or-flight, mobilization), or a dorsal vagal state (immobilization, shutdown, freezing).

Primary emotions: Feelings that are softer, clear, and at the core of your experience (like pain, sadness, hurt, and loneliness)—also known as core emotions. Although primary emotions can be difficult to identify, they bring your partner closer to you, helping them understand your more vulnerable parts, while secondary emotions tend to push them away.

Projection: The (often unconscious) mental process where you attribute your own thoughts, feelings, and internal experiences to others. For example, if you are highly self-critical, you may believe that other people are highly critical of you.

Pursue-defend cycle: This is a type of negative cycle between partners where one partner pursues for connection while the other partner defends or shuts down, only to result in a cyclical pattern of negative affect and unmet needs and longings.

RAIN: From psychologist Dr. Tara Brach, using this acronym can help bring acceptance to difficult and painful experiences. Start by *recognizing* what is happening. *Allow* the experience (your thoughts, emotions, bodily sensations) to be there, just as they are. *Investigate* your experience with curiosity and openness, avoiding judgment. Finally, offer something *nurturing* to yourself: What would you say to a dear friend from a place of compassion and kindness?

Repair: The act of returning to a difficult moment with your partner and taking ownership for how you contributed to the difficult moment. Repair is the acknowledgment that your relationship is more important than your individual ego and the need to be right. Even if you did not intend to hurt your partner, repairing acknowledges the impact that your behavior had on the other person. This act is essential to building healthy and strong relationships.

Reparent: Learning to meet the needs of your inner child, either physically, emotionally, or spiritually, through daily actions and behaviors.

Although your parents may not have been able to meet these needs in your childhood, as an adult, you can now practice meeting your own needs.

Repetition compulsion: The unconscious need to reenact early childhood traumas and unhealthy relationship dynamics as a way to overcome or work through them.

Scapegoat: An individual who is blamed for everyone's mistakes and faults. When you are not willing to take responsibility for your contribution to your own problems, you put problems onto the other person to alleviate your own distress.

Secondary emotions: These are emotions about emotions. Secondary emotions, like anger and frustration, are often more confusing and are not related to your core experiences. Secondary emotions act to protect you from feeling more vulnerable primary emotions and keep your partner at a distance.

Self: In Internal Family Systems therapy, the Self (noted with a capital *S*) is a deep inner resource of consciousness that reflects your true essence. The Self is characterized by the 8 C's: curiosity, compassion, clarity, connectedness, calm, confidence, courage, and creativity.

Self-abandonment: The process of rejecting, suppressing, or giving up your own needs and wants. This may be an unconscious strategy to prevent rejection and abandonment from others. However, this strategy is ineffective, as you may end up growing resentful and bitter toward others while feeling like you are not aligned with your own values. Self-abandonment begins in childhood when your caregivers do not meet your emotional or physical needs, leading to feelings of unworthiness and unlovability.

Self-compassion: This is offering the same kindness that you would to a loved one and turning it toward yourself.

Self-fulfilling prophecy: A psychological phenomenon in which you expect something to happen and this expectation comes true simply because you act in ways that end up confirming or aligning with your belief.

Self-regulation: The ability to go from a state of hyperarousal or dysregulation to one of calm using different self-soothing strategies. Healthy strategies may include using temperature (taking a cold shower), breath, or movement.

Stonewalling: One of the "Four Horsemen," stonewalling involves withdrawing and closing yourself off from your partner. This happens when you feel overwhelmed or physiologically flooded.

Subjugation: In schema therapy, subjugation is a life trap in which you allow others to dominate you and you experience ongoing issues around feeling controlled by others and pleasing others. In this life trap, you self-sacrifice to avoid punishment or abandonment, believing that your own thoughts and feelings are not valid or important to others.

Sympathetic nervous system state: As discussed in polyvagal theory, this state is characterized by a fight-or-flight experience with an adrenaline rush that motivates you to protect yourself from danger.

Therapeutic alliance: The experience between a therapist and client with regard to how positively a client feels in the relationship with their therapist.

Trauma bond: An unhealthy pattern of attachment that develops in toxic relationships that are characterized by emotional, physical, or sexual harm. It reflects the bond that someone can feel toward a person who is causing them harm.

Triangulation: With the goal of alleviating and deflecting tension, one or both people involved in a relationship put a third person into their dynamic. This creates increased distress and tension between all relationship dynamics.

Underfunctioning: In this part of the overfunctioning-underfunctioning dynamic that occurs in relationships, you procrastinate, don't complete your fair share of household or childcare tasks, frequently ask for help, and rely on your partner for decision-making.

Validation: The act of letting another person know that their experience is real and valid. Through validation, you are helping them feel heard and understood. Validation often comes in the form of: You + a verb (*like, think, feel, desire, want, struggle*) + a description of their reality without judgment. For example, "You feel unheard when I'm on my phone," "You're struggling with your work assignment," or "You wish this were different and it's really hard for you."

Values: Akin to an internal compass, your values are the things that you believe are meaningful and important to you. Values are highly individualistic, meaning that what you find meaningful will differ from someone else. Partners often have overlapping values that drive their relationship and connection.

Ventral vagal state: Highlighted in polyvagal theory, the ventral (front) vagal part of the vagus nerve is responsible for responding to cues of safety in your environment. In a ventral vagal state, you are calm, connected, and socially engaged.

Window of tolerance: This is your ability to remain internally connected and make sense of your thoughts and feelings. Working within your window of tolerance means that you can think logically. When you are outside of your window of tolerance, you are dysregulated and flooded, and no longer able to defuse conflict.

Wise mind: Stemming from dialectical behavior therapy, when you are in a state of wise mind, you can access both reason and emotion and make choices from a place of calm and connectedness. The wise mind is able to observe emotional experiences without reactivity and practice present-moment awareness.

References

Introduction

Research now shows that loneliness and social isolation (i.e., disconnection from others) kills more people than heart attacks or cancer: Holt-Lunstad, J., Smith, T. B., Baker, M., Harris, T., & Stephenson, D. (2015). Loneliness and social isolation as risk factors for mortality: A meta-analytic review. *Perspectives on Psychological Science, 10*(2), 227–237. https://doi.org/10.1177/1745691614568352

Chapter 1

Like 80 percent of women in this type of negative cycle, Emily falls into the pursuer role: Johnson, S. M. (2004). *The practice of emotionally focused couple therapy: Creating connection.* Brunner-Routledge.

***Emotional fusion* is the opposite of differentiation:** Bowen, M. (1978). *Family therapy in clinical practice.* Jason Aronson.

Chapter 2

67 percent of new parents will experience decreased marital satisfaction for the first three years after having a baby, and the first year is often said to be the hardest: Shapiro, A. F., Gottman, J. M., & Carrère, S. (2000). The baby and the marriage: Identifying factors that buffer against decline in marital satisfaction after the first baby arrives. *Journal of Family Psychology, 14*(1), 59–70. https://doi.org/10.1037/0893-3200.14.1.59

According to *polyvagal theory*, the autonomic nervous system can react to this conflict by going into a state of mobilization: Dana, D. (2018). *The polyvagal theory in therapy: Engaging the rhythm of regulation.* W. W. Norton.

Chapter 3

Neuroscientist Dr. Jill Bolte Taylor has shown that emotions tend to flare up and fade within just ninety seconds if we identify the internal experience, name the emotions, then allow them to flow: Bolte Taylor, J. (2021). *Whole brain living. The anatomy of choice and the four characters that drive our life.* Hay House Inc.

Research shows that depression and anxiety influence relationship satisfaction and vice versa: Snyder, D. K., Castellani, A. M., Whisman, M. A. (2006). Current status and future directions in couple therapy. *Annual Review of Psychology, 57,* 317–344. https://doi.org/10.1146 /annurev.psych.56.091103.070154

Chapter 4

I shift to helping Peter understand what happens for Karine in these moments by sharing the concept of *flipping the lid,* as described by psychiatrist and author Dr. Dan Siegel: Siegel, D. J. (2011). *Mindsight: The new science of personal transformation.* Bantam Books.

Chapter 5

Either way, these couples have experienced an *attachment injury* in the relationship, in which one partner violates the expectation of providing security and care for the other partner in times of distress: Johnson, S. M., Makinen, J. A., & Millikin, J. W. (2001). Attachment injuries in couple relationships: A new perspective on impasses in couples therapy. *Journal of Marital and Family Therapy, 27*(2), 145–155. https://doi.org/10.1111/j.1752-0606.2001.tb01152.x

I have also worked with couples whose disconnection has led them to *conscious uncoupling,* a term created by psychotherapist Katherine Woodward Thomas: Woodward Thomas, K. (2009). *Conscious uncoupling: 5 steps to living happily even after.* Harmony Books.

CHAPTER 6

As described by relationship experts Drs. John and Julie Gottman, these communication styles are known as the "Four Horsemen" because they lead to the destruction of a relationship: *criticism, defensiveness, stonewalling,* and *contempt*: Gottman, J. (1994). *Why marriages succeed or fail: And how you can make yours last.* Simon & Schuster.

According to psychotherapist Terrence Real, people engage in affairs for one of two reasons: Real, T. (2022). *Us: Getting past you and me to build a more loving relationship.* Rodale Books.

CHAPTER 7

Eve Rodsky, author of *Fair Play: A Game-Changing Solution for When You Have Too Much to Do (and More Life to Live)*, describes three parts to a task within the family unit: Rodsky, E. (2019). *Fair play: A game-changing solution for when you have too much to do in life (and more life to live).* G. P. Putnam's Sons.

CHAPTER 8

However, as psychologist and author of *The Dance of Anger* Dr. Harriet Lerner puts it, women are taught to either be nice and sweep their feelings under the rug (which build unconscious anger and rage), or they are viewed as bitches for expressing and venting anger: Lerner, H. (2005). *The dance of anger: A woman's guide to changing the patterns of intimate relationships.* Perennial Library/Harper & Row Publishers.

CHAPTER 9

Anger and high conflict impact a child's brain development and their ability to self-regulate: Porter, C. L., Wouden-Miller, M., Shizuko Silva, S., Earnest Porter, A. (2003). Marital harmony and conflict: Links to infants' emotional regulation and cardiac vagal tone. *Infancy, 4*(2), 297–307. https://doi.org/10.1207/S15327078IN0402_09

The Swiss psychologist Dr. Jean Piaget asserted that between the ages of two and seven, children are developing memory and imagination but have difficulty thinking outside of their own perspective: Piaget, J. (1954). *The construction of reality in the child.* (M. Cook, Trans.). Basic Books.

The ability to see both self and other isn't fully formed until the prefrontal cortex is done developing at the age of twenty-five: Morris, A. S., Silk, J. S., Steinberg, L., Myers, S. S., & Robinson, L. R. (2007). The role of the family context in the development of emotion regulation. *Social Development, 16*(2), 361–388. https://doi.org/10.1111/j.1467 -9507.2007.00389.x

Research shows that gay couples don't tend to experience the conflicts that come from normative societal sex roles: Shechory, M., & Ziv, R. (2007). Relationships between gender role attitudes, role division, and perception of equity among heterosexual, gay and lesbian couples. *Sex Roles: A Journal of Research, 56*(9-10), 629–638. https://doi.org/10.1007 /s11199-007-9207-3

CHAPTER 10

In Dr. John Gottman's research, couples were asked to talk about a recent conflict while hooked up to physiological monitoring systems that measured markers like blood pressure, heart rate, and oxygen levels: Navarra, R. J., & Gottman, J. M. (2013). Gottman method couple therapy: From theory to practice. In D. K. Carson & M. Casado-Kehoe (Eds.), *Case studies in couples therapy* (pp. 369–382). Routledge.

This reaction to withdrawal is natural and instinctive, as shown by psychologist Dr. Ed Tronick's "still face" experiment: Weinberg, M. K., & Tronick, E. Z. (1996). Infant affective reactions to the resumption of maternal interaction after the Still-Face. *Child Development, 67*(3), 905–914. https://doi.org/10.2307/1131869

It is also supported by studies showing that suppressing your own emotions increases your partner's blood pressure: Butler, E. A., Egloff, B., Wilhelm, F. W., Smith, N. C., Erickson, E. A., & Gross, J. J. (2003).

The social consequences of expressive suppression. *Emotion, 3*(1), 48–67. https://doi.org/10.1037/1528-3542.3.1.48

I also suspect, based on Peter's personality, that he was what child psychologist Dr. Becky Kennedy calls a "deeply feeling kid": Kennedy, B. (2022). *Good inside: A guide to becoming the parent you want to be.* Harper Wave.

Research by psychiatrist Dr. Rosemary Basson has shown that the desire and arousal system is different for women compared to men, which is why female Viagra has yet to hit the market: Rosemary, B. (2000). The female sexual response: A different model. *Journal of Sex & Marital Therapy, 26,* 51–65. https://doi.org/10.1080/009262300278641

It's also important to acknowledge that for women, the desire system is nonlinear and cyclical, which is in contrast to Masters and Johnson's initial research on the linear model of sex: desire, arousal, orgasm, and refractory period: Masters, W. H., & Johnson, V. E. (1966). *Human sexual response.* Bantam Books.

Sex educator and author Dr. Emily Nagoski uses the analogy of a car to distinguish between sexual excitation (the gas pedal) and sexual inhibition (the brake): Nagoski, E. (2015). *Come as you are: The surprising new science that will transform your sex life.* Simon & Schuster.

This is also known as the dual control model of sexual response: Bancroft, J., & Janssen, E. (2000). The dual control model of male sexual response: A theoretical approach to centrally mediated erectile dysfunction. *Neuroscience & Biobehavioral Reviews, 24*(5), 571–579. https://doi.org/10.1016/S0149-7634(00)00024-5

CHAPTER 11

Play is any activity where you find yourself in a state of flow, described by psychologist Dr. Mihaly Csikszentmihalyi as the optimal experience of being completely absorbed in an activity: Csikszentmihalyi, M. (2008). *Flow: The psychology of optimal experience.* Harper.

Chapter 12

Psychiatrist and author Dr. Dan Siegel describes the difference using the example of a bicycle: Siegel, D. J. (2011). *Mindsight: The new science of personal transformation.* Bantam Books.

The personality type of an HSP, as articulated by psychologists Drs. Elaine and Arthur Aron, includes a high degree of sensory-processing sensitivity: Aron, E. N. (1998). *The highly sensitive person: How to thrive when the world overwhelms you.* Broadway Books.

As couples therapist Terrence Real describes in his book *Us: Getting Past You and Me to Build a More Loving Relationship*, each moment between you and your partner can answer the question "What path do I want to choose today?": Real, T. (2022). *Us: Getting past you and me to build a more loving relationship.* Rodale Books.

Chapter 14

One study found that in order to make the choice of infidelity seem okay, people were able to change both their view of self (how they understand themselves) and their view of infidelity (their belief that it is wrong or hurtful): Alexopoulos, C. (2021). Justify my love: Cognitive dissonance reduction among perpetrators of online and offline infidelity. *Journal of Social and Personal Relationships, 38*(12), 3669–3691. https://doi.org/10.1177/0265407521103774

Chapter 15

When our parents are unable to meet our core attachment needs (e.g., need for soothing, comfort, unconditional acceptance), we find ways to continue holding our parents in a positive light: Teyber, E. (2006). *Interpersonal process in therapy: An integrative model* (5th ed.). Thomson Brooks/Cole.

CHAPTER 19

In his study of newlyweds, Dr. John Gottman found that couples who were still married six years later turned toward each other 86 percent of the time: Navarra, R. J., & Gottman, J. M. (2018). Bids and turning toward in Gottman method couple therapy. In J. Lebow, A. Chambers, & D. C. Breunlin (Eds.), *Encyclopedia of couple and family therapy* (pp. 253–255). Springer.

CHAPTER 21

I decide to shift into emotionally focused interventions that will lead to what is known as a *blamer-softening*: Johnson, S. M. (2004). *The practice of emotionally focused couple therapy: Creating connection.* Brunner-Routledge.

CHAPTER 22

Psychologist Dr. Tara Brach uses an acronym that I find incredibly helpful for navigating difficult emotions: Brach, T. (2004). *Radical acceptance: Embracing your life with the heart of a Buddha.* Bantam Books.

CHAPTER 23

The overfunctioner must be willing to engage in what psychologist Dr. Harriet Lerner calls *hanging in*: Lerner, H. (2005). *The dance of anger: A woman's guide to changing the patterns of intimate relationships.* Perennial Library/Harper & Row Publishers.

CONCLUSION

Several studies have shown that curiosity helps us build connection and affection with each other: Kashdan, T. B., McKnight, P. E., Fincham, F. D., & Rose, P. (2011). When curiosity breeds intimacy: Taking advantage of intimacy opportunities and transforming boring conversations. *Journal of Personality, 79*(6),1369–1402. https://doi.org/10.1111/j.1467-6494.2010.00697.x

About the Author

 **Dr. Tracy Dalgleish,** CPsych, is a clinical psychologist, couples therapist, and sought-after relationship expert. For over fifteen years, she has provided direct clinical services to couples and has dedicated her time to researching, writing, and speaking about relationships. Her goal is to make the skills and tools she teaches her clients more accessible so they can build healthier relationships with themselves and with others. She is the founder of Be Connected Digital and the owner of a mental health clinic, Integrated Wellness. She lives in Ottawa, Canada, with her husband and two children.